THE MONKEY IN THE BODHI TREE

Crazy-Wisdom & the Way of the Wise-Fool

THE MONKEY IN THE BODHI TREE

Crazy-Wisdom & the Way of the Wise-Fool

Jason Brett Serle

BOOKS

London, UK
Washington, DC, USA

CollectiveInk

First published by O-Books, 2025
O-Books is an imprint of Collective Ink Ltd.,
Unit 11, Shepperton House, 89 Shepperton Road, London, N1 3DF
office@collectiveinkbooks.com
www.collectiveinkbooks.com
www.o-books.com

For distributor details and how to order please visit the 'Ordering' section on our website.

Text copyright: Jason Brett Serle, 2024

ISBN: 978 1 80341 744 8
978 1 80341 751 6 (ebook)
Library of Congress Control Number: 2023952033

A CIP catalogue record for this book is available from the British Library.

Design: Lapiz Digital Services

UK: Printed and bound by CPI Group (UK) Ltd, Croydon, CR0 4YY
Printed in North America by CPI GPS partners

We operate a distinctive and ethical publishing philosophy in all areas of our business, from our global network of authors to production and worldwide distribution.

Other Books by the Author

KISSING ACHILLES' HEEL:
The Joyful Unmasking of Delusion

"Kissing Achilles' Heel" is a collection of 63 short pieces —
parables, fables, stories, commentaries, poems, letters and
conversations, that all in some way present a challenge to our
unquestioned assumptions about the nature of existence. Unlike
many other books that share a similar theme, "Kissing Achilles'
Heel" aims to bring a little playfulness and humour to the all
too serious task of seeking. It is, at best, a finger pointing to the
Transcendental, and at worst, a temporary calm respite to the
sometimes stormy search for the Self.

"KISSING ACHILLES' HEEL is a lovely little book, full of wit
and wisdom, not to be read in a hurry like a novel. The longer
you take, the more you will enjoy and gain."
— RAMESH S BALSEKAR
ISBN: 978-1-32981-492-9

ABIDE AS THAT: Ramana Maharshi & the Song of Ribhu

There are some writings that transcend time and tradition
and speak to the ever-present heart of the human experience.
Simple yet profound, challenging yet compassionate, the Song
of Ribhu is one such example of this. In the same tradition as the
Bhagavad Gita or the Ashtavakra Gita, the Ribhu Gita, literally
the Song of Ribhu, represents the highest declaration of Advaita
Vedanta, spoken by the enlightened sage Ribhu to his disciple
Nidagha on the slopes of Mount Kedara in the Himalayas.

Some 2,500 years later, another awakened master, Sri Ramana Maharshi, was touched by these same words, considering them to be one of the most sublime expressions of the awakened state that humanity had ever produced. He spoke of it reverently and would even give copies to his devotees to read.

The version that follows is a selection, made by Sri Ramana Maharshi himself, of 45 verses that capture the very essence of the Ribhu Gita — an essence that this fresh and masterful modern translation manages to communicate in simple and elegant English, perfectly adapted to the Western reader.

The book also contains the story of Ribhu and Nidagha as told by Sri Ramana Maharshi, as well as excerpts from informal talks with his students to further clarify the themes.

"The Ribhu Gita is a timeless classic, a bliss bomb of intuitive spiritual utterances, insights and revelations condensed into pill form. Jason Brett Serle's elegant and easy to absorb translation is a gift to all earnest seekers of Truth."
— MOOJI

ISBN: 978-1-78904-234-4

Contents

There is in human nature generally more of the fool than of the wise.
— FRANCIS BACON

The psychotic drowns in the same waters in which the mystic swims with delight.
— JOSEPH CAMPBELL

He saw God's foot upon the treadle of the loom, and spoke it; and therefore his shipmates called him mad. So man's insanity is heaven's sense; and wandering from all mortal reason, man comes at last to that celestial thought, which, to reason, is absurd and frantic; and weal or woe, feels then uncompromised, indifferent as his God.
— HERMAN MELVILLE, *Moby Dick*

Though this be madness, yet there is method in't.
— WILLIAM SHAKESPEARE, *Hamlet*

PART I

1

CRAZY-WISDOM

There is no great genius without a touch of
madness.

— ARISTOTLE

Introduction

There is, at times, a fine line between the wise man and the
madman and history is replete with examples of both as well as
people who have been one and yet taken to be the other — crazy
men elevated to the stature of sages and sages taken for mere
crazy fools, usually by those who are neither truly crazy nor
truly wise. But the fact remains, although many have perhaps
been merely mad, others have demonstrated a certain method in
that madness — a method reflecting a self-development beyond
the constraints of logic and reason, and a method of teaching
designed to break one out of their habitual thinking patterns so
as to see the world anew, even if only momentarily. Due to this
fine line between genius and madness, as well as the paradoxical
nature of genuine spirituality and the fact that the trans-rational
by definition is not rational, we find in almost every one of the
Great Wisdom Traditions, a current that has often been termed
"crazy-wisdom". Within it are adepts and masters who embody
this peculiar and unconventional mode of being and teaching,
as well as those drawn to it as a means of self-transcendence
within the context of an authentic spiritual path. Of the many
paths up the mountain, that of crazy-wisdom, although one of
the lesser travelled, presents a dramatic and formidable climb
to those that are so inclined. It can, in another light, be seen
as an integral part of any and all paths, for as they reach the
peak, they must necessarily converge for the final few steps.

This is perhaps why the more elevated the point of view of the sage, the less he is understood by those who remain at the base, mapping the paths to the top with logic and reason without ever going beyond them by actually climbing the mountain. The awakened man standing at the peak with a privileged 360 degree view will make little sense and no doubt sound like a madman to those at the base when he cries down to them that there is ocean, desert, forest and fertile plain at the base of the mountain when they can only see one or the other, depending on which side they stand. The "either/or" reasoning, so useful at the foot of the mountain, must necessarily give way to a realisation that transcends this two-valued Aristotelian system when stood at the summit. The view from the top allows one to see logic and reason for what they are — useful tools — whilst at the same time, recognising their limitations. In this sense, crazy-wisdom should not be misconstrued as being something against reason, or at odds with rationality and logic. It is simply beyond them — trans-rational and post-logical rather than merely irrational or illogical. I use the word "merely" because statements made from this transcendent perspective can indeed be, at times, illogical and irrational — just not merely so. But just as the transcendent statements of sages are often mistaken to be merely the ramblings of an unhinged mind, often the babblings of madmen have been elevated to the status of wisdom by those who are unaware of this subtle difference and unable to discern the irrational from the trans-rational — the crazy from the crazy-wise. For this reason the world of crazy-wisdom, divine madness, holy fools and rascal gurus can be something of a minefield for neophytes and spiritual novices, strewn as it is with frauds and charlatans. Too often what passes for crazy-wisdom is nothing more than narcissism dressed up as spiritual altruism, perversion justified as liberated equanimity or unacknowledged pathology relabelled as a manifestation of the transpersonal.

As a fool striving to elevate his wisdom to the level of his craziness, this book is my attempt to help set the record straight. Rather than waste precious ink and paper on denouncing the fakers and phonies, I have instead attempted to shine the light of awareness on the authentic ways of the wise-fool and the ageless archetype of the genuine crazy-wisdom master — the monkey in the Bodhi tree. In order to do this, I have approached the subject from two broad perspectives: the theoretical and the practical. Part I deals with the *theory* and tries to answer such questions as: What is crazy-wisdom? Where did it come from? How is it embodied and expressed? Who are its greatest luminaries and expositors? And why should anyone care anyway? Part II deals with the *practice* and aims to demonstrate crazy-wisdom in action. To this end, I have collected 151 teaching tales from around the world to illustrate the methods of the great masters and adepts; stories that not only give practical insight but also, like Zen *koans*, can be used as contemplative tools to illuminate and provoke epiphany.

This work is in no way intended to be an exhaustive study. So numerous are the sects and adherents of even India alone, that they would fill volumes in a detailed investigation. Instead, what draws my pen inexorably onwards is twofold: to help bring some measure of clarity to the radically different perspective that is afforded by the view from the mountain-top; and to arouse and inspire the abandonment of comfortable base-camps to risk it all on the climb. To this end I have summoned help from those less foolish than I — those great crazy-wisdom adepts and masters from all Traditions who have pointed the way and encouraged my own ascent. This is their book, and to them it is humbly dedicated.

The Teaching Tales

The stories that make up Part II have been gathered from books, articles, and oral accounts from people all over the world, my primary task being to select those that possessed the rare qualities of crazy-wisdom and that demonstrated the ways of the wise-fool — tales that could take one beyond the self and its claustrophobic conditioning in order to glimpse, if only for a moment, one's own folly and a way out of it. My secondary task was to render these tales into the more familiar flow and format particular to a native English speaker. Having read over the years every collection of such stories that I could get my hands on, I was always struck by the storytelling manner particular to the cultural and linguistic milieu of the author. Language not only defines the idiosyncratic landscape of our communication but also its frontiers, its borders and limitations. The fact that Spanish speakers have two different verbs for "to be" whereas English has only one, or three spatial adjectives to refer to an unspecified object whereas English has only two — "this" and "that" — leads the native speakers of any language towards certain propensities and considerations that are unique to the language in question. This often only becomes truly apparent when one acquires a certain proficiency in any other language other than their native tongue. Even the well-known Mulla Nasruddin anthologies of Idries Shah, whose grasp of the English language certainly cannot be faulted, exhibit a distinctive Eastern flavour, not in the grammar or the vocabulary nor even in the story itself, but rather in the more subtle aspects of storytelling and emphasis or lack thereof that is an inescapable part of being raised with one or another native tongue. Here, rather than improve upon what has come before, I presume only to make the stories more relatable to Western, and in particular, native English-speaking sensibilities and tendencies, whilst at the same time maintaining their archetypal essence and essential wisdom. The fact that these stories are reflections of the human condition and deal with existential questions of universal import, I believe, allows for cross-cultural translation without any appreciable loss of vital insight and spiritual potency. Indeed, the most difficult task in all of this has been to salvage and transmit this underlying essence. In doing so I have chosen a rather more classic and timeless formulation of the English language as the most effective means through which to achieve this. I can only hope now, for your sake, that I have succeeded more than I have failed in this endeavour.

Wise and Otherwise

The knowledge beyond knowledge is my knowledge.[1]

— KABIR

Although at a glance the term "crazy-wisdom" appears to be an oxymoron, a deeper analysis will reveal it to be anything but. Of course, the key to it being a contradiction in terms or not depends entirely on how we choose to define the two terms. In its simplest and most conventional sense the two terms do contradict one another. The word "crazy" is derived from an old English word meaning "full of cracks" and implies that one's thinking faculties or mind is somehow broken and not functioning correctly, whereas "wisdom" as conventionally understood implies not only the correct functioning of the mind, but indeed the optimal functioning of the mind. A person with wisdom is judicious, perspicacious, astute and intelligent and displays the best things a mind has to offer. So how can one possibly be both crazy and wise? Are the two not mutually exclusive?

Perhaps the best way to bring greater clarity to this issue is to grasp what the modern spiritual philosopher Ken Wilber calls the "pre/trans fallacy". If we consider such things as "rationality", "logic" or "conventionality" it is not hard for us to recognise that there exists a state that is pre-rational, pre-logical and pre-conventional. We only have to look at a baby, a toddler or young child to observe this fact. They have not yet developed

7

the capacity to reason and rationalise or to determine a logical argument, neither have they learnt the often unspoken rules and conditions of conventional behaviour. What is perhaps a little more difficult for many people to realise, although all of the Great Wisdom Traditions of the world have alluded to it in a more or less direct manner, is that being rational, logical or conventional does not represent the final step in one's possible development. Rationality is a small window through which to view the world. Just as there is a stage before reaching the rational, logical or conventional, there is also a stage after.

If we take any logical progression — *All men are mortal, Socrates is a man, therefore Socrates is mortal* — we can see that it is much like a single path which we precede down step-by-step. Now imagine, instead of standing on one of these paths viewing the logical conclusion of just one of these progressions, our perspective is now raised up so as to look down from above. From here we can see multiple paths of logic, each dealing with a specific aspect of a single larger theme. Instead of merely dealing with a step-by-step process leading to a logical conclusion, we are now able to contemplate simultaneously a multitude of logical conclusions dealing with different aspects of the same theme, weighing the pros and cons of each and thereby reaching a meta-conclusion — an embracive macro-conclusion drawn from multiple micro-conclusions. And the higher our perspective, the more logical paths that can be included in our consideration. Like a fabric woven from individual strands of different colours, this meta-conclusion would transcend each of the individual logical paths that it had been drawn from and would perhaps even appear illogical, when compared to any single one of them. This ability to consider multiple paths of logic simultaneously is known as "vision-logic" and although not yet trans-logical or trans-rational it is a useful illustration of how certain thinking modalities go beyond the limitations of others.

Although much of modern science is at pains to admit it, and many contemporary approaches to spirituality admit it perhaps too eagerly, there do exist cognitive modalities on the other side of rationality and logic. And so just as there are pre-rational and pre-logical modes of thinking, there are also trans-rational and trans-logical modes — inspiration, insight, intuition, contemplation, revelation, and in fact true wisdom, all lie not in the pre-rational, nor even in the rational realm, but on the other side of rational: the trans-rational. What was Christ's call to repentance if not a call to transcend the mind's rational and logical limitations? The word translated from the Ancient Greek as "repentance" is *metanoia*, literally "going beyond the mind". The meditation of the Buddhist, Hindu and Jain, the *wu-wei* of the Taoist, the *koan* study of Zen, the *dhikr* of the Sufi and the contemplative prayer of the Christian mystic are all practices designed to take the practitioner beyond themselves into trans-personal and trans-rational cognitive dimensions. Perhaps this threefold distinction is what the controversial guru, Osho, was referring to when he said: "Before you are wise; after you are wise. In between you are otherwise".[2] The pre-rational toddler is guided by the wisdom of instinct and the awakened adept is guided by the integrated wisdom of trans-rational intuition and insight. Only the conventional man of reason in the middle has just his limited thinking mind to guide him — out of touch with his true instinct on the one hand and not yet in touch with his trans-rational intuitive faculties on the other.

However, the tendency for us to see things dualistically is a powerful one, fostered by oversimplification of the world and the conventional categories of language that we most commonly use to describe it. Day/night, black/white, big/small, short/tall — it splits an infinite variety of phenomena into two neat little categories and leads us into a mental muddle whenever we do so. This two valued, "either/or" Aristotelian system of reasoning, when faced with something that appears to not be logical, sees only the illogical — something that is not rational is considered irrational. And at a glance, this twofold model appears to pose no real problem. It is convincing and coherent. Only when we realise that there are two radically different sides to "illogical", "irrational" and "unconventional" can we begin to grasp the immensity of the error of forcing these things to conform to our dualistic propensities.

As is often the case, the problem here arises from defining things by what they are not, rather than what they are. In the category of "plants", for instance, are ferns, oak trees and daisies. Although very different in many ways, they also have certain things in common other than merely their label of categorisation — they are all carbon-based life forms, they grow, photosynthesise, require water and so on. But in the category of "non-plants" one could list pelicans, pearls, pencils and a whole host of other things with perhaps little or nothing in common other than the fact that they are not plants. In much the same way, in the category of "logic" are all the things that share the quality of being logical whereas that which is "illogical" is predicated on no shared quality other than that generated by the label of classification. We confuse the common lack of a shared quality for a shared quality in itself, which it isn't.

So while both the small child and the sage may demonstrate behaviour or ideas that are unconventional and that appear illogical or irrational, when we start to tease apart the confusion of our own systems of categorisation, we can begin to see that their "irrationality", "illogic" and "unconventionality" is itself of two very different types. The small child is pre-rational, pre-logical and pre-conventional and has yet to understand and embody these things; he or she is moving towards grasping them as they grow and learn. The sage, however, acts from a cognitive space that is trans-rational, trans-logical and trans-conventional. They have learnt, understood and embodied these things. They know when to apply them and when they are appropriate. They are also not limited by them and have moved beyond them into more expansive cognitive realms. This is just what was meant when the contemporary crazy-wisdom master, Chögyam Trungpa, said:

> crazy wisdom does not occur unless there is a basic understanding of things, a knowledge of how things function as they are. There has to be trust in the normal functioning of karmic cause and effect. Having been highly and completely trained, then there is enormous room for crazy wisdom. According to that logic, wisdom does not exactly go crazy; but on top of the basic logic or basic norm, craziness as higher sanity, higher power, or higher magic, can exist.[3]

This confusion of before and after; the "pre" with the "trans" phases; the inability to distinguish between them and realise their differences; the collapsing of these two into a single homogenous "non" category, is the basis of the pre/trans fallacy.

Crazy-wisdom then is not logical, not rational and not at all conventional — it is beyond them. Those caught in the grasp of the pre/trans fallacy though are blind to this and instead will tend to do one of two things — they will either glorify or denigrate the "non" category in its entirety depending on their own perceptual prejudice.

And so, on the one hand we have the reductionists such as Freud and his followers, as well as most of modern academia, philosophy and science. To them, rationality and logic are the pinnacle of human development and so all "trans" stages are reduced to being just "pre" stages and with this reductionism, all mystical, transcendent, trans-personal or non-dual states are downgraded to mere infantile, pre-personal regressive states of narcissistic, undifferentiated adualism. When presented with the elevated pronouncements of a true crazy-wisdom master, they hear only the babblings of a madman or the nonsense of a child. On the other hand, we have the elevationists such as Jung and his followers, as well as many of the Romantic philosophers and much of the modern spirituality movement. So enamoured are they with the mystical, transcendent modes of being that they see only that, everywhere. Unwittingly they elevate all "pre" stages into "trans" stages and will often be heard advocating for the return to a childlike or primitive state, seeing that as somehow beyond mere logic and rationality. In turn, they, when presented with the babblings of a madman or the nonsense of a child, may well insist that it is a pure utterance of crazy-wisdom.

As we can see, once familiar with the pre/trans fallacy, both perspectives contain a grain of truth. However, their paradigms are lacking an essential distinction and are flawed by the inability to discern between the before and after of rationality and logic, instead lumping them all together into one category and then either raising it up to be praised or tearing it down to be cursed.

Crazy-wisdom is not worldly wisdom. It is not logical, not rational and not at all conventional. It is not the pre-conventional, pre-rational gobbledegook of the small child or the illogical ravings of a madman; nor is it the carefully considered logical declarations of the philosopher or scientist. Crazy-wisdom dwells above all of these. It is the grey area beyond black and white — the place of nuance, context, perspective and appropriateness (or complete lack thereof should that be appropriate). It has no clear-cut and pre-agreed rules. It is fluid, spontaneous and extemporaneous. It lacks all familiar landmarks and has no safe harbour. It is the pure natural flow of the universe manifest through man, inspiring awe or fear, wonder or bewilderment, depending on the observer's proximity and perspective; much like a raging sea or a mighty storm. And like a force of nature it is uncontrived, unconstrained and ultimately, unpredictable.

It is the place of transcendence, growth and expurgation — of purification in the fire of merciless authenticity. Forever outside of one's comfort zone, crazy-wisdom remains the domain of only the select spiritual connoisseur who is willing to play the fool so as to not fool himself any longer.

> Having achieved the power of conceptual thought,
> man is called upon to go beyond it.[4]
>
> — WEI WU WEI

The Crazy-Wisdom Adept

The term "crazy-wisdom" is generally attributed to the twentieth-century Tibetan Buddhist master, Chögyam Trungpa, although the essential idea it encapsulates is far more ancient. Trungpa was himself a modern embodiment of crazy-wisdom for many and, as can be expected, much controversy still surrounds his life and teaching methods. The English term was his translation of the Tibetan *drubnyon* — a philosophy that according to one Buddhist scholar "traditionally combines exceptional insight and impressive magical power with a flamboyant disregard for conventional behaviour".[5]

Although the philosophical foundations of *drubnyon* can be traced back to the Indian adept Padmasambhava (credited with having brought Buddhism to Tibet in the eighth century and the founder of the Nyingma or "ancient" tradition) it perhaps found its fullest expression in the lives and teachings of the tenth-century *mahāsiddhas*, or Great Adepts, the founders of the Kagyu lineage, another of the four main schools of Tibetan Buddhism. Tilopa, Naropa, Marpa, Milarepa and Gampopa, also known as the "Five Founding Masters" of the Kagyu school, would all no doubt be considered to be stark raving mad were they to be judged by modern standards of conventionality and morality. Their fierce dedication to their guru's instructions and spiritual practices as well as their uncompromising

13

authenticity so exceeded any of the considerations that normally cause people to mask their true intentions or suppress their natural inclinations, that the result was at times terrific and at other times terrifying. Fascination, awe, adulation, fear, disgust, confusion — their presence would arouse anything but indifference. Their rejection of both religious and societal norms in the service of truth, authenticity and the ultimate freedom of realisation made them targets for the established institutions of their time. To the status quo they posed a present and real threat and were dutifully marginalised by all those who simply wished to perform their rituals, repeat their mantras, and go through the motions of their chosen practices in peace.

This Tibetan-styled crazy-wisdom found its precedents within the Indian tantric tradition and the even earlier *mahāsiddhas* such as Saraha, Nagarjuna and Maitripa. They too were the outcasts and spiritual misfits of their time; flouting the rules of the rigid caste system, living in charnel grounds and renouncing the comfortable life of a respectable religious in favour of condemnation from all quarters. Their realisation, instead of being silently written down in sutras or quietly spoken in discourse, was sung in spontaneous songs or *dohas*. Amongst them were not only kings, princesses and Brahmins, but also cobblers, potters, shepherds, hermits, cooks and housewives. In fact, the only thing that this motley bunch had in common was their unwavering dedication to Truth. This was their only qualification and the only one they needed. They were indeed the very embodiment of crazy-wisdom.

In *Journey Without Goal*, Chögyam Trungpa defines crazy-wisdom as:

absolute perceptiveness, with fearlessness and bluntness. Fundamentally, it is being wise, but not holding to particular doctrines or disciplines or formats. There aren't any books to follow. Rather, there is endless spontaneity taking place.[6]

And in his book *Crazy Wisdom* he tells us:

> Crazy wisdom knows no limitation and no logic regarding the form it takes. A mirror will not compromise with you if you are ugly. And there is no point in blaming the mirror or breaking it. The more you break the mirror the more reflections of your face come about from further pieces of the mirror.[7]

The crazy-wisdom adept as teacher must use any means at his disposal to confront the student with their own folly. They must do whatever it takes to dissipate their illusions, break down their conditioning and shake the novice awake, sometimes violently. There is a Zen saying that "a tactful teacher is no teacher at all". Just as a student who is not prepared to have their sensibilities offended is no student at all, a teacher who is not prepared to offend the sensibilities of their students, is not an effective teacher. The job of waking up is not, for the most part, the acquiring of new knowledge but rather the tearing down of all the false knowledge that one currently takes as real and useful. As Rumi once said: "Recognise that unlearning is the highest form of learning". Or as Idries Shah bluntly put it: "You must empty out the dirty water before you fill the pitcher with clean". Giving up what one has striven to acquire, whether possessions or knowledge, is no easy task. Giving up what one has, or more importantly, what one takes themselves to *be* is what the ego fears the most and the resistance is at times fierce. Therefore it takes one who is equally fierce and prepared to go to whatever lengths necessary to tame the wild beast of imaginary selfhood.

As for the crazy-wisdom adept, Trungpa tells us:

> A description for a crazy-wisdom person found in the scriptures is: 'He subdues whoever needs to be subdued and destroys whoever needs to be destroyed'. The idea here is that whatever your neurosis demands, when you relate with a crazy-wisdom person you get hit back with that. Crazy wisdom presents you with a mirror reflection.[8]

The crazy-wisdom teacher is seemingly crazy because life is crazy and his student, crazy — although most of their own craziness is initially unacknowledged. How else can someone be shown their own face, warts and all? Just as it is not the wart in the mirror that is ugly but rather the one on the face being reflected, the behaviour of the adept is not to be blamed as it is only a mere reflection, shown for the sake of glimpsing one's own madness and folly.

Although the term has come to us as a translation of a Tibetan concept, crazy-wisdom is a universal phenomenon that can be found throughout all of the world's Great Wisdom Traditions. It can be found amongst the Zen and Taoist masters, the Holy Fools and Fools-for-Christ of Christianity, the Old Testament prophets and Hasidic masters of Judaism, the Sufis of Islam, the *tantrikas*, *mahāsiddhas*, *bāuls*, and *avadhūtas* of India as well as the Hellenistic Greeks. In fact, it is difficult to find a spiritual tradition where it has not raised its crazy head. It is also a common thread that runs through the world's mythology and folklore in the archetype of the Trickster; from Hermes of the Greeks to Loki of Norse mythology or Coyote of the Native Americans. The Trickster in his more mundane manifestations is the unrestrained and untameable spirit of spontaneity, creativity and freedom; the champion of the common folk who makes a mockery of senseless rules and unconscious behaviour, as well as the authorities who wish to establish and impose these conventions for their own benefit. In his more refined aspects, the Trickster is the crazy-wisdom adept whose transgressions of the societal norms are due to having transcended them. He is the unintentional spokesperson for the non-dual vision of Reality — an all-embracing perspective that sounds like madness to all those still stuck in the dualistic mire of selfhood. Crazy-wisdom then is used here in its broader sense — one that pays no allegiance to any one particular tradition. It is deeper and more universal than that; a result of the transcending of personhood and its limitations no matter what language and terms are used to describe it. In this sense, crazy-wisdom can be defined simply as "an authentic manifestation of wisdom that defies or contradicts conventional logic and decorum". Although there are many things that defy or contradict conventional logic or decorum, few of them represent true manifestations of crazy-wisdom, and so, scattered across the broad crazy-wisdom landscape we are apt to find many casualties: madmen, substandard imitators, as well as those who are looking to justify their own antinomian indulgences and dress them up as something more elevated than the base animalistic urges that they are revealed to be on deeper analysis. To help further discern the true crazy-wisdom adept from the rest, we can distil their essence into five key elements:

1. Statements and behaviour that appear to be irrational, illogical, unpredictable or paradoxical.
2. An apparent disregard for conventional norms and at times an outright transgression of them.
3. An overarching benevolence towards others with a genuine concern for their wellbeing.
4. An explicit or implicit concern with matters of a spiritual nature; God, the Divine, the Absolute, the transcendent, and so on.

5. Attainment on the chosen path such as redemption, liberation, awakening, enlightenment, and so on.

Perhaps the essential defining factor of crazy-wisdom is the notion, held by others, that the person has attained to the heights of spiritual accomplishment and therefore that their behaviour cannot be adequately judged by conventional standards. Without that clear distinguishing feature of "wisdom", as might be expected, the person is generally considered to be merely "crazy" with nothing of value in their bizarre behaviour. I would also add that the true crazy-wisdom adept is one who unites in their very being these five key elements. Hence if only the first two are present, you may simply be dealing with a crazy man and if only the last three are present, you may simply be dealing with a wise man. At any rate, should one or more of these elements be missing, then proceed with caution. And if all five of these elements are present, then proceed with utmost caution — your very sense of self may be at stake.

Divine Madness

So then the ancients testify to the fact
that god-sent madness is a finer thing than man-
made sanity.[9]

— PLATO

Closely related to crazy-wisdom and often taken to be synonymous with it, is "divine madness". Known to the ancient Greeks as *theia mania* it refers to the spontaneous, unconventional or outrageous behaviour manifested by someone under the influence of a deep religious or spiritual experience and usually combines and expresses the first four elements of crazy-wisdom. What is often missing however is the fifth — the stabilised abiding in a higher cognitive state demonstrated by the crazy-wisdom adept. Divine madness then is often demonstrated by those still on the Path, the seekers of Truth and those desperately yearning after God, and is often marked by moods of profound interior absorption, ecstatic frenzy or extreme demonstrations of love and devotion. In his dialogue *Phaedrus*, Plato clearly distinguishes "two kinds of madness, the one caused by sicknesses of a human sort, the other coming about from a divinely caused reversal of our customary ways of behaving".[10]

Through the voice of his master, Socrates, he describes this second kind, divine madness, as the condition of being possessed by a god and describes four different types: prophetic frenzy, mystical revelation, poetic inspiration and ecstatic love, depending on the god in question — Apollo, Dionysus, the Muses and Aphrodite respectively. He is also careful to distinguish this divine madness from its mundane namesake and elevates it, not only above conventional madness but even above "man-made sanity".

In this he is in keeping with our earlier assertions that crazy-wisdom, like divine madness, is not merely unconventional or irrational, but rather trans-conventional and trans-rational. As we shall see, the two are closely aligned, sometimes confused and often difficult to discern one from the other. Ultimately their differentiation lies in the most difficult to ascertain of the five elements stated above — the spiritual attainment of the one in question. When Diogenes roamed the streets of Athens in broad daylight with a lighted lamp in search of "an honest man", was he in the grips of divine madness or were these the shock tactics of a crazy-wisdom adept? We will almost certainly never know. When Ramakrishna scandalised his fellow Brahmins by ecstatically anointing and worshipping his own wife as the Divine Mother rather than the Kāli statue in the temple, was it intentional — the act of a crazy-wisdom master — or was he lost in a divine rapture? No doubt it is impossible to say. For this reason, the two terms are often interchangeable and the difference between them is sometimes very difficult to discern, depending ultimately on attainment. Hence the crazy actions of a practitioner lost in an ecstatic swoon or under the influence of an intense transpersonal experience would more appropriately be called "divine madness", whereas the crazy actions performed from a stabilised abiding in a non-dual state, with complete control over one's faculties, would here be considered to be the truest manifestation of "crazy-wisdom".

The Great Chain of Being

I died as mineral and became a plant,
I died as plant and rose to animal.
I died as animal and I was Man.
Why should I fear? When was I less by dying?
Yet once more I shall die as Man, to soar
With angels blest; but even from angelhood
I must pass on: all except God doth perish.
When I have sacrificed my angel-soul,
I shall become what no mind e'er conceived.
O let me not exist! For Non-existence
Proclaims in organ tones "To him we shall return!"[11]

— RUMI

To further illustrate the difference between these two terms it would help for us to map out more clearly the spiritual terrain of which they are features. All of the world's Great Traditions have spoken, if not explicitly then implicitly, about what has been called the "Great Chain of Being". Arthur Lovejoy in his magnum opus of the same name tells us:

the phrase which I have taken for the title was long one of the most famous in the vocabulary of Occidental philosophy, science, and reflective poetry; and the conception which in modern times came to be expressed by this or similar phrases has been one of the half-dozen most potent and persistent presuppositions in Western thought. It was, in fact, until not much more than a century ago, probably the most widely familiar conception of the general scheme of things, of the constitutive pattern of the universe.[12]

Although knowledge of it can be found wherever human culture has developed, the idea was most explicitly developed by Plato and Aristotle, reaching its fullest expression in the work of Plotinus and the Neo-Platonists. Simply stated, it recognises that reality is composed of an interwoven hierarchy of discrete and distinct levels, planes, or realms, each with their own unique qualities and nature, and that the universe unfolds in a series of discrete stages with each senior level transcending but including the elements of the junior; uniting and organising those elements to bring about a qualitative quantum leap — a novel emergent whose properties differ entirely from its predecessor. From matter, to body, to mind, to soul, to Spirit — each higher level enfolds or envelops the lower, bringing increased organisation and complexity as well as a radically novel nature. And so, although the animal body includes matter in its constitution, it also brings forth the emergent qualities of sensation, feeling and emotion. The human mind includes sensation, feeling and emotion but brings forth reason and logic, something not found in rocks, plants or animals. The soul, in turn, includes the mind in its makeup but brings forth native intuition, transcendent vision, illumination, archetypes and so on, with none of these found in any of the previous levels. There is a Kabbalistic aphorism that makes this same point in a far more concise and poetic manner: "a stone becomes a plant; a plant a beast; the beast a man; a man a spirit; and the spirit a god". There are many ways in which the universe uses this hierarchical, or holarchical structure — a term used by Arthur Koestler as each level is composed of holons or "whole parts" (whole at their own level, but parts of the level above them). Whether fundamental particles, atoms, molecules, and elements; or cells, organs, bodies, families and societies, the Great Chain of Being is everywhere. Even the most ancient and archaic cultures had their own formulation of this in the threefold hierarchy of Earth, Man and Heaven. This is a conception of the Great Chain we are only too familiar with today thanks to the marvels of modern marketing whose successful repackage has made it into a household brand with the catchier slogan of "Mind, Body and Spirit", or rather Body, Mind and Spirit to present it in its correct order.

Earth, Man, Heaven; body, mind, spirit; physical, psychological, spiritual; matter, mind, soul; gross, subtle, causal — this threefold conception is the most common and indeed the simplest categorisation of the Great Chain of Being and when understood in this context, it is quite clear that Man is a multidimensional being whose sweep and scope reaches both down into the discrete, quantifiable solidity of the physical realm of matter, and up into the subtle and ungraspable perceptions of the psychological realm of the mind, as well as the transcendent illuminations of the soul and apperceptive witnessing of pure causal Spirit.

What Goes Down Must Come Up

The implications of this are far-reaching and one of them in particular inspired Plato and the Neo-Platonists to write volumes in an attempt to refine their understanding of it. In all cases, the Great Chain of Being is represented as a vertical hierarchy — whether the macrocosmic *scala naturae*, or "ladder of being", Jacob's Ladder, the Kabbalistic Tree of Life, or the microcosmic chakra system whose "ladder" is the spinal column. This vertical *axis mundi* permits a flow or flux of influence that is of two kinds — the first is a Descent, an effluence of the One into the Many, of Spirit into matter, of unity into multiplicity, from the causal to the subtle to the gross. The second is an Ascent, a return of the Many to the One, of matter to Spirit, of multiplicity to unity, from the gross to the subtle to the causal. In Genesis we are told that "the earth was without form, and void" until "the Spirit of God moved upon the face of the waters" (Genesis 1:2) and descended to bring forth the world and everything in it. In the Vedic tradition this descending animating force is the Divine Mother, *Shakti*, much like the *Shekhinah* of Judaism that issues forth from Transcendent Spirit — the *Ein Sof* — and animates in its descent the ten *sephiroth*, or emanations, of the Kabbalistic Tree of Life, becoming progressively denser until reaching *Malkuth*, the world of physical matter. Without this Descent, there would be no world and without Ascent, there would be no point in having a world. After all, it was God's descent to earth as Christ that gave rise to the possibility of redemption and the return or Ascent back to God. Up and down, Ascent and Descent, the two go hand-in-hand; they are inseparable, as the awakened sages and non-dual traditions of every persuasion have duly noted. The *Heart Sutra* states: "Form is emptiness, emptiness is form",[13] but what is "form" if not "this-worldly" and what is "emptiness" if not "otherworldly"? Essentially it tells us that these two, are in reality not two. As does Shankara's famous threefold declaration: "The world is an illusion; only Brahman is real; Brahman is the world",[14] which leads with two otherworldly statements before transcending them both in its third and final affirmation of non-duality, saying essentially, like the *Heart Sutra*, "the otherworldly *is* this-worldly" — "Brahman is the world". And when we analyse the laconic Zen aphorism, "First mountains are mountains, then mountains are not mountains, finally mountains are mountains again",[15] we can see that once again, its three parts represent the Descending, Ascending and Transcending perspectives respectively.

Unfortunately, for the most part, history has been written by the dualists and reveals a long-running and ongoing philosophical battle between them. On one side, the Ascenders, the advocates of otherworldliness whose aim is to transcend this illusory realm of shadows and escape into their idealised otherworld of *nirvana*, heaven, or paradise; and on the other side, the Descenders, the advocates of this-worldliness whose idea of spirituality is to live more fully, deeply and viscerally down here in the physical realm, in these animal bodies with their passions and pleasures. To the Ascenders, God is transcendent, above and beyond this realm of pain and suffering, whereas to the Descenders, He is immanent, beneath and within every stone, flower, breeze and ray of sunshine. He is this very world — its joy and delight. Of course both of them are right in their assertions, and only wrong in their partiality. They err then by considering God as essentially absent from the world in the otherworldly view and by considering there to be no God beyond this immediate world in the this-worldly view.

Although the struggle between the Ascenders and Descenders has been ongoing since time immemorial, the Ascenders have had the louder voice and, as Lovejoy rightly points out, their otherworldly position:

> has, in one form or another, been the dominant official philosophy of the larger part of civilized mankind through most of its history.[16]

This predisposition towards otherworldliness should come as no surprise. After all, if this world is full of suffering, pain, separation and death, it would make sense to seek the remedy to those things elsewhere. To the Christians this means Heaven; to the Muslims, *Jannah* or Paradise; to the Jews, "The World to Come"; to the Buddhists, *nirvana*; to the Jains, *siddhaloka*; and so on. It is safe to say that mankind has struggled for millennia to escape what is. And it is this struggle to Ascend, and equally the struggle to Descend, that when taken to extremes has been labelled "divine madness". Hidden beneath this blanket term then are actually two different types of divine madness, each the result of extreme spiritual strivings in opposite directions. The first of these — "otherworldly divine madness" — manifests as acts of fanatical asceticism and self-abnegation, such as St Daniel the Stylite's 33 years spent atop a pillar in the desert; or acts of devotion that go beyond what might be considered appropriate or normal, such as Naropa's offering to his guru, Tilopa, of a *mandala* made with his blood and severed fingers. The second of these — "this-worldly divine madness" — instead appears as extreme hedonism or perversion, such as the debaucheries and sexual practices of *tantrikas*; or acts that to most people are simply disgusting, such as Swami Nityananda's penchant for eating cowpats. The first is motivated by the desire to escape the here-and-now in order to find God, and the second, by the desire to find God even in the deepest, darkest depths of the here-and-now. One thing common to both are bouts of either ecstatic exhilaration when God's presence is felt or dejection and despair at His absence.

Just as these two forms of divine madness arise from a temporary imbalance in one's spiritual disposition, crazy-wisdom instead arises from perfect balance and is the result of harmony between the Ascending and Descending currents. Crazy-wisdom is the natural disposition of the Awakened One who has transcended all limitations, restrictions and restraints and who sees through the multitude of dualisms that govern the life of the common man. It is the liberated play of one in perfect harmony. It is, however, impossible to speak of one without the other as many of the saints and sages who ended up as crazy-wisdom masters, passed through the fires of divine madness on their way to Perfection. We might well say then that crazy-wisdom is forged in the fires of divine madness and is for those lucky enough to have made it through.

From Foolery to Mastery

If thou hast never been a fool, be sure thou wilt never be a wise man.

— WILLIAM MAKEPEACE THACKERAY

An astute observation made by the founders of NLP (Neuro-Linguistic Programming) is that there are four stages to the learning of any new skill or the acquiring of new knowledge. They are: unconscious incompetence, conscious incompetence, conscious competence and unconscious competence.

If we consider any acquired skill such as learning to play a musical instrument, it can be observed that prior to ever having picked up the instrument, the budding musician-to-be will tend to seriously underestimate the task at hand and equally overestimate their ability to perform. This is perhaps due to having seen just how easy it looks for trained musicians to play their instruments and noticing the ease with which their fingers find the correct notes. This is the phase of unconscious incompetence — we are incompetent at playing the instrument and absolutely unaware just how incompetent we are. Then comes the time for us to play the instrument for the first time. Quickly our illusions are shattered as we struggle to force our fingers to obey our will. The instrument feels awkward rather than the natural extension of our limbs we imagined it to be, and from it we manage only to elicit a very inharmonious din. In doing so, we become aware of just how bad we are, hence the second phase — conscious incompetence. Over time and through persistent application, we start to begin to actually play the instrument, but clumsily. Initially we have to play from our head, thinking about our posture, our fingers, the notes, the chords, the timing, all at the same time. It involves struggle and is taxing and tiring. Although we start to acquire some competence, it is all very cerebral, very conscious. It lacks ease and naturalness and only comes through great exertion, but at least we can play, sort of. This is the stage of conscious competence — we are beginning to be competent but only with great conscious effort. Finally, once we have mastered something we arrive at the stage of unconscious competence where we no longer have to think about what we are doing. It is all done of its own accord — completely unconsciously. We can look up from the instrument, talk or sing whilst playing, and our unconscious mind takes care of the rest. The important point to note from this fourfold observation of how we learn, is that for the first two and potentially three stages, we must accept that we will at times look, and more importantly feel, foolish. During these stages we will make many mistakes, we will feel incompetent and stupid, and if we are not prepared to look and feel like a fool, we will never become a master. When it comes to the acquisition of a new language, it is well known that the greatest stumbling block to doing so is embarrassment. We so hate to look like fools but simply must if we are ever to do anything worthwhile whatsoever. We must fail many times to get good at anything. In fact, the master has failed more times than the beginner has ever tried. This is often a hard truth to face and one that has perhaps made all of us, at one time or another, choose inaction and avoidance, over expansion, growth and progress; the safety of opting out, over the inevitable moments of looking like a complete idiot. If on the other hand, we are completely at ease with idiocy and being seen by others to be a fool, then a whole world of possibilities opens up to us. From then on, the path to the mastery of anything whatsoever is merely a case of application and persistence. Perhaps this is what William Blake meant when he wrote: "If the fool would persist in his folly he would become wise".[17]

For those who choose the path of the wise-fool then, the sky is the limit. Only those who care nothing of what others may think of them are utterly free to become masters. Only those that can first go beyond their petty limitations will be able to transcend the more consequential and significant ones later. If the common man lives in dilemma, then one must be prepared to be something other than common in order to escape the dilemma, and for the most part, this something "other" to the common man appears to be weird, extreme, strange or foolish.

Further to the mere acceptance of looking a fool to others and establishing equanimity in the face of public opinion, is the staged and contrived attempt to arouse and even incite the scorn and derision of one's peers. We can see this most clearly in the behaviour of the Fools for Christ or the practitioners of the Sufi Path of Blame (to be discussed later). As a practice to denigrate and negate the importance of the self, they bring the negative judgement of others upon themselves so as to intentionally develop this equanimous fortitude rather than merely leaving it to chance. If the persistent idea of selfhood is what stands in the way of the ultimate flow state of divine union, then the self, or at least the sense that there is one, must be done away with at any cost. What better way to do this than by cutting ties with everything that makes having a self worthwhile. Approbation, respect, esteem, status, appreciation, praise, acceptance, approval, admiration — these are the building blocks of the self, the very things that give rise to its existence and lead to its persistence. They lead to pride, conceit and arrogance in their most extreme forms and self-satisfaction and vanity in their milder forms; all of them toxic to the purification process of an authentic spiritual path.

When it comes to the religious or spiritual impulse then, it follows that one must go beyond standard religious dogmas if real progress is to be made, for if liberation were to be found in those exoteric doctrines, then we should see more cases of awakened individuals within their ranks — and we do not. For this reason the Sufis have a saying:

> None attains to the Ultimate Truth until a thousand honest people have called him an infidel.[18]

Words, Words, Words

The purpose of words is to convey ideas.
When the ideas are grasped, the words are forgotten.
Where can I find a man who has forgotten words?
He is the one I would like to talk to.[19]

— CHUANG TZU

All the world's Great Wisdom Traditions recognise that real knowledge and true spiritual insight cannot be effectively transmitted via the medium of words and language. When it comes to the clear communication of transcendent realisation, words fail miserably at the task, but in the day-to-day of our lives, they have become our world. We can only share the thoughts in our heads with each other if we have a common language in which to communicate them, which of course seems obvious until you take a moment to reflect on what our world would be, not if we were merely struck dumb, which is only the loss of expressing language, but if we were struck language-less and knew not a single word. What would become of our inner lives? For the most part, words have taken on such importance for us that we live not in the world, but merely in our own personal description of the world. The words we call something are, more often than not, of more importance to our actual lives than the nature of the thing itself. It is no wonder that there is a close etymological connection between the words *spell* and *grimoire* to *spelling* and *grammar*. For these reasons we too often fall into the error of ascribing to them an independence and character far beyond their merit and only when we stop to really think does it become quite clear that words are not the things they represent. Or as Zen Master Chi Hsien so elegantly put it: "A cake drawn on paper can never satisfy hunger".[20]

But although the map is not the territory and the menu is not the dish, when caught up in life, we are almost fooled into thinking they are. Meanings are interdependent, differing from person to person and even fluctuating within the same person from moment to moment with passing moods. For practical purposes, words rarely pose too much of a problem, however, the more abstract and subjective the communication, the more they fall victim to misinterpretation. Of what use could they possibly be then in evoking and expressing the subtle and sublime, the mystical and metaphysical, the Eternal or the Absolute? Plato had this to say on the matter:

> But this much at any rate I can affirm about any present or future writers who pretend to knowledge of the matters with which I concern myself, whether they claim to have been taught by me or by a third party or to have discovered the truth for themselves; in my judgement it is impossible that they should have any understanding of the subject. No treatise by me concerning it exists or ever will exist. It is not something that can be put into words like other branches of learning; only after long partnership in a common life devoted to this very thing does truth flash upon the soul, like a flame kindled by a leaping spark, and once it is born there it nourishes itself thereafter.[21]

And the great sixth-century Christian monk, Pseudo-Dionysius, was even more emphatic when in his *Mystical Theology* he wrote:

> The fact is that the more we take flight upward, the more our words are confined to the ideas we are capable of

forming; so that now as we plunge into that darkness which is beyond intellect, we shall find ourselves not simply running short of words but actually speechless and unknowing... But my argument now rises from what is below up to the transcendent, and the more it climbs, the more language falters, and when it has passed up and beyond the ascent, it will turn silent completely, since it will finally be at one with him who is indescribable.[22]

Even the greatest love poetry comes nowhere near to the feeling of being hopelessly in love. In fact, the extent to which it can arouse one's own latent amorousness is directly proportional to one's lived experience of love. In this then, words serve as mere reminders rather than transmitters of something new. In the same way, the richer one's palette of spiritual experience, the more effective the signifiers that attempt to communicate and elucidate the more subtle and abstract referents of the spiritual domain. In this, as in other fields, the deeper one's knowledge, the deeper the words may penetrate and the less likely they are to mislead. Unfortunately — and this is where most of the trouble starts — the opposite of this is also the case. The novice, due to unfamiliarity with the referents, unwittingly twists words and distorts context, making a hermeneutical hash out of a text that a more seasoned practitioner can quite easily grasp. It is this very principle that has led masters of all persuasions to guide their students towards truth in an indirect manner. Such is the fickle nature of language that something shared with a novice may at times sound like a lie from the point of view of the initiate and vice versa. The path to adeptship then, entails a progression from untruth to truth, from deception almost, to clarity. The field of modern science has done little to tiptoe around this issue, instead choosing to call it outright a "lie-to-children" — a simplified explanation of a complex subject as a means of imparting the basic idea to laymen and newcomers.

As defined by the creators of the term, it is "a statement that is false, but which nevertheless leads the child's mind towards a more accurate explanation, one that the child will only be able to appreciate if it has been primed with the lie".[23]

Just as the instructions given to a baby learning to crawl, bear little to no resemblance to those given to a toddler learning to walk, the pointers on the path are stage-specific, or at least they are meant to be. Any attempt to do otherwise would be to confuse, confound and even arrest the natural developmental process. In making this same point in his own delightful style, Wei Wu Wei tells us:

> ...in early stages teaching can only be given via a series of untruths diminishing in inveracity in ratio to the pupil's apprehension of the falsity of what he is being taught.[24]

For this reason Christ spoke to the common folk only in parables and reserved the deeper, more direct teachings for his disciples, in private. Many traditions stagger their teachings through a series of initiations that are only given when the teacher considers the student to be ready, and in the Western Esoteric Tradition a similar method of damage control is achieved through a system of progressive grading with the teachings of the higher grades even forbidden to those still at the lower ones. The Tantric tradition of India even went so far as to invent a new language in an attempt to keep sacred knowledge from the profane — a "secret language, that great convention of the yoginis, which the sravakas and others cannot unriddle"[25], the *Hevajra Tantra* states. Known as *saṃdhyā-bhāṣā*, or "twilight language", this secret, polysemic symbolic system was reserved for their most confidential teachings and understood only by initiates. Despite these precautions, we now have at our fingertips, accessible to serious practitioners and frivolous dabblers alike, the complete corpus of world scripture and religious writings. Modern technology and translation efforts have liberated them from the grip and guidance of their guardians and the controls and contexts of the living traditions they were once exclusively a part of, and now we are free to access knowledge that is beyond our ken with all the consequent dangers and delights that this entails.

In *The Gateless Gate*, a collection and commentary on 49 *koans* by the Buddhist Ch'an master, Mumon, *koan* number 25 quotes the master Kyozan as saying: "The truth of Mahayana is transcendent, above words and thoughts. Do you understand?" Mumon's commentary tells us: "When he opens his mouth he is lost. When he seals his mouth he is lost. If he does not open it, if he does not seal it, he is 108,000 miles from truth".[26] In another instance Mumon tells us even more bluntly: "When the mouth opens, all are wrong".[27]

And herein lies another element of the sage's madness — his reliance on words to say what words cannot say. It is no wonder that paradox abounds in the writings they have left us. Nevertheless, when one begins to understand the nature of language, its limitations and scope, it can be turned from a stumbling block into a stepping stone and a means to elevate one's vision.

The Way of Affirmation

The first and most common form that language takes is that of affirmation. Known theologically as the *via positiva*, or the cataphatic way, this involves giving positive statements as to the nature of God or the divine. It tells us what something *is*; the Gospel of John tells us *God is love*; Brahman is *sat-chit-ananda* or *Being-Consciousness-Beatitude*; the transcendentals — the properties of Being — are *the Good, the True and the Beautiful*. All of these statements while explicitly affirming certain qualities, also at the same time, implicitly negate others. By saying that Being is *Good, True and Beautiful*, is at the same time saying that it is not Bad, False and Ugly and while this may be a useful aspect of affirmation when talking about the world of gross objects, it becomes more and more misleading when we move from the gross to the subtle and the causal. If I say "the water is hot" I do actually wish to say, by implication, that it is not cold. There is an explicit affirmation and an implicit negation, and both of them are true. At other times, however, what is implicitly negated can be misleading. While "the tail of the peacock is blue" is a true statement in itself, if it is not also explicitly affirmed that it is "green", "yellow", "iridescent" and so on *as well*, then our initial statement is more misleading than it is enlightening. Just think then what errors arise when speaking of God either as the Great One who embodies all things — which by necessity includes their opposites — or as the Absolute, which utterly transcends all attributes and categories of classification.

The Way of Negation

For these reasons, many saints, sages and adepts have preferred the use of the *via negativa* or apophatic way — the way of negation. Pseudo-Dionysius, in the penultimate chapter of his *Mystical Theology*, quoted above, tells us:

> The Cause of all is above all and is not inexistent, lifeless, speechless, mindless. It is not a material body, and hence has neither shape nor form, quality, quantity, or weight. It is not in any place and can neither be seen nor be touched. It is neither perceived nor is it perceptible. It suffers neither disorder nor disturbance and is overwhelmed by no earthly passion. It is not powerless and subject to the disturbances caused by sense perception. It endures no deprivation of light. It passes through no change, decay, division, loss, no ebb and flow, nothing of which the sense may be aware. None of all this can either be identified with it nor attributed to it.[28]

One of the primary practices in Jnana yoga, the Indian path of knowledge, involves the use of the Sanskrit formula for negation, *neti, neti*, "neither this, nor that", found in the *Upaniṣads* and elsewhere. Applied to all of the contents of consciousness as they arise, it can be used as a means to establish a keener sense of *atman*, the Self, or applied to all phenomena, it can be used to refine one's understanding of *Nirguna Brahman* — the formless Absolute beyond all qualities and attributes. The Buddhist concept of *nirvana* is apophatic, meaning literally "to become extinguished", and is spoken of in negatory terms such as the "void" or "emptiness", as is *anatta*, or "not-self" — the negation of an abiding self. In the same sense the Sufi uses the term *fanā* — "passing away" or "annihilation". These traditions, while clarifying what something is not, unfortunately leave us helplessly lost when we attempt to grasp just what anything actually *is*. Although that perhaps is their very point.

Silence Is Golden

Words then can present us with quite a dilemma. They can misinform and mislead, can be misunderstood and mistranslated, and often miss the point entirely. Even in the best-case scenario, they cannot communicate Ultimate Truth. Sadly, they are all we have. Well, almost. There is one other way to avoid being misunderstood and that is to not speak at all. This simple commonsense technique has been put to good use by practitioners and adepts of every persuasion. If words can mislead and are unable in any case to transmit Truth, then simply to not use them at all, or at least to severely restrain their use, would seem like a sensible solution. In all monastic traditions, gossip and idle chatter are frowned upon if not explicitly forbidden, and in general, silence is preferred to speech. And even in this atmosphere of cultivated quiet, many monks take formal vows of silence for extended periods. The Indian practice of *satsang* meaning "in the company of truth", consists of practitioners gathering with their teacher and, for the most part, sitting together in silent meditation and contemplation. The contemporary Indian master, Ramana Maharshi, was renowned for having done his most eloquent teaching in silence, his very presence communicating the radiance of Realisation as no combination of words could ever do. In the Western Esoteric Tradition, of the four powers of the Sphinx, the fourth is the most important — to Know, to Will, to Dare and to Keep Silent. Even the philosophers, hardly known for ever being at a loss for words, have come up against the same impenetrable barrier as the sages when their thoughts have soared too high. The final two propositions in Wittgenstein's meditation on what is knowable and unknowable, the *Tractatus Logico-Philosophicus*, read:

> My propositions are elucidatory in this way: he who understands me finally recognizes them as senseless, when he has climbed out through them, on them, over them. (He must so to speak throw away the ladder, after he has climbed up on it.) He must surmount these propositions; then he sees the world rightly. Whereof one cannot speak, thereof one must be silent.[29]

The *Tao Te Ching* tells us in its opening paragraph: "The way that can be spoken of is not the constant way; The name that can be named is not the constant name".[30] Why then, it must be asked, is Lao Tzu even attempting to write a book about "the way" when the very way itself cannot be spoken of? In his defence, it is quite clear that the Taoist sage had no intention of writing down anything for posterity. If the legends surrounding him are to be believed, he was a man of very few words. One such illustration of this is an event that took place one morning, on one of his daily walks. Oftentimes a nearby neighbour would follow along but this time the neighbour had brought a guest who happened to be staying with him. Although the neighbour was aware of Lao Tzu's reluctance to talk, his guest seemingly was not, and as time passed, the silence began to weigh on him. He began to feel awkward, burdened by the lack of conversation. Finally he could bear it no longer. "What a beautiful day!" he said, but no one replied and they returned home again in silence. Once back, Lao Tzu took his neighbour aside and said to him, "Please don't bring this man again. He is a chatterbox". If only the poor man had had access to Lao Tzu's one and only book he would have had fair warning. In it he would have also read: "To use words but rarely is to be natural"[31], and again, "One who knows does not speak; one who speaks does not know".[32]

One might well ask that if this last statement is true, why would he even want to write a book? Well ... he actually didn't. The fact is the only reason the *Tao Te Ching* even exists is due to the well-intentioned extortion of some border guards. As an old man, having grown weary of the moral decay in Chengzhou where he lived, Lao Tzu decided to leave but was held at the border; the guards none too keen to let their greatest sage wander off into the sunset never to be seen again. They gave him an ultimatum — they would let him go only after he had written down his wisdom for the benefit of generations to come. Maybe the first verse was a middle finger to the guards who were still naive enough to think that he could actually tell them something of real value. Or maybe he was just writing it as a disclaimer for those with too high an expectation. Unfortunately we'll never know. The words, as is so often the case, do not tell us.

It should come as no surprise then that what makes perfect sense to the initiate seems nothing but craziness to the outsider. To the common man, words are robust and reliable things that one can depend upon year in, year out. To the adept, they are evanescent and volatile, precarious and inconsistent, morphing and mutating with every sentence and dependent upon multiple factors such as context, experience and knowledge, to say nothing of the tone, intention, mood and gesture of the speaker. To use them effectively is an art, as what is said for the benefit of one may even be detrimental if said to another.

But like the proverbial finger pointing to the moon, the linguistic pointers of even the most eloquent sage are the lesser concern. No matter how well he points, if the other does not turn away and look, then for all intents and purposes, there is no moon. If on the other hand, the student's realisation is deep, then even the most cursory nod in the general direction of the moon is enough. For this reason, in one of his early talks, the Graeco-Armenian mystic and spiritual teacher, George Ivanovitch Gurdjieff, warned his students:

> In order to be understood by another man, it is not only necessary for the speaker to know how to speak but for the listener to know how to listen. This is why I can say that if I were to speak in a way I consider exact, everybody here, with very few exceptions, would think I was crazy.[33]

We are left then with a strange paradox, and one that has been fertile ground for crazy-wisdom throughout the Great Traditions: although words cannot transmit Truth, Truth can be transmitted with words. That is to say, with a speaker who knows how to speak and a listener who knows how to listen. Or to put it another way, with the right teacher, the right student and the right words at the right time, progress can be made. When one or more is missing, then as Zen master Teh Ch'eng tells us:

> A good sentence is a stake to which a donkey can be tethered for ten thousand aeons.[34]

2

A CRY IN THE WILDERNESS

For the wisdom of this world is foolishness in
God's sight

— 1 CORINTHIANS 3:19

The Prophets of the Old Testament

Open any book of scripture and amongst the sublime revelations
of the human spirit, one can almost always find certain
puzzling passages whose meaning is obscure and interpreted
by scholars and laymen alike in a whole host of different ways.
Many of them give accounts of what, by today's standards,
would be considered very bizarre behaviour. What are we to
make, for example, of the strange verse in the Old Testament
where God commands Ezekiel to prepare bread with "wheat,
barley, beans, lentils, millet, and spelt",[1] to bake it with "dung
that cometh out of man",[2] and then lie down on his left side for
390 days. If that were not enough, he was then instructed to lie
on his right side for a further 40 days. Although this may be
interpreted as some form of peculiar penance, what are we to
make of the following chapter where poor old Ezekiel, as if he
hadn't suffered enough already, is then commanded to shave
his head and beard with a sword, weigh the hair on scales so as
to be divided up into three equal parts of which one was to be
burnt, another struck with the sword and the third scattered
to the wind! The Old Testament prophets were no doubt an
eccentric bunch in their undivided enthusiasm for fulfilling
the will of God, at least as they saw it. Indeed their behaviour
knew no bounds if instigated at the behest of divine revelation
and inspiration.

Although we are not told if he obliged eagerly or reluctantly, Hosea was commanded to "Go and marry a prostitute, so that some of her children will be conceived in prostitution".[3] A strange request perhaps, but hardly stranger than the name he was told to give their first-born daughter — Lo-Ruhamah, which means "not loved" — a difficult demand for any father to submit to and a perplexing psychological burden for the poor child growing up.

And while he would have been quite at home with the naked *sadhus* or Jain Digambara monks of India, the prophet Isaiah's three years of wandering, naked and barefoot, would have most likely been frowned upon in most places both then and now, where nakedness and religiosity are almost considered to be at opposite ends of the spectrum.

Intense religious fervour is known to make people act in very strange ways and confer upon the adept almost superhuman abilities to sustain extreme feats of penance, renunciation and self-abnegation. Whether as a result of it, or in search of it, crazy-wisdom no doubt played an important role for both Ezekiel, Hosea and Isaiah in enduring their hardships.

There is though a fine line between genius and insanity and whilst the Old Testament prophets are generally considered to have been blessed with the former, many of their villainous counterparts were not so lucky and instead were cursed with the latter. The sin of hubris led to Nebuchadnezzar's seven years of naked wandering in the wilderness during which "he began eating grass like cattle, and his body was drenched with the dew of heaven until his hair had grown like eagles' feathers and his nails like birds' claws".[4] King Saul was driven insane out of hatred for David and Balaam went mad for rebelling against God. There is a simple lesson to be learnt from all this — he who fulfils the will of God receives in return the trans-personal genius of crazy-wisdom, whilst he that goes against it just gets the crazy bit. Wisdom it seems, makes all the difference.

It is interesting to note that the Greek word translated as "sin", which can be found in the earliest copies of the New Testament texts, is *hamartia* which means literally "to miss the mark", as when an archer's arrow fails to connect with its target. In this sense, any action or attitude that keeps us from living up to our divine potential; anything that keeps us from moving closer to God, can be considered a "sin". It is anything that causes us to forget who we truly are. Any moralistic interpretations we may ascribe to it are only due to their capacity for leading us astray from the One True Path — the One leading away from crazy, and towards wisdom. Or crazy-wisdom as the case may be.

Fools for Christ's Sake

Continuing in the tradition of the earlier Old Testament prophets are the Fools for Christ's Sake, the Holy Fools or Blessed Fools of Christianity. The term comes from the First Epistle of St Paul the Apostle to the Corinthians where he tells them:

> For I think that God has exhibited us apostles as last of all, like men sentenced to death, because we have become a spectacle to the world, to angels, and to men. We are fools for Christ's sake, but you are wise in Christ. We are weak, but you are strong. You are held in honour, but we in disrepute.[5]

He returns to this idea of fools and foolishness several times throughout this first letter and states clearly and unequivocally a common theme throughout crazy-wisdom teachings — that somehow conventional thinking must be turned upside down if one wishes to go beyond worldly tendencies and glimpse the realms of the divine:

> Let no man deceive himself. If any man among you thinks that he is wise in this age, he must become foolish, so

41

that he may become wise. For the wisdom of this world is foolishness before God. For it is written, 'He is the One who catches the wise in their craftiness'; and again, 'The Lord knows the reasonings of the wise, that they are useless'.[6]

The two quotes are from the Old Testament (Job 5:13 and Psalm 94:11) perhaps to lend greater authority to his own words and establish them in the greater context of the Judeo-Christian tradition, but also showing us just how this idea was nothing new at the time, preceding both the New Testament texts as well as the teachings of Christ and placing its genesis at least as far back as the ancient prophets of the Old Testament as we have already seen, if not earlier.

The Madness of Christ

However, the supreme model of the Holy Fool within the Christian tradition is, of course, Christ himself, who embodied many of the principles of holy foolishness and demonstrated them both in his life as well as his teachings. This is perhaps not initially obvious when confronted with only the expurgated version of Jesus that conventional, exoteric Christianity has made of him, but only a summary look at the evidence is enough to overturn this contrived and sterilised caricature. Theirs is the meek and mild Jesus, subdued and sanitised for the sake of acceptance by a wider audience and far from the uncompromising God-man on a single-minded mission — unapologetically fulfilling "the will of Him who sent Me"[7] and seeking "to save that which was lost".[8]

When he had returned to Galilee and began teaching in the synagogues, on one occasion he quotes from Isaiah to further clarify his aims: "to preach the gospel to the poor", "to proclaim release to the captives and recovery of sight to the blind", and "to set free those who are oppressed".[9] These were radical statements to be made at a time of religious conservatism and conformity and even more so when clearly identifying himself with the prophet Isaiah and risking the obvious charges of blasphemy.

The exoteric, conventional Jesus, however, is not so much a lie, it is just such a partial view as to be considerably misleading. If we consider that the true realised adept has moved beyond logic and reason, we can only expect certain elements of their behaviour and teachings to reflect this and escape conventional classification. Their statements will seem contradictory at times; their words and actions paradoxical. Unfortunately, for the most part, their followers do not dwell in the same enlightened state as they do, but as heirs to the teaching, find themselves responsible for its transmission and propagation. The tendency, in all cases, is for the teaching to become systemised and in order to do this, it must be made coherent and consistent — completely at odds with the original intentions of its originator, whose aim was to shake people out of their habitual ways of seeing and take them beyond all systems of thought and categorisation. Needless to say, the same thing has happened with the life and teachings of Jesus Christ. While we are all familiar with the image of the peaceful Jesus, the pacifist-at-all-costs while "turning the other cheek" and "going the extra mile" have even made it into our day-to-day colloquialisms as expressions of goodness and compassion, how many are familiar with the other, less palatable side of Jesus? For good reason, sermons and Sunday schools everywhere conveniently skip over such shocking passages as can be found in the Gospel of Matthew where Jesus reveals to his disciples:

> Do not think that I came to bring peace on the earth;
> I did not come to bring peace, but a sword. For I
> came to set a man against his father, and a daughter
> against her mother, and a daughter-in-law against her

mother-in-law; and a man's enemies will be the members of his household.[10]

How can this be explained in conventional terms? The truth is it cannot. It can only be dealt with by transcending conventional terms and as such, stands as a clear and concise example of Christ's crazy-wisdom. The same passage even ends with one of the classic crazy-wisdom techniques — a direct inversion of reality — the turning upside down of what would be the common understanding:

He who has found his life will lose it, and he who has lost his life for My sake will find it.[11]

In a similar vein, in the Gospel of Thomas, Jesus spoke to his disciples saying:

Perhaps people think that I have come to impose peace upon the world. They do not know that I have come to impose conflicts upon the earth: fire, sword, war.[12]

When reading the above passages, one is perhaps reminded of the figure of Manjusri, one of the oldest and most important bodhisattvas of Mahayana Buddhism and one of the Four Great Bodhisattvas of Chinese Buddhism, who is almost always depicted as wielding a flaming sword in his right hand to represent the realisation of transcendent wisdom used to cut through ignorance. And yet even Manjusri it seems underwent some revision in around the eighth century when depictions of him began to show a ceremonial sceptre in his right hand instead of the flaming sword. Perhaps, like Christ, an attempt was made to distance Buddhism from violent imagery and align it more closely with the developing narrative of the exclusively peaceful nature of Buddhism and Buddhists.

Many of these more controversial aspects of Christ's teachings are often called the "hard sayings" of Christ, hard as they are to either follow or understand. The term is taken from a response to one of Jesus' more bizarre statements:

Truly, truly, I say to you, unless you eat the flesh of the Son of Man and drink His blood, you have no life in yourselves. He who eats My flesh and drinks My blood has eternal life, and I will raise him up on the last day. For My flesh is true food, and My blood is true drink. He who eats My flesh and drinks My blood abides in Me, and I in him.[13]

Several of the disciples, after hearing this, respond "This is a hard saying; who can hear it?"[14] Who indeed.

Who, other than a holy fool, is really prepared to follow Christ all the way when we are told that "none of you can be My disciple who does not give up all his own possessions".[15] Or that "If anyone comes to Me, and does not hate his father and mother and wife and children and brothers and sisters, yes, even his own life, he cannot be My disciple".[16]

No doubt the typical reaction to these things would be much like the young man in Matthew, who is told to sell his possessions and give them to the poor. Far from heeding the advice he merely "went away grieving; for he was one who owned much property".[17] Surely only a fool would be mad enough to do such a thing.

His extreme renunciation of possessions and his readiness to undergo harsh austerities such as his 40-day fast in the desert; his willingness to associate freely with the outcasts of society — prostitutes, criminals, the sick and abjectly poor — his flouting of conventional religious observances to even the extent of direct confrontations with the established religious customs of the time, such as the overturning of the money-changers' tables before driving them out of the temple. All these were classic outward manifestations of the crazy-wisdom impulse, an outpouring of the awakened disposition into a world that was for the most part too asleep to understand it. A quote generally attributed to Nietzsche states: "And those who were seen dancing were thought to be insane by those who could not hear the music". So while Christ danced, his head in the clouds beholding the heavens, the people puzzled, deaf to the divine melodies that moved him, their feet on the ground, their eyes cast down seeing only the earth beneath them. Like two worlds colliding: the heavenly and the earthly, the noumenal and the phenomenal, the Absolute and the relative, the divine and the mundane. And although one could not understand the other, the other could understand the one only too well.

The Desert Fathers

Following the example of Christ, the ideal of the blessed fool spread first to the early Desert Fathers, extreme as they were in their renunciation of worldly possessions and concerns and resolute in their rejection of societal norms. Beginning around the third century, these hermits, monks and ascetics fled to remote parts of the desert around Egypt so as to pursue lives of solitude, simplicity, austerity and prayer. It was the gradual aggregation of these hermits and anchorites into informal communities that unintentionally lay the foundations for the more formalised Christian monasticism to come.

Paul of Thebes is generally considered to have been the first of these early desert monks. At the age of 16, after losing his parents and becoming embroiled in a dispute over inheritance with his brother-in-law, he retreated to a cave in the desert where he lived for almost 100 years, surviving solely on spring water and the fruits from a palm tree that grew near his cave. His memory survives thanks to Anthony the Great, known as the Father of All Monks and the man recognised as the founding Desert Father, who sought out the old hermit after he appeared to him in a dream. Anthony discovered the old man in his final year, at the age of 113, absorbed in prayer and clothed only in palm leaves.

Like Paul, Anthony too lost his parents when still just a young man. Shortly after this, one day whilst listening to a sermon, he was moved by the words of Christ to "go, sell what you have and give to the poor",[18] and after doing just that, he retired to the desert where for a period of 20 years he lived a life of complete seclusion in the ruins of an old Roman fort, surviving almost entirely on bread, salt and water.

Most of what is known of St Anthony comes from the *Life of Anthony*, a fourth-century book written by the Greek, Athanasius of Alexandria, who from his early youth maintained close relations with many of the desert monks and later became the Archbishop of Alexandria. His book portrays Anthony as a holy, though illiterate man, a recurrent feature amongst the holy fools of Christianity, who, if not actually illiterate, would often feign illiteracy in their rejection of worldly knowledge, relying solely on purification and prayer as the means to move closer to God. In the upside down tradition of crazy-wisdom, Anthony suggests to us that the true madman might not be quite who we think:

A time is coming when men will go mad, and when they see someone who is not mad, they will attack him saying, 'You are mad, you are not like us'.[19]

In the *Lausiac History*, written in the fourth century by Palladius of Galatia, who was the bishop of Hellenopolis and disciple of St John Chrysostom, we are given brief glimpses into the lives of many of these ascetics and holy fools, the book being "a record of the virtuous asceticism and marvellous manner of life of those blessed and holy fathers, the monks and anchorites which inhabit the desert".[20]

In it we are told of an Egyptian monk, Sarapion the Sindonite, who took Jesus' advice to even greater lengths than Anthony. Not content with merely doing away with all his possessions, he even went as far as to sell himself as a slave in order to donate the money to the poor. In time, through his selflessness and piety, he converted his masters to Christianity and they made him a free man once more.

We are also told of a young nun named Isidora at the Tabenna monastery in Egypt "who feigned madness and possession by a demon".[21] She wore a rag on her head, in sharp contrast to the standard monastic cowls the other sisters wore, and they would insult and abuse her. She would intentionally seek out the most menial tasks, the dirtiest jobs that the others would try to avoid, and survived solely on the crumbs she wiped from the tables and the dirty dishwater from the cooking pots. And yet, even with this harsh self-abnegation, as well as the constant cruelty and mistreatment from her fellow sisters, we are told, "Never did she insult any one nor grumble nor talk either little or much, although she was cuffed and insulted and cursed and execrated".[22] Inspired by an angelic vision, a highly reputed anchorite called Piteroum was guided to visit the nunnery in search of a saintly woman "wearing a crown on her head".[23] Having demanded to see all the sisters and not finding the promised saint, he told them: "Bring me all, for there is one lacking".[24] After forcibly dragging Isidora from her chores in the kitchen, Piteroum fell to his knees and pleaded with her to bless him, whereupon Isidora too fell at his feet in the same manner. At this display, and filled with remorse, the sisters all began confessing their sins against her and begging for forgiveness. After just a few days of this newfound status and "unable to bear her glory and the honour bestowed by the sisters, and burdened by their apologies, she left the monastery".[25] Where she went, where she ended up, and how or where she died, no one knows, but in true holy fool fashion, she turned upon their head the mundane wishes and aspirations of the conventional, worldly life.

Simeon the Holy Fool

A common characteristic of the holy fool that differentiates their state from one of true madness is their purposeful flouting of society's conventions; their deliberate employment of shocking and unconventional behaviour so as to challenge accepted norms and shake people awake from their spiritual slumber. Sometimes used as a method for incurring the scorn of others so as to avoid praise and prestige and to overcome pride (to annihilate the ego and denigrate the self) or merely as a way of keeping others at bay so as to be left alone to pursue prayer and contemplation in peace, whilst a true madman cannot escape his state of madness, the holy fool's feigned madness is used as a tool for purposes that only one in the same state could perhaps fully appreciate.

The case of Simeon the Holy Fool, a Byzantine monk, hermit and saint who lived in the sixth century, clearly illustrates this. After almost 30 years living on lentils in a remote cave by the Dead Sea, he returned to civilisation, entering the gates of the city of Emesa dragging a dead dog behind him on a rope. When not blowing out the candles in church and throwing nuts at the congregation, running naked into the women's quarters at the local bathhouse, tripping people up in the street or dragging himself around on his buttocks, he was unobtrusively performing selfless acts of charity and kindness, the likes of which only became known publicly after his death. Even miracles were attributed to him, such as the turning of vinegar into wine so as to aid a poor mule driver in establishing a successful tavern. During his life, he was considered by most to be an obscene and scandalous madman, but after his death, his virtue and holiness were recognised and the truth of his feigned insanity became clear. It also came to light that his crazy persona ceased entirely when in the presence of his friend John, the deacon of the church in Emesa, demonstrating conclusively complete control over his faculties.

The Yurodivy

Perhaps nowhere has the character of the holy fool been so enthusiastically embraced and enacted as within the Eastern Orthodox tradition. Out of the 42 Christian saints who lived their lives as holy fools, 36 of them belonged to the Russian Orthodox Church. As one hymn would have it, the blessed fool or *yurodivy* strives "with imaginary insanity to reveal the insanity of the world".

The most loved and revered of them is St Basil the Blessed, whose mortal remains lie buried in the brightly coloured cathedral that bears his name in Red Square in the heart of Moscow. From the tender age of 16, in the summer heat or the biting cold of the Russian winter, he could be seen wandering the streets of the city barefoot, wearing little to no clothing at all, and bound in heavy chains. A common trait of the holy fool is a complete absence of the worries and fears that plague most of us. Fearing only God and the damnation of their soul, they have no concerns with lesser sufferings or even death. One such story of Basil tells how during Lent, when all Russians were keeping a strict vegetarian fast, he presented Tsar Ivan IV with a cut of raw beef and asked him "Why abstain from meat when you murder men?" This, to many, would have seemed an extremely reckless act and even suicidal, for the Tsar was known as Ivan the Terrible for good reason, and had killed men without a thought for far lesser offences. Nevertheless, even the Tsar held Basil in high esteem and would allow no harm to come to him. He would occasionally send presents that Basil would give away to those in need, and when the saint died, Ivan served as one of his pallbearers and saw to it that a chapel be built over his grave, annexed to the great cathedral he had built some years before.

St Francis of Assisi

Even many of Christianity's more well-known characters that have been sanitised over time reveal their own peculiar eccentricities and moments of madness when investigated further. St Francis of Assisi, the nature-lover and founder of the Franciscan order of monks, was known to preach the gospel to flocks of birds and on one occasion tried to convince a wolf to stop attacking the local townsfolk. To his credit, it must be said that the birds remained still as if listening as he wandered amongst them, and the wolf, from that moment on, ceased his attacks and even became a pet to the locals who would ensure that he was always well fed. Peculiar behaviour by most people's standards but perhaps not as shocking to religious sensibilities as another event in his colourful life. While at a dilapidated church outside the gates of Assisi, he heard Christ on the crucifix above the altar command him to repair the crumbling building. Not wasting any time, he ran home, took some fine cloth from his father's shop, and rode to the local marketplace where he sold both the cloth and the horse to raise funds for the repair work. His father, furious on discovering the theft of the cloth, dragged his son before the bishop of Assisi, demanding that the money be returned to him. Not content with merely returning the money, Francis stripped off all of his clothes and returned them to his father, declaring that from now on the only father he recognised was his Father in heaven. The astonished bishop hurried to cover his nakedness with a cloak, whereupon Francis ran off into the woods singing praises to the Lord. It is said that the first men he met on the road were a band of thieves who attacked him and stole even his cloak. Not one to be so easily discouraged, he got up from his beating and skipped away still singing his praises to God.

In *The Imitation of Christ,* second only to the Bible as the most widely read Christian devotional work and written by Thomas à Kempis in the fifteenth century, we are given the essential formula of the holy fool:

> Then it will be seen that the man who learned to be a fool and to be despised for Christ's sake was the one who was wise in this world.[26]

The authentic way to God — living one's life for the sake of Christ, in the technical language of Christianity — is the only true wisdom. It requires a complete inversion of the concerns and ambitions of the world and so appears as nothing but insanity to secular society. For this reason, Christianity is replete with divine madness and holy fools going all the way back to Jesus Christ himself, and beyond to the Old Testament prophets and the founding fathers of the People of the Book.

The Hasidic Masters

> When I had risen in prayer, and was standing in the hall of truth, I begged God to grant me that my reason might never proceed against his truth.[27]
>
> — RABBI MIKHAL

From the Old Testament prophets, the Judaic torch of crazy-wisdom passed to the Hasidic masters, whose own imitable brand of divine madness rekindled its glowing embers into a flame worthy of its prophets of old. This spiritual revival that swept across Europe in the eighteenth century was not defined in particular by any new doctrines or religious theories but rather by its emphasis on certain ideas that had been an integral part of Judaism for thousands of years, ideas that had become increasingly marginalised due to the prestige and predominance of scholarship and scriptural study. It can also be seen in a broader context as part of a worldwide revivalist trend that rejected rigid religious hierarchies in favour of a more simple and direct relationship with the Divine — a trend that it shared with the rise of Pietism in Germany, the Russian Old Believers, Wahhabism in Arabia and the Evangelical Revival that swept Great Britain and New England in the 1730s and 1740s.

Like many other mystics and mad saints, the Hasidim were a grassroots movement representing all those everyday men and women who felt the yearning and presence of the One God without recourse to the sophisticated Hebraic terms to describe it. While traditional Judaism was seeking God in scripture and the detailed study of the Hebrew alphabet, the Hasidim were finding Him in the birds, trees and flowers. As orthodox Judaism tended evermore towards the Way of Ascent favouring the "World to Come" over the world that is, it was only natural that a movement should arise to counter the imbalance and re-establish some measure of harmony. As is so often the case with reactionary groups, initially the movement was defined as much by their rejection of the prevailing religious tendencies of the time as they were by their own natural inclinations. Thus, in order to set themselves apart from the rest, the Hasidim often demonstrated a strong tendency towards the Way of Descent, overemphasising the immanence of God in the world with the same zeal as their more orthodox counterparts were overemphasising His transcendence of it. Their underlying philosophical stance reflected this by placing little emphasis upon ascetic practices and fasting, and while scriptural study was engaged in and encouraged, it always remained subordinate to fervent prayer and one's capacity for *kavvanah* or "holy intent". Martin Buber in his *Tales of the Hasidim* sums up the work of the Hasid as follows:

If you direct the undiminished power of your fervor to God's world-destiny, if you do what you must do at this moment — no matter what it may be! — with your whole strength and with kavvanah, with holy intent, you will bring about the union between God and Shekhinah, eternity and time. You need not be a scholar or a sage to accomplish this. All that is necessary is to have a soul united within itself and indivisibly directed to its divine goal. The world in which you live, just as it is and not otherwise, affords you that association with God, which will redeem you and whatever divine aspect of the world you have been entrusted with. And your own character, the very qualities which make you what you are, constitutes your special approach to God, your special potential use for Him. Do not be vexed at your delight in creatures and things! But do not let it shackle itself to creatures and things; through these, press on to God. Do not rebel against your desires, but seize them and bind them to God. You shall not stifle your surging powers, but let them work at holy work, and rest a holy rest in God. All the contradictions with which the world distresses you are only that you may discover their intrinsic significance, and all the contrary trends tormenting you within yourself, only wait to be exorcised by your word. All innate sorrow wants only to flow into the fervor of your joy. But this joy must not be the goal toward which you strive. It will be vouchsafed you if you strive to 'give joy to God'. Your personal joy will rise up when you want nothing but the joy of God — nothing but joy in itself.[28]

As can be seen, there is an overarching emphasis on the world "just as it is", its "creatures and things" and the ability to find God there, even in its contradictions and one's own desires. These ideas are all characteristic of the Way of Descent — the life-affirming path of finding God in the here-and-now. This, in a world where the prevailing religious attitudes of the time were otherworldly and Ascending, was in itself unconventional and was seen by many to be unholy, transgressive, foolish or mad. Above scholarship they valued heartfelt, fervent prayer and were known for their emotive outpourings. It is said that Rabbi Yitzhak's whole body would shake with uncontrollable tremors when he prayed. He was wont at times to make demands of God and even went as far as to hurl threats at Him as if negotiating with an equal. Much of their religious activity centred around feasting and religious discussion, and as well as prayer, music accompanied by frenzied dancing was their preferred method of worship, something the more orthodox communities looked at in dismay. The founding master of Hasidism, the Baal Shem Tov, once said: "If a man falls into the mire and his friend wants to fetch him out, he must not hesitate to get himself a little dirty".[29] The same sentiment was echoed by the later Rabbi Shelomo when he said:

> If you want to raise a man from mud and filth, do not think it is enough to keep standing on top and reaching down to him a helping hand. You must go all the way down yourself, down into mud and filth. Then take hold of him with strong hands and pull him and yourself out into the light.[30]

It is this lack of disgust and even acceptance and embrace of the "mud and filth" of the world that led the followers of orthodox Jewry to reject the Hasidim and brand them as heretics and dissidents. No doubt their reaction towards this new religious movement had been negatively coloured by certain other messianic heretic groups that were already active at the time like the Sabbateans and Frankists, whose doctrines were indeed unholy, transgressive and highly questionable. Far from these antinomians however, the Hasidim were the revivalists of the Descending current at a time defined almost exclusively by Ascent. They were the bringers of mirth and play to solemnity and study, the new stewards of the ancient crazy-wisdom vision of their forefathers.

3

CHOP WATER, CARRY WOOD

There are things that even the wise fail to do, while the fool hits the point. Unexpectedly discovering the way to life in the midst of death, he burst out in hearty laughter![1]

— SENGAI

Taoist Nobodies

The China of the sixth century BC was a place of turmoil and upheaval. It was a time characterised by warfare and the consolidation of power and at the cusp of a turbulent new era that came to be known as the Warring States period. Yet in the midst of this societal chaos, the Golden Age of Chinese philosophy flourished into the Hundred Schools of Thought — Confucianism, Legalism, Mohism, the Logicians, the School of Yin-yang — all seeking to make sense of the senseless and establish man in his proper relation to the cosmos. The atrocities of war are known to make thinking men reflect deeply upon the human condition, and the absurd contradictions of men who with not the slightest sarcasm called themselves "civilised", were painfully obvious to anyone who had not been likewise swept away by the same hysteria that had captured their hearts and minds. As the very philosophy of the *tao* would predict, whenever nature is pushed too far in one direction, an impulse arises that pulls it back in the other in an attempt to restore balance. In this case that impulse took the form of a series of crazy-wisdom masters who were to turn the conventional wisdom of their time on its head. While the other philosophical schools focused primarily on the nature of the social order and the question of how people were to coexist harmoniously — who was to reign over them, with what laws and which ethical principles — the Taoist masters went to the heart of the problem, to the nature of reality itself. While the general populace sought prosperity, notoriety and esteem, these men championed the ways of austerity, anonymity and obscurity. While the Mohists and Confucianists were urging people to honour men of worth, Lao Tzu was telling them the contrary: "Not to honour men of worth will keep the people from contention",[2] he writes in the *Tao Te Ching* — considered the foundational text of Taoism. While everybody was struggling to be a somebody, the Taoist masters were demonstrating the supreme value of being a nobody.

Tao, most commonly translated as "the way", is a symbol for many things. On the one hand it refers to the free and unaffected flow of nature and the perfect harmony of its processes where each apparent part is surrendered to the will and wellbeing of the whole, utterly devoid of self-interest or personal motive. At the same time, it is the transcendent ground and goal of this phenomenal effluence — the noumenon, beneath, above and beyond all of it. It is at once the pattern and power that orders "the ten thousand things" and gives rise to "the myriad creatures", and also the ineffable void from whence they came and to where they shall all return. *A Source Book in Chinese Philosophy* tells us:

> it is the One, which is natural, eternal, spontaneous, nameless, and indescribable. It is at once the beginning of all things and the way in which all things pursue their course. When this Tao is possessed by individual things, it becomes its character or virtue (te). The ideal life for the individual, the ideal order for society, and the ideal type of government are all based on it and guided by it. As the way of life, it denotes simplicity, spontaneity, tranquillity, weakness, and most important of all, non-action (wu-wei). By the latter is not meant literally 'inactivity' but

rather 'taking no action that is contrary to Nature' — in other words, letting Nature take its own course.[3]

The *tao* is the perfection from which the practitioner takes his cues and learns his lessons and is utterly removed from the conventional world of men; of struggle, force, acquisition, accumulation and ultimately, discontent. The Taoist sage then does not look to stand out, and values neither greatness nor victory. His idols are neither heroic men nor great kings. But like the puzzle pieces of the natural world that dovetail effortlessly and seek nothing more than to fulfil their proper function within the grander scheme, the Taoist sage seeks nothing more than to be like the wind when it blows or like the trees that sway with its touch. His only action is non-action, *wu-wei*, an effortless and spontaneous movement that arises from being immersed in the flow of the universal current, untouched by the personal cravings of selfhood. Through non-action, all things are accomplished — "The way never acts yet nothing is left undone".[4] His only seeking is an end to seeking. His only care is to cast off the constraints of the self with all its artifice and hypocrisy, and assume his rightful place within the harmonic flow of things. His heroes are the flowing water that yields in order to overcome; the gnarled tree, so twisted that no one cares to take an axe to it. To be conventionally useful is to tempt others into exploiting those talents or merely being jealous or envious of them. To accumulate wealth or power only captures the attention of those who would too eagerly take them from you. The *tao* is unassuming but overcomes all. Wind cannot be caught, stolen, trapped or harmed, but still has the power to fell trees. The Taoists reasoned that the greatest power lay in having none. The highest aspiration was to have no aspiration. The boldest adventure was in its perfect absence, for even the simplest, most mundane moments are brimming with the *tao* — "Without stirring abroad one can know the whole world;

without looking out of the window one can see the way of heaven".[5]

Perhaps as an antidote to the contrived atrocities they saw committed all around them, the Taoist masters saw it most beneficial to reject what was man-made and instead cleave to nature.

The founding crazy-wisdom master of this way of nature was Lao Tzu which seems to have been an honorific title meaning "Old Master". He was a man of few words and his only book, the *Tao Te Ching*, sometimes called the *Lao Tzu*, is known as "the book of five thousand characters" due to its brevity. Although just a short text, it is the most translated Chinese text in history with more than 250 translations of it into Western languages alone. Composed of 81 short pieces — reflections on the nature of the *tao* — it abounds with metaphors from the natural world and is written in a straightforward and sober aphoristic manner. However, as he himself tells us: "Straightforward words seem paradoxical".[6]

And although he assures us that "My words are very easy to understand and very easy to put into practice",[7] the nature of the subject matter and the manner in which it goes against the grain of conventional wisdom has made it the subject of lively debate for more than two and a half millennia.

His heir to the Taoist inheritance and the second of the two most renowned Taoist masters was Chuang Tzu. Although the two never met, Chuang Tzu took up the baton from the Old Master due to his depth of realisation and his ability to communicate the essence of the *tao*. His one book, the *Chuang Tzu*, however, was markedly different and employed a writing style that was far more playful and whimsical than his predecessor, replete with complex wordplay and parables infused with satire, sardonic humour, irony and irreverence. Almost everyone has heard the story of the man who dreamt of being a butterfly and, on awakening, questioned whether he was really a man who had dreamt of being a butterfly or whether perhaps he was actually a butterfly now dreaming of being a man. Far fewer know that the man, or butterfly in question, was Chuang Tzu. Although perhaps more accessible than the *Tao Te Ching*, the *Chuang Tzu* is just as uncompromising. Its shared contempt for conventional knowledge and the soporific psychological comfort zone it establishes and guards zealously is dissected and its presumptions extirpated in no uncertain terms; however its lightness and mirth, like the sugar in a medicine that disguises an unpleasant taste, makes it easy to swallow. But as much as one would like to develop a clearer intellectual notion of the *tao*, Chuang Tzu is relentless in providing nothing of the sort to cling to. In one such story, the personification of Knowledge is roaming around the country looking for answers to the questions:

> 'By what system of thought and what technique of meditation can I apprehend Tao? By what renunciation or what solitary retirement may I rest in Tao? Where must I start, what road must I follow to reach Tao?' Having searched north and south he finally receives an answer from the Emperor Hwang Ti at his palace:
> To exercise no-thought and follow no-way of meditation is the first step toward understanding Tao. To dwell nowhere and rest in nothing is the first step toward resting in Tao. To start from nowhere and follow no road is the first step toward attaining Tao.[8]

As for the Taoist philosophy, Chuang Tzu sums it up by saying:

> To regard the fundamental as the essence, to regard things as coarse, to regard accumulation as deficiency, and to dwell quietly alone with the spiritual and the intelligent — herein lie the techniques of Tao of the ancients. Kuan Yin'

and Lao Tan (Lao Tzu) heard of them and were delighted. They built their doctrines on the principle of eternal non-being and held the idea of the Great One as fundamental. To them weakness and humility were the expression, and openness and emptiness that did not destroy anything were the reality.[9]

Like other non-dual, apophatic traditions, the Taoists were intent on pointing out the nothing rather than the something, the absence instead of the presence, the ground as opposed to the figure. The figure is what is obvious, it is where our attention is naturally drawn, whereas realisation requires the undermining and transcending of this innate one-sidedness. Chapter XI of the *Tao Te Ching* reads:

Thirty spokes share one hub. Adapt the nothing therein to the purpose in hand, and you will have the use of the cart. Knead clay in order to make a vessel. Adapt the nothing therein to the purpose in hand, and you will have the use of the vessel. Cut out doors and windows in order to make a room. Adapt the nothing therein to the purpose in hand, and you will have the use of the room. Thus what we gain is Something, yet it is by virtue of Nothing that this can be put to use.[10]

To see the presence of the wheel, the clay vessel and the room is the basis of conventional knowledge. To see the emptiness between the spokes, the space contained by the clay vessel and the absence that constitutes doors and windows — the very things that make them functional — is to see the *yin* with the *yang* as coterminous; as the ongoing interplay of apparent opposites whose eternal flux and flow is the *tao*. This is the beginning of what appears to outsiders as craziness and to adepts as true wisdom. Indeed, these are such strange themes to the common man and woman that it is no surprise that Lao Tzu told us:

When the worst student hears about the way he laughs out loud. If he did not laugh it would be unworthy of being the way.[11]

But to see this clearly and unequivocally is the only worthwhile endeavour. As for knowledge, honour, prosperity, esteem, ethics or accomplishment, to the Taoist masters it was all merely worthless straw to be burnt up in the fire of true realisation. "The perfect man", Chuang Tzu tells us, "has no self, the holy man has no merit, the sage has no reputation".[12]

As the *buddhadharma* travelled eastward from India to China, it found an accomplice in the tradition of the Tao that was already there and flourishing. As the two paths joined and found their commonalities, a new current of the perennial wisdom was slowly birthed: the Ch'an of China and the Zen of Japan.

Mad Zen Masters

Although at times the displays of crazy-wisdom are flamboyant, at others they are far more restrained; sometimes wild, sometimes subdued; sometimes shocking and at other times, merely puzzling. There is a story told of the Buddha in his later years that perfectly illustrates this more sober side of crazy-wisdom. On one occasion, as his students gathered for their customary sermon around the edge of a quiet pond, the Buddha instead of speaking to them, reached into the water and pulled out a lotus flower that he silently held up for them to see. For the most part he was met with blank stares, but his cousin, Mahakashyapa, who had been with him for many years, began laughing. According to tradition, it was at this moment that Zen was born; its name being the Japanese pronunciation of the Sanskrit word *dhyāna* meaning something akin to "meditation", "contemplation" or "absorption", and known as *Ch'an* in China. The story represents the first instance of the silent transmission of mind and Mahakashyapa went on to become the Buddha's successor.

A similar story with a far more dramatic ending is told of the Zen master, Gutei, who, whenever he was asked what his teaching was, would simply hold up one finger without saying a word. One day a visitor to the monastery asked one of Gutei's attendants about his master's teaching, to which the young man responded by raising one finger in the same way as his master. On hearing about this, Gutei called for the attendant and without warning, cut off his finger. As he ran away screaming, Gutei called out to him and the boy stopped and turned around, at which point Gutei raised his finger. It is said that at that moment, the attendant became enlightened. Gutei's one-finger Zen was a powerful tool of transmission if in the right hands (pardon the pun), but before he died, he revealed that the technique was not his own but had rather been passed on from his own teacher. His last words were: "I attained my finger-Zen from my teacher Tenryu, and in my whole life I could not exhaust it".[13] Unfortunately history is silent on whether Gutei's attendant was successful with his own fingerless finger-Zen, an even deeper transmission perhaps than his predecessor.

Savage Kindness

At times the violence within the Zen tradition reaches levels that are shocking to Western sensibilities and perhaps not always bring about the desired results. I am sure Gutei's anonymous attendant would have been quite happy to trade his lost finger for the magnificent jewel of enlightenment, but others have not been so lucky. In his book, *The Empty Mirror*, Janwillem van de Wetering, who spent several years living in Zen monasteries in Japan in the 1960s, relates one such unfortunate event that occurred to a stubborn and conceited young monk in one of the monasteries in Tokyo. In one of the early morning interviews with the master in which, as usual, he was being obstinate and argumentative, he was beaten so severely with the master's stick that he died. The stick in question is the Zen stick or *kyosaku* sometimes called amusingly (and without the slightest sarcasm I might add) the Stick of Compassion, and is used to strike the monk across the shoulders when in sitting meditation should they begin to doze or drift off.

A similar story is told of the Japanese Zen master Ekido, a very severe teacher who was much loved by his admirers from afar but also greatly feared by his monks up close. One of them, whose duty it was to strike a gong as a means of signalling the time, accidently skipped a beat as his attention was caught by a beautiful woman who passed by beyond the temple grounds. The monk, oblivious to the fact that Ekido was just behind him, received a single blow from his stick and was killed instantly. Nothing was done about the incident, Ekido himself never so much as mentioned it and life went on as normal in the monastery. Though it may seem madness to the modern secular mindset, the vocational monks — rather than the ones sent merely to accrue merit for their families or ancestors — are engaged wholly and exclusively in the Great Work of enlightenment. And they must either get there or die trying. And just as only a handful of seeds fall on fertile ground and bring forth fruit, the vast majority "die trying". Most are eaten by birds, or choked by thistles, or fall on stony ground, or in these rare cases, are killed by their master's "compassion stick". To his credit, it is said that during his time as a teacher, Ekido produced ten enlightened successors, a very extraordinary number indeed.

The Threat of Violence

Violence in the service of awakening is no doubt a dangerous weapon to wield, but it must also be said that the fear of the weapon — the mere threat of violence — can be a magnificent motivator, allowing the student to access otherwise inaccessible reservoirs of attention, energy and effort. There is a story told where Bodhidharma uses this fact to great effect during an encounter with the emperor of China. The emperor, a refined and cultured man, is anticipating the imminent visit of the great Buddhist master to his country, but his lofty expectations are dashed to pieces when Bodhidharma arrives with a shoe on one foot and the other on his head, and then goes on to insult him and offend his sensibilities in a variety of different ways. The emperor, much to his credit, takes the abuse calmly and without complaint. Although bewildered and shocked by the encounter, he persists in what seems to be a genuine attempt to glean some wisdom from this strange man he has heard so many great things about. Finally, in response to the emperor's exasperation at his inability to stem the constant flow of thought, Bodhidharma tells him to come again early the following day, but this time alone, without his assistants and guards and his familiar entourage. At the appointed time, Bodhidharma sits down and bids the emperor to sit in front of him. He then shows him a large stick and tells him that if he is seen hanging onto a single thought, instead of simply allowing it to pass away, he will be struck across the head with it. Removed from the safety net provided by his attendants, far from familiar surroundings, and with the threat of being beaten about the head with a hefty wooden stick by this mercurial madman, the emperor was able to gather his faculties and focus, and bring them to bear in an act of supreme willpower like never before. By the time the sun had risen, the countenance of the emperor had changed — he had experienced *satori*, the apperception of one's own Buddha-nature and the apprehension of the true nature of reality.

Suiwo, one of the most renowned students of the great Zen master Hakuin, used the ultimate threat of violence in order to catalyse the awakening of one of his own students who was struggling to make a breakthrough with his *koan*. Having wrestled for three years with the question "What is the sound of one hand clapping?" without success, the student approached Suiwo in tears, asking to be dismissed so as to return to his village. Suiwo convinced him to stay just a week more and continued to do so in weekly increments until once again the student was in a desperate state and begged to take leave. At this, Suiwo gave the young man his last piece of advice — meditate for just three more days on the *koan* and if, at the end of the third day, it had not been resolved, then he should kill himself. Although the student left in a hopeless state, on the second day he became enlightened. There seems to be little doubt that some people just work better under pressure.

Kill the Buddha!

The fierce Chinese Ch'an master Lin-Chi (Rinzai in Japanese) was another teacher famed for his use of shouting and striking as effective means to train his students. His now infamous phrase: "When you meet a Buddha, kill the Buddha; When you meet a Patriarch, kill the Patriarch",[14] has shocked, perplexed and caused all manner of controversy ever since it was delivered to a group of monks over a millennia ago. What could he possibly have meant? "Surely the Buddhist's are peaceful fellows!" come the cries from outsiders. "We are!" respond the orthodox Buddhists, "We would never kill the Buddha!" Both, of course, have missed the point. We are, after all, talking of crazy-wisdom, not conventional wisdom. Lin-Chi's intentionally provocative statement is to be interpreted in the same context as the Sufi saying mentioned earlier: "None attains to the Ultimate Truth until a thousand honest people have called him an infidel".[15]

Truth realisation, enlightenment, awakening, deliverance, salvation, redemption — abiding non-dual awareness — always lies on the other side of reason, conventionality and orthodoxy, outside of any box intended to contain it and beyond any systematic attempt to pin it down or clearly define it. It is like water that flows unhindered through any attempt to grasp it or stem its natural flow. As Tsung Kao, one of the later masters from Lin-Chi's own school of Ch'an Buddhism tells us: "If you want to grasp it, it runs away from you, but if you cast it away it continues to be there all the time".[16]

Lin-Chi's admonishment then is just another pulling of the rug from beneath us, so as to not get too comfortable and complacent. If we look beyond the proverbial pointing of the Buddha's finger or those of the patriarchs that came after him, then all is well and good. However, as soon as any of them become the focus of our attention, rather than our attention being directed towards, and fixed upon, the inexpressible Truth that lies beyond them — the Truth that we are duty-bound to realise for ourselves — then we fall into error. Then, in Lin Chi's analogy, it is time to kill the Buddha. This idea, that even the Buddha must be surrendered in the interest of enlightenment, has become an integral part of Zen. It is the essence of the *koan*, "Where buddhas dwell, don't stop. Where buddhas don't dwell, hurry past",[17] and in *The Gateless Gate*, the great Zen work on *koans* from the thirteenth century, Mumon tells us in his commentary to the first *koan*, (*Joshu's Dog*): "If a Buddha stands in his way, he will cut him down; if a patriarch offers him any obstacle, he will kill him; and he will be free in his way of birth and death".[18] A hundred years later, echoing these sentiments, the Korean Zen master Taego said, "Here, if buddhas come, I will hit them; if patriarchs come, I will hit them".[19] And The Great Pearl, Ch'an master Hui Hai, expressed the same sentiment in an altogether more gentle manner when he said: "Sages seek from mind, not from the Buddha; fools seek from the Buddha instead of seeking from mind".[20]

Although perhaps framed in a more forceful manner, these sentiments merely reaffirm what the Buddha himself taught. In a conversation with his disciple Subhuti, recorded in the *Diamond Sutra,* he compares his teaching to a raft that must be discarded once it has carried one to the other side of the river. In a similar vein, the great contemporary Indian sage, Ramana Maharshi, when asked about the usefulness of the concepts he was using in his teaching, replied that our situation was like having a thorn in our foot and that he was merely using some other thorns to help remove the one that seemed to be troubling us. Once the thorn had been removed, however, all of the thorns can then be thrown away. Likewise, the Buddha, the patriarchs or any other provisional aid to Seeing can all be done away with when one actually Sees for themselves. And prior to this moment, we must constantly be reminded that the Seeing is what we are here for. Those pointing to what we must See are trivial and inconsequential in comparison. They are only a means to an end and should never become an end in themselves. This disdain for idols and religious fetishism is a prevalent attitude throughout the crazy-wisdom traditions of the world and receives particular emphasis in the Chinese Ch'an tradition and the later flowering of this into Zen in Japan.

But perhaps the first prize for shocking our sensibilities of reverence and devotion would have to go to the Chinese Ch'an master Yunmen, who took the theme of killing the Buddha to another level in the following exchange with a monk. Part of the incredible mythology surrounding the life of the Buddha claims that when he was born, he took seven steps, looked in the four directions, pointed with one hand to the sky and the other to the ground before calmly declaring, "Above and beneath heaven, I alone am the Honoured One". When asked by a student what this meant, Yunmen responded by saying, "If I had seen him at the time, I would have cut him down with my staff, and given his flesh to dogs to eat, so that peace could prevail over all the world".[21] This was the same Yunmen who became enlightened when his teacher broke his leg by slamming a door on it. It makes you wonder.

Burn the Buddha!

Another story that illustrates a similar contempt for contrived piety is told of the Chinese Ch'an master, Tan-hsia, although several similar versions exist with other great masters playing the role of protagonist. Whilst staying the night in a temple in the middle of the winter, and unable to sleep due to the biting cold, Tan-hsia decided to burn a wooden statue of the Buddha in order to keep warm. When the temple priest caught him delighting in the dying embers of the fire, he began to berate him for sacrilege and defilement of the Buddha.

"I'm burning it to get the sacred relics out", Tan-hsia replied in his defence.

"What relics?" the priest retorted. "It's just a piece of wood!"

"If it's just a piece of wood", said Tan-hsia, "then what is the harm in burning it?"[22]

Some versions of the story then have the recalcitrant master ask the temple priest for the two attending statues to burn as well so as to keep him comfortable for the rest of the night. Sadly, posterity remains silent as to whether he did or not.

In the section "Buddhas for Burning" in his book *Why Lazarus Laughed*, Wei Wu Wei nicely sums up this whole theme in his own inimitable style:

Men and women who seek doctrines, study them, endeavour to follow them, are impeding their own progress. The Masters, from the Buddha down, in their frequent condemnation of 'discoursing' have made that clear, and in declaring that there must be no attachment to, or identification with, the *Dharma* itself (or any *dharma*), that even the teaching of the Buddha himself must be discarded, have left no room for doubt on that score.

Doctrines, scriptures, sutras, essays, are not to be regarded as systems to be followed. They merely contribute to understanding. They should be for us a source of stimulation, and nothing more.

We must create each his own dharma, understanding, and may use those of others to help us to that end; they have no other value for us. Adopted, rather than used as a stimulus, they are a hindrance. As the Zen master stated to the monk whom he found studying a sutra, 'Do not let the sutra upset you — upset the sutra yourself instead'. Some Masters expressed themselves more forcibly, as when they recommended that Buddhas (statues of) were for burning and on a cold day used one as firewood, and in advising, 'If you meet the Buddha, turn aside and look the other way'.[23]

Hakuin's Poison Words for the Heart Sutra

Whereas conventional commentaries on religious scripture inevitably adopt a tone of reverence and praise, highlighting and extolling the positive aspects of the text and generally ignoring or underplaying any shortcomings, Zen master Hakuin's *Dokugo shingyō*, or *Poison Words for the Heart*, a commentary on the revered Buddhist classic, the *Heart Sutra*, not surprisingly takes a decidedly different approach. The *Prajñāpāramitāhṛdaya* or *The Heart of the Perfection of Wisdom*, better known simply as the *Heart Sutra*, was composed in India around the seventh century and though one of the shortest works in the Buddhist canon, less than a page of text, it is arguably the most popular, with thousands of pages dedicated to commentary and exegesis. It is the original source for such classic Buddhist aphorisms as "Form Is No Other Than Emptiness, Emptiness No Other Than Form", to which Hakuin has this to say:

A nice hot kettle of stew. He ruins it by dropping a couple of rat turds in. It's no good pushing delicacies at a man with a full belly. Striking aside waves to look for water when the waves are water.

And at the mention of Shariputra, one of the Buddha's chief disciples, to whom the sutra is directed, Hakuin says:

Phuh! What could a little pipsqueak of an Arhat with his measly fruits possibly have to offer? Around here, even Buddhas and Patriarchs beg for their lives.[24]

Hakuin's commentary abounds in these acerbic comments and condemnations, designed on the one hand to stifle any tendency towards excessive veneration, as well as shock the student out of their predispositions towards the customary interpretations of these well-known verses, forcing them to rely on nothing but their own unique and idiosyncratic understanding. Far from being a curiosity within the Zen corpus, Hakuin's work follows a highly respected and established tradition that began with such texts as the *Blue Cliff Record* (*Pi-yen lu*) and *The Gateless Gate* (*Mu-mon-kan*).

The Three Hermits of Tientai

From its inception, Zen has effortlessly integrated the fine arts into its own austere and minimalist aesthetic, developing them as a means of practice, and a medium for the preservation and transmission of *dharma*. As well as enlightened masters, over the years it has also produced some of the East's finest poets, painters and calligraphers. Not surprisingly, a few of them were a little mad.

One such vagabond-poet-monk who blurred the lines between Zen and Taoism — blending the terminology and ideas from both into his unique style of poetry — was Cold Mountain (Han-shan), named after the mountain where he lived for many years in the far east of China. Portrayed as wearing a birch-bark hat, a patched robe, wooden clogs and carrying a pigweed staff with a crazy look on his face, his poems were found written on rocks and trees in and around the cave to which he fled after being sought out to be honoured by a high official. When not at his cave retreat or wandering the wilds, he could be found at the Kuoching Temple at the foot of Mount Tientai, a day's hike to the northeast. There he met his two sidekicks, Big Stick (Feng-kan) and Pickup (Shih-te) — both of them poets in their own right and equally shrouded in mystery — who, along with Cold Mountain, became known as the Three Hermits of Tientai. As one of his poems has it:

> I usually live in seclusion
> but sometimes I go to Kuoching
> to call on the Venerable Feng-kan
> or to visit with Master Shih-te
> but I go back to Cold Cliff alone
> observing an unspoken agreement
> I follow a stream that has no spring
> the spring is dry but not the stream[26]

When at Kuoching, he lived on the fringes of monastic life, going about his own practices, poking fun at the other monks and generally causing mayhem. On one occasion Cold Mountain was herding oxen past the temple, singing to himself, "I have a jewel / inside my body / but nobody knows". He saw some monks giving a lecture to a group of novices on the precepts and led the oxen over to them. "What a throng! What's all this milling about?" he said, and laughed as the animals wandered amongst them. "You stupid lunatic!" one of the monks shouted at him angrily, "You're interrupting our lecture on the precepts!" Laughing, Cold Mountain replied, "No anger. That's the precepts. When your mind is pure, then you're a monk. Our natures are one. There's no distinction in the light of the Dharma".[27]

A poem by Big Stick further illustrates this playful contempt they shared for the common standards of monkhood at the time:

> By and large the monks I meet
> love their meat and wine

instead of climbing to Heaven
they slip back down to Hell
they chant a sutra or two
to fool the laymen in town
unaware the laymen in town
are more perceptive than them[28]

It was said of Big Stick that he appeared one day, riding through the front gate of the temple on the back of a tiger. He was exceptionally tall and instead of a shaved head, he wore his hair long, hanging down over his eyebrows. Like Cold Mountain, he came and went as he saw fit and followed his own schedule, usually spending his days in the kitchen hulling rice and his nights chanting the sutras. When asked about Buddhism, he would simply shrug and say "Whatever". One day, while walking along one of the temple trails, he heard crying in the bushes. On investigation he came across a 10-year-old boy who had been abandoned by his parents. Big Stick picked him up (hence the name with which he was to be known for the rest of his life) and after an unsuccessful attempt to locate his parents, he was taken in by the temple custodian. Although initially put to work in the main shrine hall, after several incidents, including eating the fruit left as an offering to the statue of the Buddha, he was moved to the kitchen. Outside the kitchen was a statue of the temple's protector god. His awareness made keen with the recent fruit-looting incident, he noticed how the birds, in the same way, would make off with the food offerings left before it. Grabbing a stick, he proceeded to go outside and beat the statue. "If you can't protect your own food, how can you protect the temple?" he shouted at it. During the night the protector god appeared to the monks in a dream to effectively snitch on Pickup and the beating he had received at his hands. The following morning, after the monks had all shared their strange dream, they went outside to check the statue, and sure enough, they found it damaged. The incident was reported to the prefect whose only response was to say: "Worthy men conceal their traces, bodhisattvas show many faces. It is only proper to acknowledge them. Let Pickup be called a worthy man".

Nevertheless, it was here in the kitchen that Pickup found his place in the temple monastery and it was here in the kitchen that he met his lifelong friend, Cold Mountain. A poem by Pickup describes their friendship:

We slip into Tientai caves
we visit people unseen
me and my friend Cold Mountain
eat magic mushrooms under the pines
we talk about the past and present
and sigh at the world gone mad
everyone going to Hell
and going for a long long time[30]

A poem by Big Stick gives further insight into the friendship of the three of them:

Whenever Cold Mountain stops to visit
or Pickup pays his usual call
we talk about the mind the moon
or wide-open space
reality has no limit
so anything real includes it all[31]

Like many of their crazy-wisdom compatriots, the Three Hermits of Tientai were not great fans of book-learning or formal practice. Although obviously well acquainted with both Buddhist as well as Taoist scriptures, they considered them to be only provisional aids, to be put aside for real spiritual work, certainly not things to become too attached to, or revere too highly. This theme weaves a constant thread throughout their poetry, as another of Cold Mountain's poems tell us:

Whoever has Cold Mountain's poems
is better off than those with sutras
write them up on your screen
and read them from time to time[32]

And again:

I met a brilliant scholar once
learned and shrewd without peer
his examination fame echoed through the realm
his regulated verse surpassed that of others
his judgments excelled all those of the past
how could he follow in someone else's dust
now rich and honored he chases wealth and beauty
what can you say about broken tiles or melted ice[34]

Transient, impermanent, subject to the same deterioration and entropic decay as tiles when they break or ice when it melts "learning" is, as Pickup would have it too, mere "dust":

I sigh when I see learned men
wasting their minds all day
babbling away at a fork in the road
deceiving whoever they can
creating more ballast for Hell
instead of improving their karma
impermanence suddenly comes
and all their learning is dust[34]

The Three Hermits were dedicated to the Truth at all cost and to personalities such as these, conventional knowledge too often acts as a stifling influence, satisfying the ego into thinking that progress is being made as new knowledge is accumulated, and bolstering it with the development of an identity that is "wise" or "learned", in order to earn the respect and admiration from others that such identities engender. Truth, however, is not an edifice built of accumulated knowledge, it is rather the hole left behind when all false knowledge has been destroyed. Although at pains to admit it — or perhaps even recognise it in the first place — most conventional seekers are not after Truth at any cost. They crave the edifice and abhor the hole. They seek what most others seek — recognition, status, attention, the admiration of their peers — and many Buddhist monks of the period were no different. They had signed up to monkhood to accrue merit for themselves and their families; their dedication was to the same egoic games as the rest of the population, just at a more subtle level. Rather than accrue treasures in order to be rich, they would gather knowledge in order to be a wise — different playing field; same game. To crazy-wisdom adepts such as the Three Hermits, however, the deception was clear. And they were all too familiar with the dangers of pointing it out to those still unwilling to see their own artifice:

Cold Mountain speaks these words
as if he were a madman
he tells people what he thinks
thus he earns their wrath
but a straight mind means straight words
a straight mind holds nothing back
crossing the River of Death
who's that jabbering fool
the road to the grave is dark
and karma holds the reins[35]

Even though they did little to encourage it, and much to discourage it, soon their fame as genuine crazy-wisdom masters spread beyond the confines of Kuoching and a high official sought them out to pay his respects. When he found them, in the kitchen, standing in front of the stove talking and laughing, he bowed in reverence. Cold Mountain and Pickup burst into laughter and ran out of the monastery never to be seen again. One of Cold Mountain's many poems found written on the rock wall of his cave would seem to make reference to this event and his final renunciation of monkhood:

> Wise ones you ignore me
> I ignore you fools
> neither wise nor foolish
> I'll disappear henceforth
> at night I'll sing to the moon
> at dawn I'll dance with the clouds
> how can I still my mouth and hands
> and sit up straight with all this hair[36]

Crazy Cloud

One of the most iconoclastic and controversial poets of Japan is the monk and Zen master, Ikkyū Sōjun, also known by his sobriquet, Crazy Cloud. A master, not only of Zen and poetry, but also of calligraphy and ink wash paintings, Ikkyū was a pivotal influence in defining the emerging artistic milieu of the fifteenth century, at a time when much of Japanese society was in turmoil due to fires, famines, peasant uprisings and the political power struggles of its leading dynasties. Within this atmosphere of war and upheaval, Japanese art blossomed: a new style of poetry, *renga* verse, was born; the classical dance drama of Noh theatre became established; the aesthetic of Chinese ink painting and calligraphy was refined into its final form, as was the quintessentially Japanese tea ceremony.

Ikkyū, a wanderer between worlds, participated in all of it. As an artist, he influenced many of the foremost artists of the time — Noh actors, painters, poets and tea masters — he moved in their circles and many of them were his students. As a respected master of Zen, he also made a deep impression upon Japanese Buddhism, helping to steer it away from its dry disciplinarianism and rigid systematisation, to instead infuse it once more with the spontaneous awakened impulse of the earlier T'ang masters.

Having spent the first half of his life, from the age of 5, in Zen monasteries undergoing formal training, he spent the second half as a wanderer — a vagabond and hermit — as much at home, alone in the wilderness, as in the midst of monks in monasteries, or visiting the bars and brothels of the inner cities. One of his poems that scandalised the polite Japanese society of the time tells us:

> Crazy madman stirring up a crazy style
> Coming and going amid brothels and wineshops.
> Which of you patch-cloth monks can trip me up?
> I mark out the south, I mark out the north, the west and
> east.[37]

As a Zen master, he was the first to deal with the themes of sex and romantic love — his poetry reaching from the dry peaks of abstract Buddhist philosophy to the humid valleys of sensual eroticism — inspired both by his own Zen practice, as well as his romantic encounters. One such poem, of the erotic kind, about Lady Mori, a blind singer and the love of his later life, tells us:

> My hand, how it resembles Mori's hand.
> I believe the lady is the master of loveplay;
> If I get ill, she can cure the jeweled stem.
> And then they rejoice, the monks at my meeting.[38]

The thinly veiled reference to his "jeweled stem" should be quite clear.

Perhaps no other Japanese poet has brought together such philosophical abstraction and earthy sensuality, such scathing social criticism and tender appreciation of nature. As a Zen purist he would aggressively denounce both the syncretists and their attempts to blend Zen with other systems, as well as the growing Zen aristocracy and their concern with wealth and prestige over truth and awakening. One such poetic attack on conventional monkhood reads:

> With kōans and old examples, arrogant deception grows;
> Everyday you bend your back to meet officials in vain.
> Proud boasters are this world's Friends of Good Knowledge;
> The young girl in the brothel wears gold brocade.[39]

At the time, a monks ceremonial dress displayed gold brocade, the implication being that just like the "young girl in the brothel", they too were merely in the business of selling you something.

However, not all his critiques were written down, some were acted out in classic crazy-wisdom fashion. One amusing anecdote tells of how he once strutted around Sakai with an enormous wooden sword strapped to his waist. When stopped by passers-by, reacting to the incongruous sight of a monk with a sword, he told them:

> "You don't know it yet, but these days the world is full of false wisdom that is just like this wooden sword. As long as it is kept in the scabbard, it looks as good as a real blade, but if it is drawn out from the scabbard, it is seen to be only a sliver of wood. It cannot kill people, much less make them live."[40]

Ikkyū had no time for the empty formalisms of institutional Zen, and when presented with his seal of enlightenment from his master, Kasō, he rejected it. The seal was given to a lay follower for safekeeping but when Ikkyū found out, he took it and tore it up. After some well-intentioned disciples pieced it back together, finally Ikkyū burned it. To the Crazy Cloud such things were less than worthless. This uncompromising and unconventional attitude shone throughout his poems in such memorable opening lines as: "The scriptures from the start have been toilet paper",[41] or "Those who keep the rules are asses, those who break the rules are men".[42]

In many ways, Ikkyū was a man of the people, more in touch with the unassuming ways of farmers and fishermen than the contrived airs and graces of those at the top of the social hierarchy, both Buddhist and secular, and he is credited with being one of the first to popularise *kana hōgo* — the delivery of sermons in everyday, colloquial Japanese.

After many years living the life of a simple hermit, Ikkyū was invited to become the abbot of Nyoian, a sub-temple within the larger Daitokuji complex, where he had trained as a young man. It was the thirteenth anniversary of his master's death, and he felt somewhat obliged to accept. His abbotship, however, did not last. The following poem was posted on the wall of his residence before he left, addressed to the principal abbot:

Ten days as an abbot and my mind is churning.
Under my feet, the red thread of passion is long.
If you come another day and ask for me,
Try a fish shop, tavern, or else a brothel.[43]

A mere ten days was all he could bear before returning to his vagabond lifestyle. Many years later, at the age of 82, he was once again invited back to Daitokuji, this time as the principal abbot, to help rebuild the complex after it had been destroyed by fire in the Ōnin War. With the very survival of the monastery and its lineage at stake, Ikkyū took the position, but with some reservation, and even a certain amount of shame, as the following poem attests:

> Daito's descendants destroyed his remaining light.
> Hard to melt the heart in song on an icy night.
> For fifty years, a wanderer with straw raincoat and hat,
> Shameful today, a purple-robed monk.[44]

Ikkyū's charisma and connections with all manner of people soon brought the required donations; the monastery was restored and the Daitokuji lineage preserved. Having embodied the awakened spirit of its founders for so long, he had now also ensured the physical means to propagate it. His task now complete, Ikkyū passed away whilst sitting in meditation at the age of 88.

4

THE DHARMA OF THE INSIDERS

First, the root of faults is nothing other than your
    ego-clinging,
the attitude of deluded fixation, so cut the ties of
    ego-clinging!
Cast away the fixation on enemy and friend!
Forsake worldly concerns!
Abandon materialistic pursuits! Engage in nothing
    but the Dharma from the core of your heart! [1]
               — PADMASAMBHAVA

Padmasambhava

Within the broad and diverse landscape that is Buddhism,
the Mahayana tradition of Zen and the Vajrayana tradition
of Tibet are the two that have embraced crazy-wisdom most
enthusiastically. Not surprisingly, their founders epitomised
these principles themselves and were as eccentric as they were
enlightened, and as crazy as they were wise, their unique and
iconoclastic visions forging systems of spiritual development
that continue to inspire and elevate millions of people around
the world.

Bodhidharma, credited with bringing Buddhism to China
in the fifth century and the first patriarch of both Ch'an and
Zen, was so one-pointed in his mission of awakening that he
is usually depicted with huge bulging eyeballs, having ripped
off his own eyelids in order to no longer fall asleep whilst in
meditation. Padmasambhava, another Indian master who
brought Buddhism to Tibet in the eighth century, was no less
unique a character. When asked by the people who he was, he
told them:

I have no father and I have no mother.
I have no teacher nor do I have a master.
I have no caste and I have no name.
I am a self-appeared buddha.[2]

And on another occasion, gave an equally mysterious reply:

My father is wisdom and my mother is voidness.
My country is the country of Dharma.
I am of no caste and no creed.
I am sustained by perplexity;
and I am here to destroy lust, anger and sloth.[3]

Padmasambhava was invited to Tibet by King Trisong Detsen
to supervise an ambitious translation project of sacred Buddhist
writings into Tibetan. He came with another great Buddhist
master, Shantarakshita, who oversaw the translation of sutras
(the oral teachings of the Buddha) while Padmasambhava
supervised the translation of the tantras — the esoteric teachings
of the Buddha. This was known as the "early diffusion" that
brought with it the "ancient tantras" and established the
Nyingma or "ancient" tradition, the oldest of the four schools
of Tibetan Buddhism.

A great deal of fanciful myth and legend has grown up
around the character of Padmasambhava, known affectionately
by his followers as Guru Rimpoche (Precious Guru), so much
so that it is now difficult to establish any reliable historical
facts. From his instantaneous birth from a lotus flower, hence
the name *padma*, "lotus flower" and *sambhava* "born from",
to his epic battles with demons in order to subdue them and
convert them to the *buddhadharma*, his entire life has become
a fantastic saga of miraculous events and spiritual triumph.
Whoever he was, he deeply impacted the Tibetan psyche
and was foremost in establishing an entirely new branch of

Buddhism — the Vajrayana, or *Diamond Vehicle* — a tradition rich, colourful, profound, and peppered with crazy-wisdom masters. However, Vajrayana is unique in its bringing of crazy-wisdom to the masses; to the common man and woman. While Zen's crazy-wisdom is usually reserved for monks, serious students and seasoned practitioners, in Tibet and Bhutan, there are whole towns painted with huge, brightly coloured phalluses in celebration and veneration of their most loved crazy-wisdom master, Drukpa Kunley.

Drukpa Kunley — The Madman of the Drukpa

People say Drukpa Kunley is utterly mad –
But in madness all sensory forms are the Path![4]
— DRUKPA KUNLEY

When not awakening the innate Buddha-nature of one of his "five thousand girlfriends" with his "flaming thunderbolt of wisdom", or getting drunk on *chung* — a crude but powerful rice wine — he was generally shocking the sensibilities of all those who came in contact with him and causing all manner of mayhem in the name of the sacred *buddadharma*. In his "secret biography", *The Divine Madman*, translated from the Tibetan by Keith Dowman, we find the following charming anecdote:

At the temple of Ramoche, he found the monks engaged in metaphysical discussion, and thinking that he should not lose this opportunity to teach them how to laugh, he asked, "What are you doing, O monks?"

"We are cleansing our spiritual perspective of doubts and disharmonies", they told him.

"I know a little bit of metaphysics myself", said the Lama, grabbing a handful of his own flatulence and thrusting it under their noses. "What came first, the air or the smell?" he demanded.[5]

Some *koan*. However, as one might expect, Drukpa Kunley's flatulence was not of the ordinary kind. On another occasion he is serving *chung* to some monks in a monastery. Walking into the middle of the assembly hall, he breaks wind "like a dragon", but rather than causing a foul smell like any other mere mortal, we are told that "the whole room was filled with a pleasant odor". Even now, the assembly hall is said to have a "holy smell".[6]

Although Drukpa Kunley's paternal family had controlled a monastery and ample estates for the best part of three hundred years, whilst Drukpa was still just a boy, a struggle for power erupted that left his father dead and his family in disarray. Perhaps for his own safety, he was taken away by his paternal aunt's husband and served as an attendant to the ruling family of Tsang for six years before leaving, at the age of 19, to begin his wanderings. During this time he took the vows of a novice monk in a monastery in southern Tibet; took his full ordination vows at another monastery; served as the abbot of yet another monastery; returned his vows as a monk; took a wife and had a son; then took a second wife and had another son, all the while training himself in meditation, and other Tantric practices such as *tummo* (the cultivation of the inner fire) and receiving the complete teachings of *Mahāmudrā* (The Great Seal) and *Dzogchen* (The Great Perfection), as well as such transmissions as *The Six Cycles of One Taste* and *The Profound Inner Meaning*. By this time Drukpa Kunley had become a master in his own right, but no ordinary master. He had become the most famous of the *smyon pa* or "mad yogis" and shared the epithet with two other crazy-wise contemporaries: Kunga Zangpo, the Madman of U, and Tsang Nyon, the Madman of Tsang. Together they are known as The Three Madmen (*smyon pa gsum*) and were all considered masters in the Kagyu tradition, one of the four main schools of Tibetan Buddhism, which traces its genesis back to the tenth-century *mahāsiddhas*, or Great Adepts of India.

Apart from his penchant for obscenity and powerful alcoholic beverages, Drukpa Kunley also liked to make love. A lot. His biography is replete with his conquests of women from all walks of life including nuns and married women, both young and old. On one of his journeys to Ralung, he came across a 16-year-old nun called Tsewong Paldsom. After merely asking her where she is going he "caught her by the hand, laid her down on the side of the road, and consummated his desire for her three times".[7]

On another occasion, he came across a husband and wife living in a small shack. Upon seeing that the wife "had all the signs of a Dakini", and was of "excellent spiritual descent", he sang a song to her:

Pale blue monkey swinging in the dry peach tree,
Don't hanker after peaches neither sweet nor sour.
Come and enjoy the goodies in uncle's pocket!

Charmed perhaps by his direct approach, she sends her husband on an errand to collect firewood, whereupon the mad lama continued with his song:

It would seem by the size of your buttocks,
That your nature is exceedingly lustful.
It would seem from your thin, pert mouth,
That your muscle is tight and strong.
It would seem from your legs and muscular thighs,
That your pelvic thrust is particularly efficient.
Let's see how you perform![8]

Having assessed her performance and successfully awakened her spiritual potential with his "flaming thunderbolt of wisdom", he sent her to meditate in a cave where a year later she found enlightenment.

Although Drukpa Kunley's sexual escapades might at first seem gratuitous and self-serving, upon investigation, it is quite clear that there is far more to it. Were he just a lecherous womaniser, he would no doubt take advantage of women's sexual receptivity at every opportunity rather than rejecting their advances. However, several excerpts from his life show this not to be the case. On the road to Kongpo he comes across five girls who proceed to flirt with him. Even though the conversation becomes sexual, instead of turning on his no-frills charm and exploiting the situation for his own ends, he rebuffs their advances and leaves them deeply offended. On another occasion, having seduced "an extremely beautiful lady called Loleg Buti", he tells her bluntly: "Raise your skirt and open your legs". However, after "looking between her thighs", he has a change of mind and tells her: "It seems that we are not suited to one another. You need a triangular organ, and I need a round aperture. Obviously we can't do business!"[9]

A merely lustful man, if faced with the same situation, would almost certainly lack the same restraint. Drukpa Kunley, however, like other wise-fools and crazy-sages, is completely unpredictable and surprises us by both his flamboyant transgressions as well as his composure and temperance. It seems that just when you are expecting the one, he does the other.

Considered in the light of tradition, Drukpa Kunley's seemingly madcap antics are merely the overflowing spontaneity of the authentic man; of one who has transcended the manipulative contrivances of selfhood and the unexamined ulterior motives that fuel the day-to-day actions of so-called normal people. "Crazy wisdom is just the action of truth",[9] Chögyam Trungpa has more recently reminded us. The life of the mad yogi then is the particular that escapes the common rules of classification and judgement that apply to the general. He is the exception to the rule. If madness is considered to be a deviation from a consensual psychological norm then the crazy sage is, as his name suggests, crazy. However, if what truly counts is the extent to which one has transcended the limitations that lead us to all act in a standardised fashion, then it is the bumbling masses — those cloned by falsehood — who are truly insane. To them, the crazy-wisdom master is a thorn in their side, like the bucket of icy water thrown to arouse the drunkard from their slumber or the slap in the face of one in the grips of a hysterical fit. To those wishing to shirk their divine duty and continue to bury their heads in the sand, the mere existence of the crazy-wisdom master is a threat, often an existential threat of such monstrous proportions that stubborn men have stopped at nothing in their crusade to silence them. Just ask Jesus.

Hence, in his unpredictable behaviour there is something to offend everyone's sensibilities, for in that very offence lies the potential for insight. His lack of affectation highlights the pretentiousness in others: their vanity and conceit. His authenticity agitates the insincere. The wise will take note of this agitation and they will learn from it. The foolish, however, will double down in their efforts, and instead project their agitation onto the perceived source of it. And so, for the puritan, Drukpa Kunley is vulgar and lewd and comes off as the embodiment of unbridled lust; for the pious ecclesiastic bound by his sense of moral superiority, Drukpa Kunley is a wanton sinner; for the one tied to his precepts and sutras and the dry veneration of scripture, he is profane and sacrilegious. Of course, in truth, he is none of these things. Or at least he is all of these things to the extent that he ends up being none of these things in particular. Ironically it is only his audience who remain bound by such concerns, the crazy-wisdom master having transcended them entirely. But for our sake he holds up the mirror to those places within ourselves that for the most part, we don't even dare to go. And with fierce compassion, he takes us there, kicking and screaming if needs be, shouldering the blame, suffering the tantrums and receiving thanks only after enduring insults and abuse. This seems to be a recurring theme in Drukpa Kunley's life, but somehow, he always emerges from the ordeal unscathed; his outlandish means and methods victorious over the distrust and incredulity of his doubters, and their faith is restored.

One such story is his meeting with an old man named Apa Gaypo Tenzin, whose children have grown up and left home and who now has little left in his life except his daily devotions. Lama Kunley teaches him a Refuge Prayer and tells him to recite it as often as he can. The only problem is that the prayer is full of lewd words and sexual references which shock and offend his wife, and his constant recitations lead to him being banished to the loft and shunned by the rest of his family and friends. They deride the Lama as a phoney and dismiss the old man as having gone stark raving mad. One day, the murmur of the old man's constant prayers cannot be heard by his family. They begin to worry and the daughter is sent up to the loft to investigate. Throwing the quilt from his bed, the old man is nowhere to be seen and all that remains is "a sphere of rainbow light with the syllable AH in the centre of it, shining white and radiant".[11]

She calls down to her family who come running, and when gathered in his room they watch as the sphere of light flies off into the western sky trailing the voice of the old man saying:

> Drukpa Kunley has delivered me into the Potala Mountain Paradise of the Bodhisattva of Compassion. You prudish people must stay here! Give the Lokthang Kyamo to the Lama as an offering.[12]

Needless to say, the family repented for their lack of faith and their foolishness in dismissing the Lama's divine recommendations, and instead became staunch devotees. Tradition tells us that when the Lama returned, he built a *stupa* over the spot where

Apa had died and left the old man's rosary there as a relic. Sometime later a monastery was built around the *stupa* which still stands and is known as the Khyimay Temple.

Often referred to as *naljorpas*, meaning "he who is tied to serenity", "he who adheres to an authentic personal reality" or "he who is an embodiment of the union of male and female principles",[13] but more commonly understood as an ascetic with magical powers, The Three Madmen and others like them were revered as living gods. Another epithet they were given which makes this even more explicit is *Heruka*, so named after a category of wrathful deities, who though fierce in appearance, embody only bliss and emptiness, and strive for the wellbeing of all sentient beings. The *Heruka* then, is one who has completed certain practices so as to become identical in power and awareness to the deity. With these kinds of credentials, it is not surprising that those who encountered them were wont to tolerate their bizarre antics, though often only after having tested them by fire — sometimes quite literally.

Kunga Zangpo — The Madman of U

While travelling through Kathmandu, Kunga Zangpo, the Madman of U, stopped at some burial grounds where, for reasons known only to himself, he damaged and desecrated some of the statues of Hindu deities by dancing on their heads and urinating over them. As can be imagined, the locals were not too happy about this and so, in retaliation, they kidnapped him and spent several days torturing him before chopping him to pieces with an axe and roasting the pieces over a fire. You can imagine their surprise when he reappeared the following day dancing wildly in triumph, and all in one piece. What better way to gain people's everlasting respect and admiration.

What we know of his life comes primarily from a biography written in two parts: the first by one of his own disciples when the master was still alive, and the second by another author five

years after his death. With a title every bit as epic as its subject —
*The Life Story of the Noble Kunga Zangpo, Glorious Holy Lama,
the Preeminent Siddha Whose Practice Is Totally Victorious in All
Respects, Called "That Which without Restriction Gives Goosebumps
of Faith"* — it tells of his birth into a heavily-indentured farming
family and a challenging childhood; the death of his mother;
physical assault by a drunken local lord; and the ongoing
injustices of a poor family trying to make ends meet within a
tyrannical feudal system. Faced with these hardships it is no
wonder that, as a young man he decided to dedicate his life so
wholeheartedly to escaping the mire of *saṃsāra* and, much to
the dismay of his family, fled home in order to become a monk.

He spent the following years under the tutelage of several
eminent gurus and quickly mastered the preliminary tantric
teachings and ritual empowerments, as well as the Six Dharmas
of Naropa. A keen student, he subjected himself to extreme
asceticism and intensive practice until attaining, we are told, a
state of supreme and perfect enlightenment. It was at this point,
in his mid-20s, that his life took an unexpected turn. Standing
before a statue of the Buddha one day, he removed his monks'
robes and smeared his body with the ashes of a corpse before
donning a tiger-skin skirt and a cloak made from human skin.
To this he added a necklace made from pieces of human bone
and, as prescribed by some of the early tantric texts such as
the Hevajra Tantra, he also began carrying a human thighbone
trumpet, a cup made from a skull, and a tantric staff engraved
with skulls known as a *khatvanga*. This radical change of
appearance also marked a radical change in behaviour. His life
as a monk had ended as swiftly as it had begun. From now on,
Kunga Zangpo's life would be an uncompromising embodiment
of the supreme deity *Heruka*, his only practice being the
Unexcelled Yoga Tantra — the tantra beyond tantra; the yoga
beyond yoga; the practice beyond practice. Certainly not one to
do things half-heartedly, for the remainder of his life, he would

alternate between extreme retreats in complete solitude and bouts of radical crazy-wisdom teaching in the midst of men. And like many of the adepts we have already discussed, Kunga Zangpo was no fool, there was much method in his madness. When not desecrating sacred statues, threatening powerful lords or urinating on the heads of minor kings, he was rubbing shoulders with members of the ruling Rinpung family, as well as Donyo Dorje, who was effectively the ruler of Tibet at the time. Through these mutually beneficial associations, he was able to establish monasteries throughout Tibet and instruct a multitude of monks and laymen in the *buddhadharma*, crazy-wisdom style.

Tsang Nyon — The Madman of Tsang

Like his crazy compatriots, tradition tells us that while still a young boy, Tsang Nyon developed a strong disgust for the endless cyclic suffering of *saṃsāra*, as well as a deep compassion for all sentient beings. At a young age he joined the monkhood and progressed through the preliminary practices with relative ease, all in the keen spirit of a conventional monk. Only when he had turned 21 did his penchant for more unorthodox behaviour begin to show. The first occasion was upon the visit to his monastery of some particularly prominent guests. His conduct, we are told, was so insulting and outlandish that he was expelled from the monastery and abandoned his vows so as to become an itinerant yogi. Much like his crazy compatriots, his life became styled upon the ways and practices of the Indian *mahāsiddhas*; he wore his hair long and dressed in the full garb of the *Heruka* while carrying a tantric staff and skull-cup. Like them, he also began to compose and sing songs of realisation or *dohas*. In an early song expressing his understanding of the essential *buddhadharma* he sang:

The nature of dharma
has no origination and no cessation.

Since it is not known by the learned,
I asked the dumb.
They did not know it either,
so I asked the corpses at the charnel grounds.
Their explanations are the nature of the dharma.
This is the meditation experience of a madman
in the Snow Mountains of Lapchi.[14]

For the remainder of his life he wandered from one holy site to another, often staying for several years in one place in order to meditate, and much of the time following in the footsteps of the great Tibetan yogi and poet, Milarepa, with whom he felt a particular connection. Like the other *naljorpas* herein mentioned, Tsang Nyon, beyond his bizarre appearance and behaviour, was extremely perspicacious and surprisingly socially skilled, forging important relationships with both religious and secular leaders of the time. Such was his influence that they would often summon him to act as a peace-keeper between two factions, as the parties on both sides happened to be his disciples and would heed his advice above anyone else's. During his lifetime he wrote several books and was a pioneer in the use of a wood-block printing technique that allowed numerous copies to be made and distributed all over Tibet. He is still known for his *Life of Milarepa,* which even now is regarded as the definitive biography of the Tibetan yogi-saint.

It seems quite remarkable that the three most famous mad yogis of the Tibetan Buddhist tradition also happened to be contemporaries and born with just six years between them in the decade of the 1450s. Tradition tells us that they knew each other personally and held each other in high esteem. One such spontaneous meeting on the road to Tsari — one of the most important mountains and pilgrimage sites in Tibet — is spoken of in Drukpa Kunley's biography. They travel together to Tsari and there, decide to leave behind some auspicious signs for the sake of future generations. The Madman of U decides to stamp an impression of his foot into a rock and the Madman of Tsang does the same but with his hand. Drukpa Kunley mocks them: "Even my dog has that kind of power",[15] he says to them, before taking the dog's leg and impressing its paw-print into the rock, as if it were mud. After performing other miracles and marvels of which we are not told, the three madmen parted ways.

As is quite clear after even a summary glance at the lives of these great men; the "crazy" aspects of their personality were more than adequately balanced with the "wise" aspects, the "mad" equally tempered by the "yogi". It should also be clear that there was far more to their demeanour and behaviour than mere shock value, and more to their shirking of societal and religious norms than just defiance or rebellion. Until we have mastered the same practices as they did and penetrated into the mind with the same depth, we are perhaps unequipped to truly judge their motivations in these matters. Nevertheless, they were widely respected and renowned for their accomplishments whether as masters of meditation, spiritual teachers, founders of monasteries, poets, writers or peace-keepers.

It is perhaps hard to see just why the Tibetans and especially their religious establishments tolerated the outrageous behaviour of the *naljorpas*. Only when it is realised that their conduct and lifestyle was nothing new at the time but instead formed part of a much wider and older tradition, does it begin to make sense. And so, to more deeply understand these mad yogis of Tibet we must consider them within the historical and philosophical milieu of which they were a part — a tradition of Tantric Buddhism that had been imported via the *mahāsiddhas* — the Great Adepts of India.

Tantra

What has come to be known as *tantra* most likely emerged initially as a reactionary movement to counter a growing formalism in the prevailing religious traditions of the Indian subcontinent — primarily Buddhism, Hinduism and Jainism — and exists as a current in all three. As their monastic traditions became systematised and the traditional paths to enlightenment for serious students became the exclusive domain of institutions and organised religion, there arose an ad hoc assortment of eccentrics and iconoclasts, of freaks and free spirits, sincere in their longing for liberation but unable to conform to the conventional standards of the times, nor willing to. Just as when a pendulum is pushed one way, it responds with equal force by moving the other, initially these religious rebels flouted the established norms in no uncertain terms. If monks were to shave their heads, then the *tantrikas* would leave their hair long. If the monks had proscriptions against bodily adornment, then the *tantrikas* would wear necklaces, bangles, bracelets, anklets, rings, earrings and all manner of personal ornamentations and accessories. If monks had prohibitions as to intoxicants and sex, then the *tantrikas* would indulge in them. If the monks had their sacred texts (the *sutras*), then the *tantrikas* would have theirs (the *tantras*). Over time, and with their own growing corpus of sacred writings, Tantra became formalised into an esoteric tradition of its own that can be found in all Eastern religions. One branch of tantric Buddhism, also known as Vajrayana, the *Diamond Vehicle*, first flourished in Eastern India before finding its way to Tibet in the eighth century. To better understand its philosophical foundations, consider the doctrine of the two truths, first taught by the Buddha and further developed in the third century by Nagarjuna, the great Mahayana scholar and philosopher and founder of the Madhyamaka or "Middle-way" school (and not to be confused with the later ninth-century *mahāsiddha* of the same name). Simply stated, it asserts that truth is of two kinds: the relative or conventional, and the Absolute or Ultimate. As well as being a point of contention for the unawakened, this doctrine has also led to differences of emphasis within the Buddhist community and the development of traditions that serve these different approaches. Whereas the Theravadin might be inclined towards the Absolute, to the extent even of denying the relative any *real* truth, the tantric practitioner is more inclined to use the relative as just another tool to realise the Absolute, and to realise ultimately, the non-dual nature of them both. If, in the final analysis, *saṃsāra* is *nirvana* and *nirvana* is *saṃsāra*, then accordingly there must be two fundamental orientations for the spiritual aspirant — two means by which Truth can be realised — one absolute, inwards, transcendent, nirvanic and the other, relative, outwards, immanent and samsaric — the ways of the Mystic and the Mage, of Ascent and Descent, or perhaps in this case, the monk and the tantrika. The tantric disposition then, involves the undifferentiated embrace of all phenomena as a means for realisation, regardless of any conventional biases that one may have towards them. As opposed to seeing the world as sinful, polluted or illusory, it attempts to utilise all phenomena in the service of awakening. Hence, many things that are avoided by more orthodox groups are accepted and even actively embraced by tantric practitioners — sex, alcohol, the eating of meat and other taboos — all of these are partaken of, celebrated and revered as aspects of the divine, although it must be added that they generally make up for a minor part of their practice, the greater part still requiring strict discipline, meditation and purificatory practices. They are by no means indulgences in the common sense. Nevertheless, it is perhaps easy to see why the tantric traditions in all of their manifestations became fertile ground, not only for abuses and antinomian excess, but also for true manifestations of crazy-wisdom.

RIDING THE LION

About this yogi Milarepa here,
Others ask, "Is he really crazy?"
I also wonder if I am crazy.
To tell of the crazy nature of such craziness:
The father, son, and lineage are crazy.
At the top of the lineage, Vajradhara is crazy.
The forefather Tilopa Sherap Sangpo is crazy.
The ancestor Naropa, the great pandit, is crazy.
My old father, Marpa Lotsawa, is crazy.
And I, Milarepa, too am crazy.
This lineage of the great Vajradhara
Was driven crazy by the demon of the spontaneous
    four kayas.
The forefather Tilopa Sherap Sangpo
Was driven crazy by the demon of Mahamudra.
The ancestor Naropa, the great pandit,
Was driven crazy by the demon of yogic practice.
My old father, Marpa Lotsawa,
Was driven crazy by the demon of the four sections
    of tantra.
And I, Milarepa, too am crazy:
I'm driven crazy by the demon of prana and mind.
I'm driven crazy by the view that is free from bias.
I'm driven crazy by the self-luminous meditation
    that's reference-free.
I'm driven crazy by the self-liberated conduct free
    of fixation.
I'm driven crazy by the fruition free of hope and
    fear.

I'm driven crazy by samaya that's free of deceit.[1]

— MILAREPA

The Five Founding Masters and the "Direct Lineage"

Just as the "early diffusion" of Buddhism to Tibet in the eighth century with Padmasambhava brought with it the "ancient tantras" and established the Nyingma tradition, the "later diffusion" that began in the tenth century brought with it the "new tantras" and led to the creation of the Kagyu tradition. The Kagyu or "Whispered Transmission" is said to derive its name from the highly esoteric teachings that were secretively whispered from master to disciple in an unbroken lineage that reaches back over a thousand years, to Tilopa, Naropa, Marpa, Milarepa and Gampopa — the Five Founding Masters. These tenth-century *mahāsiddhas* were highly accomplished tantric adepts, renowned as much for their profound realisation as the lengths that they went to in order to attain it.

Tilopa

Although Tilopa was said to have been born into a priestly caste, perhaps even a royal family, during an encounter with a *dakini* — in this case understood to mean a female buddha whose purpose is to inspire promising practitioners — he was advised to adopt the lifestyle of a wandering mendicant. His travels took him to many of the great masters of his time who initiated him into different aspects of practice and he soon became a holder of all the tantric lineages; the only person in his day known to have done so. After many years of meditation and practice and under the advice of one of his gurus, Matangi, he began to practise the phase of "action". For the next 12 years he worked as a pimp and bodyguard for a prostitute called Dharima in a brothel in Bengal, whilst during the day he worked grinding sesame seeds. As a master of the direct path, he is known for his Six Words of Advice which have been translated as:

No thought, no reflection, no analysis,
No cultivation, no intention;
Let it settle itself.[2]

Much of what we know about Tilopa comes from the hagiographies of his foremost disciple, Naropa. As we are about to see, he was an uncompromising teacher, utterly unconcerned with social convention and traditional morals, and from his disciples — Naropa in particular — he demanded nothing less than their utter surrender to his bizarre yet apparently effective methods.

Naropa

Much like the life of Padmasambhava, the lives of the Five Founding Masters have been enhanced and embellished with all sorts of supernatural and miraculous events, making it difficult to discover true biographical details. In some accounts, Naropa was a prince in the royal line of the Sakya clan, his father the great king Santivarman; in others, he was the son of a mixed-caste union, his father a dealer in liquor in the east of India. According to this version, Naropa began life quite conventionally, selling wood as a young man and entering into an arranged marriage with a young Brahmin girl. After eight years they agreed to dissolve their marriage and become ordained. Now 28, Naropa entered the famous Buddhist University at Nalanda, where he studied both *sutra* and *tantra* and achieved considerable repute as a scholar and debater. Like Tilopa, a chance encounter with a *dakini* changed the direction of his life. Appearing to him as an "old woman with thirty-seven ugly features",[3] she asked him if he correctly understood the *dharma*, to which he responded that he did. She then burst into tears and said that although he was a great scholar, he was also a liar, as the only one who correctly understood the *dharma* was a great adept called Tilopa. Drawn by his own spiritual intuition and intense feelings of devotion, he set out on a quest to find the mysterious master. This confrontation with the hideous hag *dakini* was the first of his 12 minor hardships — a series of repulsive and shocking visionary experiences designed to undermine his sense of purity and propriety, and prepare him for his meeting with the Guru. They included encounters with "a leper woman without hands and feet"[4]; "a stinking bitch crawling with vermin"[5]; "a man who was tearing the intestines out of a human corpse and cutting them up"[6]; "a dark man with a pack of hounds, a bow and arrows"[7] that asked him to kill a deer; two old people "ploughing a field, killing and eating the insects they found in the furrows"[8]; "a man who had impaled his father on a stake, put his mother into a dungeon and was about to kill them"[9]; and other such delights straight from the darkest recesses of the human shadow. Disgusting as they may sound, they were nothing compared to the ordeals he had to endure once he had found his guru — hardships that brought him to the brink of utter despair and suicide.

Nevertheless, after years of searching and having wandered the length and breadth of India, he had the good fortune of coming across Tilopa on the very road he was travelling. Prostrating in the dust and circumambulating him, he addressed him as Guru, inquiring after his health. "I am not your Guru and you are not my disciple", Tilopa stormed at him, and then he struck him angrily.[10]

Undeterred by this initial encounter, Naropa spent the next 12 years with his guru, undergoing 12 major hardships — initiations that included such things as jumping from a temple tower and breaking all his bones; throwing himself into a fire; the attempted kidnap of a minister's bride which ended with a severe beating; and making a *mandala* for his master with his own blood and severed fingers. On one such occasion, begging food at a wedding feast, Naropa returned to his master with a selection of exquisite dishes. Tilopa was delighted. For the first time he spoke to his disciple respectfully and sent him back for more food. Although there was a prohibition on monks returning to the same place to beg, Naropa was ecstatic at the change in his master's attitude towards him and so returned several times for more food. On his fifth visit, this time too embarrassed to beg again, he stole a final delicious dish. Spotted by some of the wedding guests, he was chased, caught, and beaten to within an inch of his life. After each of these ordeals, as Naropa lay beaten, broken, burnt, dismembered or otherwise dying, Tilopa would ask him, "Naropa, what is wrong with you?" In this last case he replied, "Thrashed like rice and like sesame crushed, My head is splitting and I suffer", to which Tilopa told him:

This twisted copper kettle of Samsāra
Deserves to be smashed, Naropa. Look
Into the mirror of your mind which is commitment,
the mysterious home of the dakini.[11]

On each of the 12 occasions, at the end of the ordeal and after he had delivered the teaching, Tilopa would miraculously heal his long-suffering student in an instant with a mere touch.

On another occasion, having first advised his student to "get a girl", he proceeded to chastise him for getting one, and then demanded the girl for himself. While Naropa beat his own penis with a stone as penance, the girl received a beating of her own from Tilopa for smiling at Naropa.

In each instance, these ordeals depict spectacularly dramatic affronts to selfhood. Any genuine spiritual practice, if not intended to directly undermine the self, is designed to improve one's ability to do so. If the mind is the tool we have to reveal the absence of an abiding self, then such practices that improve concentration or visualisation are not of any use in themselves, but only to the extent that they make the tool more powerful. The goal ultimately, in all cases, is the undermining of the sense of self that gives rise to the primal duality of self and other. It is the fundamental illusion that leads to a sense of separation and consequently, to all of our apparent troubles and tribulations. Simply stated, *saṃsāra* is the perspective of the suffering, separate self, while *nirvana* is the undivided, universal flow that results from the transcendence of the imagined separation. Naropa's 12 minor and major hardships, beyond being real-life biographical details, are fanciful allegories that highlight the deepest fears and calamities of the self. They are stories of suffering writ large, on the one hand designed to motivate the practitioner towards transcending their sorry state, as well as to give insight into the various facets of the self-sense that are to be transcended and hence include all the motifs of illness, pain, death, decay, sex, and so on that make up the visceral building blocks of selfhood. It is no wonder that from the conventional perspective, where selfhood is a given, any talk of its illusory nature sounds like the ramblings of a madman. Selfhood, after all, is the very ground of who we take ourselves to be, conventionally speaking. This unenlightened perspective, however, only demonstrates a naivety of analysis of the whole situation. It is founded upon an unexamined presumption, nothing more. Rather than demonstrate a conclusion based upon profound analysis, it reveals an assumption based upon none.

Marpa

Marpa Lotsawa, which means "Marpa the Translator", was the first Tibetan patriarch of the Kagyu tradition, sometimes referred to as Marpa Kagyu in his honour. He was the first to bring together the two currents of the "direct lineage" of Tilopa and Naropa with the "indirect lineage" of Saraha, Nagarjuna,

Savaripa and Maitripa, and made three epic journeys to India in order to seek out his teachers and study the *buddhadharma* from its purest sources. As distinct from the "direct lineage" which was primarily concerned with the four special transmissions of Tilopa and the six yogas of Naropa, the "indirect lineage" focused mainly on the teachings of *mahāmudrā*, The Great Seal. According to the *Cakrasamvara-tantra, mahā* refers to the indivisible nature of *mu*, the awareness of emptiness, and *drā*, the freedom from *saṃsāra. Mahāmudrā*, much like aspects of the Taoist *wu-wei*, is the practice of no practice — the realisation of the mind as it is. It does not strive to create any special state of mind nor interfere in any way with the presently arising contents of consciousness. It is rather the absolute surrender of striving to change anything whatsoever; the bare, unobscured awareness of all phenomena as ultimately empty and free from *saṃsāra* — always and already one with *nirvana*. It is in this respect less of a practice itself and more of an abiding state of constant awareness, engaged in, not at a specific time for a specific duration, but at all times, unceasingly. Over the course of 40 years, of which, half was spent travelling in India, he studied under a total of 13 different gurus, the two *mahāsiddhas*, Naropa and Maitripa being first and foremost.

As his name suggests, he was instrumental in translating the foundational Sanskrit texts of Vajrayana into Tibetan, and some 24 works of the Tibetan Buddhist canon are attributed to him. As a native who had studied both Tibetan and Sanskrit from an early age, he was an ideal candidate, not only for his ability to effectively accomplish the literal translation of texts, but also as an experienced practitioner to "translate" the methods and practices of Indian Vajrayana into the unique cultural milieu of Tibet, and adapt it to the distinct characteristics of its people.

From his time with Maitripa, he also learnt the art of the *doha*, or song of realisation, an extemporaneous outpouring that reveals the deeper understanding of the singer and expresses their unique insight. Traditionally these songs were delivered in a concise and obscure tantric code understood only by adepts, but with Marpa they became longer and took on the format of a narrative that used more straightforward language. This transformation of the *doha* reached its culmination with Marpa's foremost disciple Milarepa, who was known as much for his prowess as a poet as he was for his profound realisation, and through their creative adaptations, it took on the familiar format that has endured to this day. Although over the centuries these innovations have found their way into what could now be considered the mainstream of Buddhist practice, at the time the *doha* represented a considerable deviation from the conventional path of the Buddhist monk, where any type of music, song or spontaneous outburst were forbidden, and where instead, restraint and self-control were the order of the day.

And while the conventional path of the monk excluded relationships with the opposite sex and upheld celibacy as an aspect of practice, Marpa, after his initial wanderings in India, instead settled down, married, had a son, and lived the life of a householder, while at the same time tending to the first of his own students. It was at this time that he was sought out by Milarepa, desperate for instruction and help in atoning for the terrible sins he had committed in his youth.

Milarepa

The epic story of his life, as told in his most well-known biography, *The Life of Milarepa*, written by Tsang Nyon, the Madman of Tsang, tells of a childhood of privilege and prosperity, before turning to tragedy upon the death of his father. Deprived of his father's inheritance by the shady machinations and betrayal of his uncle and aunt, Milarepa, along with his mother and sister, were torn from their comfortable existence and thrust into poverty and suffering, all due to the greed and vanity of members of their own family. Urged by his mother's bitterness to take revenge, Milarepa was sent away to study sorcery with black magicians. He was evidently a talented student and one of his spells wrought its havoc on the day his uncle and family were celebrating their eldest son's wedding feast. As 35 guests gathered in the very house that Milarepa's father had built for them, the young apprentice's magic took effect and brought the house tumbling down, killing everyone inside. Much to the mother's dismay, the uncle and aunt had stepped out of the house momentarily and were saved. And so the feuding continued. Meanwhile, Milarepa, having heard the results of his sorcery, was stricken with remorse. In a desperate attempt to offset his negative karma, he sought out Marpa and pleaded with him for initiation into the *buddhadharma*. The seemingly impossible trials that followed and the abuse he endured at the hands of Marpa have become legendary and stand as a testament to the lengths some are willing to go to in the steadfast pursuit of enlightenment.

Before he would initiate Milarepa, Marpa set him the task of building a tower. When it was only half built, Marpa made him tear it down and return the rocks to their original places, before ordering the construction of another tower with slightly different specifications. Once again, before it had been built, Milarepa was ordered to destroy it. This went on several times, until Milarepa was at his wits' end. Pleading with his master to give him the definitive instructions, Marpa said to him:

> Build in this place a square white tower nine stories high with a superstructure and a pinnacle, forming ten stories. It will never be torn down. When you have finished, I will give you the secret teaching. Then you may retire to meditate and during your retreat I will provide for your sustenance.[12]

After making Marpa promise to not make him disassemble it once more, and calling for the lama's wife to be a witness to the promise, Milarepa once again began to build. What could possibly go wrong?

Whilst laying the foundations, two of Marpa's disciples happened by and helped by rolling a large boulder into place as the cornerstone. As he was finishing the second story, Marpa came and pointed at the cornerstone, asking where it had come from. Upon finding out that it had been put there by his other disciples, he ordered Milarepa to replace it, knowing full well that he could not do so without dismantling the whole building. Milarepa objected and reminded Marpa of his promise, however, Marpa insisted that he was not asking for the building to be taken down, only for the stone to be replaced as it had not been Milarepa's work. And so, once again, Milarepa destroyed the whole building, only to roll the boulder back to where it had been, and then, this time by himself, roll it back to the cornerstone position. By the time he had reached the seventh story, his body was wracked with pain and his back was full of open sores. Still, he persisted and finished the tower to his guru's specifications. However, upon petitioning his guru once more for initiation, he was rebuffed yet again:

> You made a little tower which isn't even as thick as my arm. It is hardly worth the Doctrine which I, with great difficulty, brought all the way from India. If you have the price of my teaching, give it to me. Otherwise do not stay here among the initiates of the secret teaching.[13]

Marpa then slapped him, grabbed him by the hair and threw him out. Throughout all of this, Marpa's wife, Dakmema, had been of great solace to the long-suffering student. She would try to reason with her husband on his behalf and did what she could to ease his situation by secretly giving provisions and food. This time, as Milarepa lay on the floor sobbing, she once again did her best to console him and lift his spirits.

Still unsatisfied with his student's exertions, Marpa now ordered a shrine to be built at the foot of the tower. Having accomplished this, Dakmema provided him with "a tub of butter, a piece of cloth, and a small copper cooking pot to give to the lama".[14] However, upon offering this gift to his guru, he was cursed at, kicked and thrown out again, as Marpa had recognised the gifts as being his own.

Having endured more abuse and with no initiation in sight, Milarepa left at Dakmema's instigation and with her aid. Their plan was for him to visit Lama Ngokpa, one of Marpa's advanced students, in the hope of initiation from him, and Dakmema forged a letter from Marpa to this effect. Unfortunately, without the lama's blessing Milarepa's meditations were fruitless, and shortly thereafter he found himself back at his master's feet, pleading for his blessing. Upon his return however, Marpa had changed his tune. He called for a celebration with Milarepa as the principal guest and said to those present:

If everything is carefully examined, not one of us is to be blamed. I have merely tested Great Magician to purify him of his sins. If the work on the tower had been intended for my own gain, I would have been gentle in the giving of orders. Therefore I was sincere. Being a woman, the mistress was also right not to be able to bear the situation, yet her excessive compassion in deceiving with the sacred objects and the forged letter was a serious indulgence.... Had this son of mine completed nine great ordeals, his complete Enlightenment, without future rebirth, would have been achieved without leaving any bodily residue. Since, due to Dakmema's weakness, that did not take place, there will remain a faint stain of defilement with him. However, his great sins have been erased by his eight great afflictions of mind and by his numerous small agonies. Now, I receive you and will give you my teaching, which is as dear to me as my own heart. I will help you with provisions and let you meditate and be happy.[15]

As can be imagined, Milarepa was ecstatic. His life as a disciple and practitioner had now begun in earnest. And although his days of suffering at the hands of Marpa were finally over, being the tough taskmaster that he was, his days of suffering by his own hands were only just beginning.

Who can say just what motivated Marpa's excessively harsh treatment of his student — whether it was to burn up the extreme negative karma of his past deeds, or whether it was simply an intervention that served to unburden the psychic load that he bore; a contrived penance that he could work through to psychologically expiate his sins. Perhaps it was none of these things and any attempt to logically comprehend the matter is to fail to recognise it as being beyond logical appraisal. Nevertheless, thanks to the gift of historic hindsight, we do know that Milarepa was successful in his quest for the Ultimate. We need not know how it worked to at least know that it did work.

Such hardships as he had endured stood him in good stead for the life of an extreme renunciate he was to pursue; meditating in remote caves for years on end and tending to his body with the bare minimum to survive. At one point, his sister discovers him in a cave, naked and emaciated, his eyes sunk in their sockets, his bones protruding, and his skin green from having subsisted on nothing but nettles for many years. She is shocked by his appearance and embarrassed by his nakedness. For her next visit she resolves to bring him some proper food and some cloth for him to make a cloak but rather than using the cloth as she had expected, Milarepa decided to instead fashion a hood to cover his head, as well as sewing a sleeve for each of his fingers and a sheath for his genitals. On her next visit, he parades around in his absurd attire, much to her embarrassment, and in response to her rebuke for having ruined her precious cloth, Milarepa tells her:

> I am the holy man who seeks the essential good from this precious human life. Knowing what real shame is, I remain faithful to my vows and precepts. Sister, you alone blush at my nakedness. Even if I wished to cut off my sexual organ, I dare not. I fashioned a modest covering for it just as you asked me, even though it interrupted my meditation. Since I consider all the parts of my body to be of equal worth, I made these sheaths. Your cloth has not been destroyed. But I see now that you feel more ashamed than I. If you blush at my organ, blush equally at your own. If for you it is better to get rid of an object you consider shameful, get rid of your own.[16]

Milarepa occupies a special place among the great adepts of Tibetan Buddhism. His reformation from murderous black magician to illumined poet-saint is unique in the pantheon of enlightened masters. The extreme lengths he went to in order to pursue his path, the body of exquisite, illuminated poetry he left behind and his willingness to risk everything, even his own life, in order to attain his goal of awakening have endeared him to practitioners and laymen alike. His legacy, like the tower he built under duress, still stands strong almost 1000 years later. To the Tibetans, he also represented the first home-grown, enlightened Buddhist master, who rose to the summit of spiritual attainment without ever having to travel to India or study with Indian masters. For a tradition that was still trying to establish itself and find its own way, this was no small feat. It could be said that the life of Milarepa was proof that Tibetan Buddhism had become an authentic tradition in its own right, capable of producing masters of its own. 300 years after Padmasambhava had first travelled from India to Tibet to plant the seed of Buddhism, Tibetan Vajrayana had blossomed, and Milarepa was its first flower.

6

THE LAND OF JAMBU TREES

Fools, dwelling in darkness, but wise in their own conceit and puffed up with vain scholarship, wander about, being afflicted by many ills, like blind men led by the blind.[1]

— MUNDAKA UPANISAD

Batty Bhārat

The rich and fertile soils of India have brought forth no less than four of the world's great religious traditions, which while impressive, still largely underscores the true magnitude of its spiritual effluence upon the world. Surpassing even the Middle East, nowhere but Holy Bhārat has seen such an abundant and eclectic proliferation of theology, philosophy and spiritual practice. Here, in the place that ancient scriptures call Jambudvīpa, "The Land of Jambu Trees", there are so many religious holidays that were one to celebrate them all, their calendar would permit nothing else and so many scriptures that one could not read them all in a lifetime even if reading scriptures was all they did. With several million sacred sites and more than 750,000 temples, it comes as no surprise that India has been called the land of 330 million gods. Although this last, oft-quoted "fact" is untrue (an error based upon bad translation), it nevertheless demonstrates one of the underlying presumptions of outsiders — that India just has too many gods and goddesses to comfortably get one's head around. Indeed, to outsiders and scholars the discussion as to whether the Hindu religion is pantheistic or monotheistic rages on as it has for millennia and does not look to abate any time soon. To adepts and mystics, however, the discussion is resolved by its transcendence to a higher plane of cognition. To them it is quite clearly either, neither and both, and they have little problem in seeing why. An amusing exchange between Vidagdha and the Vedic sage Yājñavalkya in the *Bṛhadāraṇyaka Upaniṣad* serves to illustrate these two perspectives:

> Then Vidaghdha, the son of Śakala, asked him. "How many gods are there, Yājñavalkya?" Yājñavalkya decided it through this (group of Mantras known as) Nivid (saying), "As many as are indicated in the Nivid of the Viśvadevas — three hundred and three, and three thousand and three".
> "Very well", said Śākalya, [son of Sakala] "how many gods exactly are there, Yājñavalkya?"
> "Thirty-three."
> "Very well", said the other, "how many gods exactly are there, Yājñavalkya?"
> "Six."
> "Very well", said Śākalya, "how many gods exactly are there, Yājñavalkya?"
> "Three."
> "Very well", said the other, "how many gods exactly are there, Yājñavalkya?"
> "Two."
> "Very well", said Śākalya, "how many gods exactly are there, Yājñavalkya?"
> "One and a half."
> "Very well", said the other, "how many gods exactly are there, Yājñavalkya?"
> "One."[2]

All that poor old Vidaghdha wants is a simple answer, just a number. If gods are entities "out there" then they can surely be weighed and measured, described and counted. Yājñavalkya the sage, knows instead that gods are not necessarily even entities "out there" to begin with, or at least, if they are, then they only are in one perspective amongst many. While Vidaghdha is bound by his single, narrow perspective and suffers accordingly, Yājñavalkya is free to navigate an ocean of them, and is bound by none. And the more intent Vidaghdha is on pinning Yājñavalkya down to a simple answer, the more Yājñavalkya slinks away to undermine his friend's simplistic notions. So, to the question "is Hinduism pantheistic or monotheistic?" the answer is "yes".

But if the 330 million gods of Hinduism errs by overcomplication, equally the term "Hinduism" errs by oversimplification. "Hinduism" is a misnomer, a geographical term that refers in a collective fashion to the peoples of the Indus valley, and a term used by outsiders in an attempt to elegantly condense in one word a tradition that thwarts all attempts to do so. The only thread that ties together an otherwise heterogeneous agglomeration of philosophical schools and religious traditions are the four Vedic scriptures: the *Rigveda*, the *Yajurveda*, the *Samaveda* and the *Atharvaveda*. In this sense, Hinduism is more properly conceived of as the religion of the Vedas and is known throughout India as *vaidika dharma*, or "the *dharma* derived from the Vedas". Within this Vedic amalgam are six philosophical schools that differ from one another in their outward signs and symbols at least as much as certain other religions differ from each other, making their underlying shared connection, at times, seem tenuous. So, should Hinduism be considered to be a single congruous religious tradition, or is it really an amalgam of different religions that simply bear a single name? As with our previous question, the answer is "yes". The trick is to not get lost in the details otherwise the details are lost. These questions, when really considered, are like asking "how long is a piece of string?" Valuable answers can only be ascertained once the questions themselves have been better understood. What is more, the answer itself lies in the correct understanding of the question. Nothing more is required. So while some hold the opinion that these six philosophical schools are separate systems, independent of one another, others consider them to be contributory rather than contradictory to one another. Others still, believe them to be like the interdependent and successive steps of a single ladder. All of course, are right. The great religion of the Vedas simply is. And whatever it is, it is broad, deep, sublime and supremely diverse. And if this were not enough, India also bore for us Buddhism, Jainism and Sikhism.

From the Middle Way of the Buddha to the furthest extremes on opposite ends of the spectrum, every spiritual experiment conceivable by the mind of mankind is either currently underway or has been tried at some point in the past. *Ahimsa*, the principle of harmlessness, has been employed by Jain monks to such a degree that their day-to-day activities are constrained by hundreds of proscriptions so as to avoid killing even the smallest living creatures; the ground before them is swept as they walk, with a peacock-feather brush, so as to avoid stepping on insects; their drinking water is strained to protect microbes; and a mask is worn over their mouths to avoid breathing in minute life forms. At the other extreme are the Thugees, a cult that so egregiously disregarded the principle of *ahimsa* to the extent of ritually murdering innocent people by strangulation as a means to worship Kāli — the ferocious and bloodthirsty goddess of death and destruction. Thankfully the Jains remain but the Thugees are no more.

Many monks follow an austere lifestyle, abstaining from sex, alcohol, drugs and a whole host of other taboo foods such as meat and fish, while other tantric practitioners instead choose to indulge in all of them. While some disregard their bodies and wander naked, subjecting themselves to the harshest of ascetic practices and self-abnegation, others dress themselves in the finest silks and pamper themselves as they would a living manifestation of God, all of course in the interest of furthering their spiritual practice. In India one can find the most balanced, sane and sensible practitioners, as well as outright raving lunatics, all seeking and surrendering themselves to the same great Divine Power, and all doing so in their very own imitable and unique way. Nowhere in the world can one find such wisdom alongside such craziness, rubbing shoulders in harmonious co-existence and peaceably sharing the same geographical space. The intersection of these two, as can be expected, abounds. From the *mahāsiddhas*, to *masts*, *bāuls* and *avadhūtas*, India has mad-saints and crazy-yogis aplenty. Drawn from its ages-old tradition of spiritual eclecticism, Tantricism and a foundational notion of the search for God being one's first and foremost concern, it is easy to see why crazy-wisdom has flourished so abundantly within its spirit-soaked shores.

The Great Adepts

To more completely understand the peculiar brand of crazy-wisdom that lived and breathed through the characters of the Three Madmen, as well as the earlier Tibetan masters such as Padmasambhava, Marpa and Milarepa, we must go back earlier still to the tradition of the *mahāsiddhas*. These legendary Buddhist masters who lived in India between the sixth and twelfth centuries were known as much for their remarkable spiritual accomplishments as they were for their unconventional behaviour and extreme teaching methods which challenged the social norms and conventions of their time. It is important to note, however, that as with other authentic crazy-wisdom masters, the *mahāsiddhas* were not simply rebels or iconoclasts. Much of their unconventional behaviour was not an end in itself, but rather a means to an end. If, in order to achieve spiritual progress, one must be willing to confront and transcend all forms of conditioning, then this too must include social norms and religious conventions. Their behaviour should be considered in this context, as the simple consequence of all considerations being subordinate to the ultimate goal of awakening. Their wisdom was to pursue enlightenment; their craziness was to do so at the expense of all else.

Unlike the more conventional approaches of other Buddhist schools of the time, these tantric masters emphasised the transformative power of direct experience, of complete immersion in the full spectrum of life experience, rather than relying solely on intellectual understanding or meditational inwardness. In this they were pioneers, and their lives and teachings offer a unique perspective on the nature of reality and the path to enlightenment. With an emphasis on spontaneity, directness, and a fearless attitude towards life, their teachings arose as a panacea to the repetitive and sheltered existence of conventional monks, whose lives had been almost entirely deprived of such things.

The term *mahāsiddha* means "greatly accomplished one" or "great adept" — the word *siddha* referring to one who had acquired one or more *siddhis*, a Sanskrit noun which can be translated as "knowledge", "accomplishment", "attainment" or "success", but more commonly understood to be the magical powers or superhuman abilities acquired through the dedicated practice of esoteric spiritual exercises. However, these mundane or lower *siddhis* such as levitation, telepathy, telekinesis, clairvoyance, or the ability to transmute physical matter, were merely by-products of their dedicated practice and certainly not the goal. The goal and the commonality they all shared was an unshakable dedication to the attainment of the ultimate or supreme *siddhi* of enlightenment. This is the common thread that weaves together the colourful fabric of their lives; however, it must be said that not all of them reached the sublime summit their sights were set on. Some failed in this great endeavour and instead of illuminating the path and its goal, their lives highlight the pitfalls on the path and stand as poignant warnings to all students of the *buddhadharma* of what not to do.

Although we have previously mentioned two of them, Tilopa and Naropa, the Buddhist Vajrayana tradition speaks of eighty-four *mahāsiddhas* in all — eighty-four being a particularly sacred and auspicious number in ancient India and featuring often throughout Buddhist scripture. The *Avatamsaka Sutra* or *Flower Ornament Sutra* tells us:

Eighty-four thousand gates of teaching do the Buddhas use to liberate beings.[3]

And the theme becomes even more pronounced and developed within the Vajrayana tradition. The *Guhyagarbha Tantra*, or *Tantra of the Secret Essence*, says:

Due to conceptual ignorance, [there are] eighty-four thousand passions; [and] the antidotes for them are eighty-four thousand categories of teachings that were taught, are being taught, and will be taught.[4]

No doubt this idea of there being eighty-four thousand dharma-doors or methods of instruction drew strength and authority from the lives and teachings of the eighty-four *mahāsiddhas* due to their radically diverse and unique personalities and the idiosyncratic paths that led them to the supreme *siddhi* of enlightenment. Their lives were a demonstration that there is no one "right" way to achieve spiritual awakening, and that any authentic path must honour the diversity of human experience, recognise that people have different strengths, weaknesses, capacities and tendencies, and cater to this fact.

Much of what we know about these Great Adepts comes from the *Caturaśīti-siddha-pravṛtti*, *The Lives of the Eighty-Four Siddhas*, written in Sanskrit by Abhayadatta in the late eleventh or early twelfth century but surviving only in its Tibetan translation. Rather than a historical text, the book reads more like a hagiography of tantric superheroes, with an almost formulaic narrative for each of its protagonists. After a brief introduction, we are then told of their own particular crisis or aspiration which then leads to a breakthrough and their first encounter with the guru. Then their methods of practice are described, as well as the duration and the *siddhis* obtained. Finally, we are told of their post-enlightenment activities, followed by their departure to the heavenly realm. Just as their lives and personalities are marked by diversity and idiosyncrasy, so too are the life-crises that lead to their meeting with a realised master. Kapalapa and Kankaripa came across their gurus in the cemetery as they grieved the loss of loved ones, while Rahula and Tantipa were already senile old men facing their own imminent demise when their teachers came to the rescue. Kucipa, a poor farmer of low caste had a swollen and deformed neck and was suffering terribly from goitre before his meeting with his guru, Nagarjuna. Ajokipa, whose name means "lazy bum", is introduced to us as a fat and idle good-for-nothing, chased out of his home by his own family. Like many of the *mahāsiddhas*, his meeting with the guru takes place in a cemetery, as he lay on his back in complete resignation. Acinta, a hermit and woodsman was so terribly poor that all he did was obsess over having wealth, while Tandhepa had gambled away everything he owned playing dice. Kamparipa, the blacksmith, was sick of his job, as was Camaripa, the shoemaker, who felt he was not where he was supposed to be and dreamt of doing other things. And less fortunate than even these two was Khadgapa, a professional thief from a low-caste family who came across his guru in a cremation ground where he was hiding out after a failed robbery attempt. In each case, the guru's appearance in the narrative is to present to them the *dharma*, not only as the solution to their current problems, but also as the solution to all problems. For others, it is not a problem that motivates them to take up the

Great Work, but rather the demonstration of new and exciting possibilities. Savaripa, the hunter, wishes only to be able to kill a hundred deer with one arrow as demonstrated to him by Avalokitesvara, the Bodhisattva of Compassion but ends up rejecting his livelihood, as well as the eating of meat, after receiving basic instruction. (Avalokitesvara also revives the deer he shot in case you were wondering. He is the Bodhisattva of Compassion after all.) Udheli's only wish is to fly like the wild geese and Bhandhepa, likewise, is inspired to practise so as to gain this ability after seeing an *arhat* fly through the sky.

Although most often the guru is portrayed as a wandering yogi — a living, breathing master of flesh and blood — at times he is superhuman, as in the case of Nagarjuna, whose teachers are Bodhisattvas, like Avalokitesvara mentioned above. At other times they are female wisdom spirits, or *dakinis*, who intervene in the destiny of the budding adept so as to strengthen their resolve or provide them with the essential insight to help them progress. Virupa had been a monk for 12 years, in which time he had recited his chosen mantra two million times, but to no avail. In disgust with his lack of progress, he tore up his rosary and threw it into the toilet. That evening, a *dakini* appeared with the rosary and returned it to him with some words of encouragement. With his confidence and determination renewed, he returned to his practice with an unshakeable trust in the process and ultimately attained the supreme *siddhi* of enlightenment.

In a similar moment of despair after jabbing his finger with a needle whilst sewing, Kantalipa, The Ragman-Tailor, was confronted by the "Dakini Vetali in the form of a woman"[5] who initiated him and instructed him in practice.

Kukkuripa, a Brahmin and renunciate who adopted the lifestyle of a wandering yogi, one day came across a starving puppy. His compassion for the sorry creature led him to feed the dog and care for it like a member of his own family. This is all the more significant when we consider that in India, dogs were considered to be unclean animals that Brahmins were prohibited to even touch. After 12 years together, living in a cave in which Kukkuripa practised his *sādhanā*, and having demonstrated his compassion and ability to disregard traditional codes of conduct that were not appropriate to the situation, his beloved dog revealed herself to be a *dakini*, and initiated him into the final teachings that led to his enlightenment.

Another story involves Luipa, a young prince with nothing but contempt for wealth and power, who escapes the palace life to live as a wandering yogi. After a fateful encounter with a *dakini* disguised as a courtesan whilst begging for food in a "house of pleasure", he is given some putrid slop which he immediately tosses into the gutter. "How can you attain nirvana if you're still concerned about the purity of your food?" she calls after him. In a flash of insight, Luipa recognises the vestige of pride and preference that remains in him. He makes his way to the river Ganges where he begins an intense 12-year period of practice, part of which involves eating "the entrails of the fish that the fishermen disembowelled, to transform the fish-guts into the nectar of pure awareness by insight into the nature of things as emptiness".[6] It was due to this seemingly repulsive practice that he was given the name Luipa, which means "Eater of fish-guts".

In the story of Kambala, unbeknownst to him until his moment of revelation, the *dakini* is his own mother. As a prince who ascends to his father's throne upon his death, his mother urges him to abdicate and become a monk. Later still, she encourages him to abandon the monastery to live alone in the jungle. Finally, she exhorts him to renounce even his fine robes, as well as his few possessions, and set out as a itinerant yogi. For 12 years he wanders "from town to town, sleeping in cremation grounds and practicing his sadhana". When finally he "gained *mahamudra-siddhi* he levitated into the sky, and suddenly he was faced with his mother and her retinue of Dakinis".[7]

Saraha

Of the many wisdom *dakinis* that feature in the legends of these Great Adepts, there are perhaps none that have had a greater impact on the tantric tradition and the flowering of Vajrayana than the two nameless young women whose encounters with the preeminent *mahāsiddha*, Saraha, brought about the defining moments of his life.

The Great Brahmin, Saraha was the consummate *mahāsiddha* and embodied the essence of the tantric ideal — eccentric, unorthodox, iconoclastic, spontaneous, creative, charismatic, fearless, bold and utterly dedicated to his spiritual quest. For Saraha, his life was his practice, the world was his altar, and his only God was the Truth Absolute. It is not even altogether certain whether he considered himself to be a Buddhist, as we are told that during the day he engaged in the religious practices of the Vedas that as a Brahmin he was born into, but at night he also practised the system of Buddhism. Even in this, he escaped the simple classifications that are a comfort to others and instead chose to seek the Truth wherever it could be found, much to the consternation of his fellow Brahmins. Whether due to their scheming or through his own experimental transgressions, he was accused of drinking alcohol (something forbidden to both Brahmins and Buddhists alike) and was brought before the king to answer to these charges. Denying any misconduct and in order to prove his innocence, he thrust his hand into boiling oil and drank molten copper to no ill-effect, which led the king to conclude quite reasonably, "If anyone who has powers like these drinks wine, then let him drink".[8]

Although obviously already a man with great wisdom, in possession of *siddhis*, he still lacked the supreme *siddhi* of enlightenment, and sought it intently. A breakthrough came one day, when at the market he came across a young woman of low caste making arrows. She demonstrated a grace and one-pointedness of action that he had never seen before and he watched her, captivated, before asking "Young girl, are you a fletcheress?" A rather strange question to ask a girl who you can quite clearly see is making arrows perhaps, nevertheless it served to open the conversation and she replied: "Noble son, the intent of the Buddha can be understood through symbols and actions, not through words and texts". At that, we are told, "the symbolic purport of this dakini came to life in his heart".[9] Suddenly the process of making arrows took on a symbolic analogy with the path to enlightenment — the cutting to size of the shaft at the top and bottom signified the necessity of cutting off *saṃsāra* and the belief in a separate self; the affixing of the arrowhead symbolised the affixing of discriminating awareness and so on. In that moment, the great and learned Brahmin stood humbled and awestruck by a simple arrowsmith girl who he recognised as the embodied manifestation of the spiritual theory he knew all too well. As a girl of low caste, even his conversing with her would have been frowned upon by his peers. Saraha, however, not one to miss the chance to set aside another dogma at the beckoning of Truth, instead took the girl as his consort and "departed with her to the cremation grounds"[10] where they lived and engaged in tantric yogic practices. So important was this event in his life, that it forged the name he would be known by forevermore. The Brahmin Rahula became Saraha — from *sara* meaning "arrow" and *ha*, "to have shot"; literally "he who has shot the arrow", the non-dual arrow that is, into the heart of duality.

As can be imagined, his peers were scandalised. "The Brahmin Rahula does not perform the time-honored rites and has given up celibacy" they said. "He indulges in shameful practices with a low-caste woman and runs around like a dog in all directions."[11] When word got back to the king, an entourage was sent to gently convince the wayward Brahmin to abandon his folly and return to his duties. Instead of having the desired effect, Saraha serenaded them with 160 verses of a spontaneous and ecstatic song of realisation, the first of his *Three Cycles of Dohas*, known as *A Song for the People*. Rather than converting him back to the path he had abandoned, he instead caused them to abandon theirs and become his followers. Upon the failure of the first expedition, a second was sent, this time led by the queen herself. Saraha welcomed them with another exquisite *doha* of some 80 verses — *A Song for the Queen* — which had much the same effect as his first. In desperation, the king himself went to coax Saraha back into the fold but was met with the third exquisite *doha* — *A Song for the King*. Just 40 verses this time was all it took, and upon hearing it, the king immediately attained full awakening. Little did Saraha know when he gave voice to those three spontaneous songs of realisation that he would be laying the foundations for a radical new perspective, as well as a new Buddhist teaching tradition: *mahāmudrā*.

Mahāmudrā

Like many other esoteric terms, *mahāmudrā* is not easily defined, nor is it used in merely one sense, but instead refers to a number of different things depending on context and usage. It is at once a body of esoteric teachings; a method of pointing to the Ultimate Ground of all things; a meditational practice; a lineage of initiates; as well as a term for Reality. Maitripa, another later *mahāsiddha* in Saraha's own lineage, who wrote extensive commentaries on his *Three Cycles of Dohas*, in answering the question "What is *Mahāmudrā*?" tells us:

It passes beyond the mind of ordinary people, it is luminous, it is without conceptuality, and it is like space.[12]

Usually translated as the "Great Seal", *mahāmudrā* refers to the fact that all phenomena are imprinted with the unmistakeable hallmark of fundamental reality. Like a wax seal on a letter, whose imprint upon the wax also conveys meaning, all phenomena are imprinted with the stamp or seal of the underlying reality that is common to all things and, to the practitioner, it conveys the ultimate meaning that the phenomena are merely modifications of this same noumenal ground. This idea when considered further, has some interesting ramifications. If all phenomena retain the great "seal" or stamp of ultimate reality — if all things are permeated with Truth — then there is nowhere to go and nothing to do in order to bring about, generate, induce or invoke realisation. There is nowhere where more of it is to be found and nothing which lacks it. There is no state of mind, no matter how sublime, that is closer to ultimate reality than any other, and no amount of mental gymnastics, no matter how sophisticated, can alter this fact. There is only the present moment awareness of this supreme stamp of reality, or the lack of it. No amount of coaxing, cajoling, begging or beseeching can increase it and no amount of elusion, evasion, aversion or avoidance can get rid of it. It just is. It is the very is-ness of what is. Therefore, it is our very attempt to seek it, to gain it or grasp it that fundamentally undermines our present moment awareness of it. Any attraction towards anything other than what is, or repulsion away from what is, represents the fundamental dilemma that is to be overcome. And yet, paradoxically, even these avoidance mechanisms shine resplendent with the Great Seal of Ultimate Reality. *Mahāmudrā* as meditation is the practice par excellence, as it requires nothing whatsoever in order to be engaged in — no sitting, no closing of the eyes, no silence, no concentrating on breath or visualised images, and no specific times. It is the moment to moment intuiting of the fundamental unifying reality behind all things and requires no change of state nor anything more than present moment awareness. It is the default meditational state and ultimately, the only meditational state, as all else involves the trance of multiplicity induced by one's focus upon distinct aspects of fragmented phenomena. *Mahāmudrā* cuts through this apparent multiplicity and fixes its focus not on the ever-changing forms of the wax, but rather the seal of Ultimate Reality that is impressed upon it. Saraha is uncompromising in his affirmation that this Ultimate Reality is imprinted upon all things without exception. Even those that are conventionally recommended to be avoided by the practitioner "have this very nature" we are told in the thirty-third verse of his *Song for the King*:

> Intellect, mind, and mental appearances have this very nature.
> All the worlds appearing in their diversity have this very nature.
> All the varieties of the seen and the seer have this very nature.
> Attachment, desire, aversion, and bodhicitta, too, have this very nature.[13]

Not surprisingly, these utterances and others like them drew scathing criticisms from both orthodox Brahmins and Buddhists alike. Attachment, desire and aversion, to them, were things to escape from, or at least to hold at arm's length with disdain. To Saraha, they were further aids to practice; signs and symbols of the very Divine and doorways to the Absolute. Had he not successfully demonstrated the truth of his assertions as well as merely stating them, then posterity would have taken a far dimmer view of him no doubt. Just another one of history's many madmen; not crazy-wise, just straight-up crazy. As it happens he was right, and instead, history smiled upon him, *mahāmudrā* was born and Vajrayana, as well as Buddhism in general, blossomed accordingly.

The second nameless *dakini* that spurred the Great Brahmin on to higher and greater things was "a fifteen-year-old house girl", most probably a servant, who he took as his wife. Having left home, they moved to another country and settled in a solitary place where Saraha was free to practice his *sādhanā* while the girl saw to their basic needs by begging for food. One day, Saraha asked the girl to make "some radishes in yogurt" but as she was preparing the food, Saraha fell into deep meditation and remained there for 12 years without stirring. Upon returning from *samādhi*, he impatiently called to the girl for his radishes. "How could I keep them?" she replied. "You have not arisen from meditational trance for 12 years. It is now spring, and there are no radishes." Perturbed by this considerable lapse, Saraha suggested he go to the mountains to meditate further but the girl continued:

A solitary body does not mean solitude. The best solitude is the mind far away from names and conceptions. You have been meditating for twelve years, yet you have not cut off the idea of radishes. What good will it do to go to the mountains?

Struck by his wife's timely insight, he took her advice to abandon names and conceptions and finally "obtained the highest siddhi of Mahāmudrā".[14]

Female Buddhas

Clearly the *mahāsiddhas* and the tantric tradition they pioneered broke with the customs and conventions of their times in many ways. The lofty spiritual status accorded to the *dakinis* and the elevation of the feminine principal in general, helped to set it apart from the mainstream of religious thought and establish its own identity within the eclectic landscape of Indian spirituality. Although the Buddha himself had done much to break down the rigid considerations of caste and saw to it that his *sangha* included both monks and nuns, the predominant cultural belief in India at the time still regarded women as unfit for buddhahood. They were free to practise and it was generally conceded that progress on the path could be made, but the supreme jewel of enlightenment would remain beyond their reach, at least in their present lives. The best they could do was to accrue merit for rebirth as a man, and only in that case could they attain final liberation from *saṃsāra*. At the time, only the Jains had openly conceded that women were capable of *moksha* by their assertion that Māllinātha, one of 24 *tīrthaṅkaras* or "ford-makers" — the fully enlightened founders of their tradition — was a woman. One in 24 was at least a start, although the prevailing attitude of the time still made its presence felt by the fact that even this concession was denied by one of its two main sects. The Digambaras, then as they do now, instead considered Māllinātha to have been a man. But to give credit where credit's due, the Śvētāmbara Jains at least had opened the door ajar to true women's liberation by acknowledging its possibility. This was the state of affairs until the arrival of the *mahāsiddhas*, who quite accustomed to doing things on their own terms, and in further breaking with mainstream spirituality, pushed the door open some more by including four enlightened women amongst their ranks: Manibhadra, the Perfect Wife; Laksmincara, The Princess of Crazy-Wisdom; and two sisters, Mekhala and Kanakhala, known as The Two Headless Sisters for having offered their severed heads to their guru as payment for his teaching as they had nothing else to give.

Manibhadra — The Perfect Wife

Manibhadra received initiation from a wandering yogi whilst still just a 13-year-old girl and took up the practices he gave her assiduously. A year later she was married and did so without complaint, continuing her practice alongside her duties as a housewife. After 12 years of performing "everything that was expected of her cheerfully and uncomplainingly, always speaking modestly and sweetly, thus controlling both her body and speech" and having raised two children, we are told that "one morning as she returned from the stream with a pitcher full of water, she tripped over a root and fell down, breaking her pot". She remained there for the whole day, until her husband finally found her, staring silently at the broken pieces of the pot. As night fell she came out of her trance and related the following verse as a testament to her enlightenment:

> Sentient beings from beginningless time
> Break their vessels, their lives ended,
> But why do they return home?
> Today I have broken my vessel
> But abandoning my samsara home
> I go on to pure pleasure.
> The Guru is truly wonderful!
> If you desire happiness, rely on him.[15]

In more recent times, we have masters like Gurdjieff, who taught his own brand of the "Fourth Way" or the "Way of the Sly Man" — the other three being the way of the fakir, the monk and the yogi, who use respectively the body, the emotions and the intellect as inroads to the Self. In addition to these three traditional paths to awakening, the Fourth Way represents the way of the householder; a path that does not involve the retreat from everyday life into a cave or monastery in order to achieve Perfection in this life. Instead it is practiced in the midst of mundane life, with duty, parenthood, family, relationship, and work, the grist for the spiritual mill — as possibility anticipated and clearly demonstrated by Manibhadra over a thousand years earlier. It was this radical innovation that made the *mahāsiddhas* a spiritual force that we have yet to fully comprehend even today; they were so ahead of their time that we are still struggling to catch up with them.

Laksmincara — The Princess Of Crazy-Wisdom

Far from this fairytale enlightenment is the story of Laksmincara, a princess who had been promised in marriage to the prince of another region. Upon arriving to be wed, she saw her groom-to-be returning from a hunting trip loaded with bloody carcasses and fainted. When she awoke, she locked herself in the chamber that her husband had provided, refusing to admit anyone for ten days. She tore off her clothes, covered herself with oil and coal dust, mussed her hair and feigned insanity, all the while unswervingly concentrating upon the essential truth in her heart.[16]

Doctors were sent to attend to her but were attacked and all attempts to engage or reason with her failed. To all appearances, it seemed she had gone mad. Finally, she escaped from the palace and spent her time sleeping in cremation grounds while scavenging food that had been thrown out for dogs. She passed seven years in this manner before attaining to the supreme *siddhi* of Truth-Realisation.

Sometime later, King Jalendra, the father of her ex-groom-to-not-be, was wandering through the forest after getting lost on a hunting expedition, when he came across her cave. He peered in and saw "a bright light inside, and in all directions he saw numberless divine maidens who were doing reverence and making offerings"[17] as she sat in meditation. He was awestruck and returned to her cave in order to seek instruction but instead, was sent by her to one of his own toilet cleaners at the royal palace, a man Laksmincara had previously initiated and instructed and who, we are told, "quickly gained the capacity of a Buddha".[18] Much to the king's credit, he somehow managed to swallow his royal pride and humbly sought out the man for instruction.

Although there is much embellishment and poetic licence as can be expected in such hagiographical literature, we can nevertheless gain an important insight into the eclectic melting pot of the early Buddhist tantric tradition and the depth and breadth of the personalities that brought it to life. In this, *The Lives of the Eighty-Four Siddhas* is unique in the corpus of spiritual writings. Nowhere has such a colourful cast of characters shared the same pages — nobility and ordinary folk alongside freaks and misfits. Indeed, one perhaps would be hard-pressed to find a more broadly representative cross section of society. Not only were they kings, ministers, Brahmins, priests, scholars and yogins, as can be expected, but also poets, musicians, cobblers, potters, shepherds, farmers, hermits, cooks, housewives and whores. Their lives continue to inspire and entertain and their teachings are now studied and practiced in all corners of the world. Many volumes have been devoted to these mad saints and many more will be written in an attempt to further unpack the wisdom they embodied and transmitted. Such was the method in their madness that it will be a long time yet before we truly understand the depths they plumbed and the heights they scaled.

The God-Intoxicated

At the crazier end of the Indian crazy-wisdom spectrum is the *mast* (pronounced like the English, "must"), from the Sufi term *mast-Allah*, meaning "intoxicated with God". These drunkards on the divine are often so inwardly absorbed as to be outwardly absent, sometimes to the extent that conventional living becomes a chore too great to successfully execute and at other times to such a degree that they would perish if not for the charity and care of others. Slipping through the cracks of Indian society, they are unfit for any of the sanctioned roles and unable to perform any of the permitted jobs that others so naturally fall into in the course of life. Like round pegs in square holes, even their religious affiliations and devotions blur the divide between traditions and are comprised of a personal blend of disparate elements, most commonly from Sufic and Vedic sources. Some *masts* then, will use the terminology of Islam and speak of Allah or Mohammed as the object of their devotions, while others will worship Krishna, Sri Caitanya or any number of other figures from the Vedic tradition. Beneath these surface considerations, however, lies a common thread of *bhakti* or devotion.

Vedic spirituality, as do others, recognises several paths to God. Of them, the two that represent the most common psychological predispositions of the practitioner are the paths of *bhakti* (devotion) and *jnana* (discernment). For the *bhakta*, emotion is primary — it is the way of the heart; for the *jnani*, the intellect is primary — the way of the head. In the Indian traditions, these two means to approach God are both highly regarded and considered equally valid paths to enlightenment. The path of *bhakti* relies primarily on faith and love for God and is marked by yearning with bouts of ecstatic exhilaration and swoons of cathartic release when one's chosen focus of devotion is felt to be responsive and heeding of their affections. Equally, the devotee can become despondent and troubled by feelings of spiritual dryness when the object of their love is felt to be distant, unresponsive or even entirely absent. The *jnani* on the other hand uses the power of intellectual discrimination to realise their true nature and therefore, the nature of God. Based purely on these basic distinctions, it is not hard to see why the outward behaviour of the *bhakta*, when taken to extremes, could give the appearance of an unbalanced mind. While the *jnani* appears more passive, inward, measured and meditational, the *bhakta* is active — their devotion is externalised through ritual and worship, and involves offerings, prostrations, prayer, dance and song. For the most part, *masts* are extreme *bhaktas* — so absorbed in the love of God as to be absent to the world. They are the epitome of this devotional divine madness.

Much of what we know about *masts* comes from the lengthy investigations of the self-proclaimed avatar of the age, Meher Baba, who spent many years travelling throughout South Asia in search of them. His view was that they represented potentially powerful conduits of the divine power that required the direction of a capable master in order for its grounding and effective transmission into the world. He considered many of them to be casualties of the spiritual path who had unwittingly awakened energies beyond their ability to contain, and as a result, were overwhelmed by an onslaught of mystical experiences that they were unable to either control or understand. Of all the cases of crazy-wisdom one can find, the *masts* are perhaps the closest to being considered outwardly crazy, their wisdom being the hardest to discern. According to Meher Baba, this was due to the confusion of two different metrics used to establish a person's degree of sanity and the inability to discern between abnormal and supernormal states of consciousness that this confusion leads to:

> According to one way of interpretation, madness is a deviation from the average mode of consciousness and behaviour; and its degree is to be measured by the amount of its departure from the average pattern. But according to another way of interpretation, madness is the incapacity of consciousness to understand or express truth; and its degree is to be measured by the extent to which it deviates from truth. If these two distinct standards are mixed up with each other and applied simultaneously, they inevitably lead to a confusion between the abnormal mad states and the supernormal mast states.[19]

Though perhaps inwardly, according to Meher Baba's second metric, the *masts* represent a fuller embodiment of truth than the saner masses, outwardly their behaviour does little to demonstrate this and more closely resembles that of a classic madman to all but the specialist in such matters. They may mutter to themselves; can be extremely capricious in their wants and obsessive in their habits; are quick to anger and can be aggressive; and are generally incapable of the day-to-day habits that maintain personal hygiene. One such *mast*, Mohammed, who stayed for some time at one of Meher Baba's ashrams in India and was considered by him to be highly spiritually developed, would "sit most of the day next to the door of the ashram, and would roundly abuse and spit on anyone who came near him".[20] He would also spend many hours of the day bending down or squatting and plucking invisible pieces from the ground. As a result of this strange habit, his fingers were rough and calloused and his nails were thick, broken and worn to the flesh. When asked what he was doing he would simply reply "I am looking at something I want"[20] and would explain that it was not done of his own free will but that he was compelled to do so by the divine power.

Meher Baba's investigations led him to distinguish between eight types of *mast*. The most common *mast*, Type Eight, which made up roughly three-quarters of the *masts* contacted, had no specific characteristics with which they could be distinguished, however, the other types — two being fairly common, three being moderately rare, one rare and one very rare — could all be classified according to their shared traits and mannerisms. Type One, known as a *jalâli*, for example:

is *always* hot-tempered, abusive to others, and talks at random. He is restless, and beats those who come near him. He is almost always dressed in rags, and lives in an environment of filth and squalor. By day, he occasionally roams hither and thither, and at night, although he rarely sleeps, he lies down usually in a particular place. When awake, he prefers to recline in a half lying posture, and occasionally rests his head on one hand. He has a habit of constantly moving his fingers and toes to and fro, has a passion for tea, and is moderately fond of tobacco.

He never asks for gifts except tea and tobacco. If given clothes, money and so forth, he at once throws them away; and though he will accept food when hungry, he may throw it away if not hungry. He is happy in crowded streets and bazaars, and sometimes enjoys the company of dogs. The presence of small children annoys him.[21]

The Type Five *mâdar-zâd* on the other hand, a moderately rare *mast*, is:

one who is born a mast. He appears to be an ordinary madman, is most of the time naked, and commonly roams about in dirty and muddy places. His tastes in food are abnormal, and he will eat even raw flesh. He is a very restless fellow, wanders about by night and by day, and seldom sits down or rests. He has no special gestures of his limbs, and he likes and dislikes everything according to his moods. He asks for anything from anyone, and takes whatever is given him, but throws it away at once, either just as it is, or after destroying it. He will accept food when hungry. As far as his choice of environment and any sort of predilection are concerned, he is so capricious that everything, and nothing, may please or displease him by turns.[22]

As can be seen, the defining features of these *masts* are really quite detailed and it is surprising to see that so many peculiarities and idiosyncrasies can all be shared by people who have no apparent relationship to one another. The resemblance between this neat behavioural classification and the classical diagnoses of mental illness are too obvious to easily dismiss, and reaffirms the idea that the *mast* dwells somewhere around the intersection of elevated spirituality and conventional madness, perhaps caused by the intense psychic experiences they have undergone, or perhaps due to the same unfortunate organic disorders of the brain and central nervous system that underlie other forms of known mental derangement. The *mast* then, is perhaps more of a curiosity within the realm of crazy-wisdom than anything else — a fascinating case of divine madness rather than the embodiment of transcendent wisdom displayed by our other subjects.

The Mad Ones

Less conventionally mad than the *masts* but with much in common are the *bāuls*. These divine troubadours are, for the most part, itinerant musicians found primarily throughout the rural areas of Bengal and Bangladesh, where they wander from village to village singing simple love-songs to God and begging their sustenance. Accompanied by an *ektārā*, a one-stringed drone instrument held in one hand, and a *ḍugi*, a small drum that hangs on the shoulder and is played with the other hand, their songs are short, simple and sung in colloquial idioms, rich with imagery from day-to-day village life and overflowing with devotional themes and declarations of their love for Bhagavān, the Lord, or the elusive divine within — the *moner mānuṣ* or "Man of the Heart".

Like the *masts*, the *bāuls* belong to a heterodox *bhakti* tradition that rejects formal religiosity and Vedic orthodoxy and instead aims to cultivate a direct and personal relationship with the divine. Ultimately, their spiritual allegiance lies not even with their own syncretic blend of Buddhist and Hindu tantra, Vaishnavism and Sufism, but rather with the thread of *bhakti* that runs throughout them all. The opening verse of a song by Lālan Shah, arguably the greatest *bāul* saint who lived in the eighteenth and nineteenth centuries, illustrates perfectly their attitude towards conventional religious distinctions:

Everyone asks: "Lālan, what's your religion in this world?"

Lālan answers: "How does religion look?"
I've never laid eyes on it.
Some wear mālās [Hindu rosaries] around their necks,
some tasbis [Muslim rosaries], and so people say
they've got different religions.
But do you bear the sign of your religion
when you come or when you go?[23]

First and foremost, the *bāuls* consider themselves to be devotees of God and care little for the outward externalities of its expression. They have no scriptures but the lyrics to the songs they sing, no temples but their own bodies, and playing music is their means of worship. Like many of their crazy-wise compatriots, they seek to transcend the common dualities that "normal" life is founded upon. Whereas to the conventional mind, any attempt to avoid praise or pleasure and welcome blame or pain, can only be seen as abnormal or insane as it goes against the most basic motivation for their day-to-day activity, to the *bāul*, both are imposters alike — mere distractions from the "eternal bliss" of their beloved and stumbling blocks on the path to perfection. As one *bāul* song would have it:

He who becomes the realizer of bhāva, the lover among
    lovers
His ways are reverse, unconventional
Who can understand them?
How does he live, the man of bhāva?
He has neither joy nor sorrow
Because he has attained the eternal bliss of love.
His eyes stream with tears, the waters of bliss.
Sometimes he laughs to himself, and sometimes he cries.
He has equal enjoyment if he smells sandal wood.
And if someone flings mud upon him.
He does not want fame, fortune, or followers.

All persons are the same to him, relatives and strangers.
He builds his castles in the sky.[24]

The respected writer on *bāuls*, Upendranāth Bhaṭṭācārya, who spent many years living with them and studying their ways, suggests that there are five principal elements to the *bāul dharma*. The first is its non-Vedic character and its affinity to other wayward sects such as the Buddhist Tantrikas and the Vedic Sahajiyās whose genesis was also consequent upon the rejection of their own orthodoxies. The second is the prominent place given to the teacher, who is seen as the ideal human being and the truest form of God. Only through faith in the teacher and surrender to him can the *bāul* progress towards the perfected state. The third element is the belief that God dwells, not merely metaphorically, but literally and physically, in the human body. In accordance with certain tantric ideas and practices, they consider the divine to exist in specific bodily fluids and their more secretive practices, often of a sexual nature, involve techniques to amplify and utilise these fluids. This immanence of the divine in the human body also helps to explain the exalted status of the guru within *bāul dharma*. The fourth element is the assertion that appearances differ from reality and that the true nature of all opposites is to be found in their union. As a consequence, the *bāuls*, like the *tantrikas* and Vaishnavites, consider the relationship between a man and a woman to be sacred, and the cultivation of their love, a divine duty. The fifth and final element is their aspiration to merge with the perfected human that dwells within — the Man of the Heart. Sometimes conceived of as God, Bhagavān, Caitanya or Muhammad, the *moner mānuṣ* is the subject of their songs, the object of their devotion, and the ultimate goal of their practice. In fact the whole of *bāul dharma* is aimed at nothing more than finding and merging with this Man of the Heart, the ever-elusive God within. This paradox of the seeming proximity and remoteness of the Man of the Heart — the abiding presence and absence of God — is a common theme throughout their songs and fuels much of their devotional fervour. *I'm Out of Touch with Myself,* a song by Lālan Shah tells us:

> The Lord is near, but seems far away. Don't you see?
> He's hidden from you like a mountain by the hair in front
>   of your eyes.[25]

The earliest references to the *bāuls* can be found in Bengali texts that date back to the fifteenth century and the name is said to be derived either from the Sanskrit *vātula*, "mad", or from the sect of Buhluliyas, named after their founder Abu Walid Ibn Amre Seiraba Khub, known affectionately by his followers as Buhlul, meaning "blockhead" or "crazy". This "crazy" epithet was no doubt earned due to their extreme unconventionality and their rejection of many of the basic tenets of Indian culture, such as the classical modes of worship in temples and mosques, as well as the caste system and the subordinate status of women. Those who are not homeless wanderers often live on the outskirts of villages, and on the fringes of society, keeping to themselves and engaging in practices that for the most part remain unknown to outsiders. Even their appearance and mode of dress differs from the population at large. Their long hair is twisted into a topknot and they wear long white or saffron-coloured upper garments and very distinctive multicoloured patchwork coats made from a variety of different fabrics. Far from rejecting this "crazy" reputation they have been given by outsiders, instead the *bāuls* have wholly embraced it, transforming its negative connotations into positive ones by affirming it to be divinely inspired — a consequence of being "madly in love" and "crazy for God". As one *bāul* song expresses it:

Mad, mad, everyone is mad.
So why are people criticized for it?
When you dive into the ocean of the heart, you see
That only the madman is truly good.
Some are mad for riches, others for people
Some grow mad from the pull of need.
Some are mad for form, and some for rasa,
And some are mad for love.
These madmen laugh and cry.
There is grandeur to this madness.
Everyone says, "Mad, mad",
On what tree does madness grow?
When you do not care for truth or falsehood
Everything is equal, the bitter and the sweet.[26]

Taking pride in their madness for God, they often affix the words
pāgol or *kṣepā* to their names, both of them Bengali words meaning
"mad" and "mad one", and used by them as terms of endearment
and respect. An amusing story that illustrates their mad behaviour,
used on this occasion to push a student beyond his own self-
limitations, is told of the *bāul*, Khepa Baba by one of his disciples:

Khepa Baba sent me to the village market to steal a goat.
He had seen it while passing and wanted that one and no
other. It was an easy thing to do. But I was resisting. He
insisted. I still refused. Then he shrugged his shoulders and
went to sleep. I felt as though I were drunk, full of anguish.
I started to vomit. Finally, covered with shame, I went out,
weeping and gritting my teeth, and stole the goat. It was not
until much later that I found out that all the goats of this
supposed merchant belonged to Khepa Baba.[27]

For the *bāul*, freedom, love and spontaneity are the true gifts
from God that form the basis of their religious impulse, not

dry, dead rituals and scriptures — the leftover remnants of another's inspiration. Instead, like true rebels and artists, headstrong and heart-centred, they tap into their own sacred source of creativity that bubbles up from within, the very same inexhaustible and living fountain of divine inspiration that crafted all the world's rituals and scriptures in the first place. As mavericks and iconoclasts within the spiritual landscape they have no doubt added to its beauty and variety in a multitude of ways and continue to provide an authentic path towards God for others like them — the round pegs in the square holes of religious orthodoxy. To the *bāul*, we are all mad, but unlike the false madmen — the majority of mankind, obsessed with the ephemeral things of the world — they consider themselves to be the true madmen, in love with the Eternal. As one *bāul* song would have it:

O crazy mind
For this reason I have not become mad
I haven't found a madman up to my wishes
I haven't found any such madman.
Only false madmen everywhere.
True madmen nowhere....
What more can I say?
The country was once full of madmen.
Where is there a madman like Ramakrishna any more?[28]

Ramakrishna

A man who has seen God sometimes behaves like a madman.[29]

— RAMAKRISHNA

One of the greatest Indian *bhaktas* and a hero to the *bāuls*, who himself passed dangerously close to the *mast* state but found salvation and enlightenment instead, was Sri Ramakrishna.

Inclined to radical mood swings in his earlier days, he was treated by many as a madman, and there were times when his behaviour became so erratic as to even give his family doubts as to his sanity. His habit of completely losing outward consciousness to deep inward states did little to help the situation, and for a long time they thought that he perhaps suffered from some terrible illness. The first time it happened, at the age of 6 or 7, Ramakrishna was walking by himself through some paddy-fields eating puffed rice. It was summer and he looked up to see dark thunder-clouds gathering overhead. Just at that moment a flock of brilliant white cranes passed in front in an enchanting contrast. The overwhelming beauty of the moment was too much for the young boy and he fell to the ground, unconscious. He was found by some villagers and carried home, but in later years, Ramakrishna described his unconscious state as a state of indescribable joy. These unconscious and semi-conscious states of spiritual absorption were to remain with him for the rest of his life, sometimes taking place at the most inopportune moments. A sight of cowherd boys crossing the river with their herd would remind him of Krishna, and he would lose consciousness. On a visit to the zoo, the sight of a lion did the same thing and he had to be taken home. When engaged in spiritual discussions with disciples, a mere word, gesture, idea, or song, would send his mind soaring and he would have to be coaxed back down to the physical plane with a whisper in the ear.

Much of his life was spent at Dakshineswar, in a temple complex on the eastern bank of the river Ganges, just a few kilometres north of Calcutta. There, his elder brother, Rāmkumār, had been appointed as the priest of a temple dedicated to Kāli, however, in due time, Ramakrishna's elevated spiritual state led the temple's administrators to cede the position to him instead. The temple complex at Dakshineswar had been recently built, around the mid-nineteenth century, and was a spectacular sight.

It was made up of a number of domed temples to Shiva and Vishnu, as well as the main temple to Kāli, all scattered over 20 acres of land overlooking the Ganges, and complete with orchards, flower gardens, two small reservoirs, music towers and a series of other buildings that served as lodgings for the priests and attendants. This was where the young man, born Gadādhar, into a humble Brahmin family, became Ramakrishna, the saint, the sage, the *avatar*. From here his influence would spread across the entire face of the earth. Before this though, he was to be forged in the fires of intense spiritual experience — experience that for a period tormented both himself, as he struggled to make sense of what was happening to him, and others, as they questioned his sanity and endured his outbursts and bizarre behaviour.

Ramakrishna's initial spiritual impulse, as we have said, was that of a *bhakta* — so much so in fact, that he would weep and plead with the Divine Mother to give him a vision of Her divine form. He would converse with Her as if talking to his own mother and would cause outrage by sitting on the Kāli statue in the temple and feeding it the food offerings with his own hands, with all the tenderness of a lover feeding his beloved. In speaking about this difficult phase in later life, he said:

No sooner had I passed through one spiritual crisis then another took its place... Sometimes I'd open my mouth, and it would be as if my jaws reached from heaven to the underworld. 'Mother!' I'd cry desperately. I felt I had to pull her in, as a fisherman pulls in fish with his dragnet. A prostitute walking the street would appear to me to be Sita, going to meet her victorious husband. An English boy standing cross-legged against a tree reminded me of the boy Krishna, and I lost consciousness. Sometimes I would share my food with a dog. My hair became matted. Birds would perch on my head and peck at the grains of rice which had lodged there during the worship. Snakes would crawl over my motionless body.[30]

During this roller coaster of recurring spiritual crises, Ramakrishna explored the full spectrum of possible relationships with the Divine, leaving no stone unturned. The Vedic tradition generally recognises five different *bhāvas*, or devotional attitudes towards God. Sometimes a sixth *bhāva* is included, that of *tanmayabhava*, the attitude of seeing God everywhere in all things, however, it differs qualitatively from the other five. Whereas the five classic *bhāvas* are relational and founded upon the illusory existence of self and other (a subject that worships and an object that is worshipped) *tanmayabhava* instead transcends this duality and is non-relational and non-dual. It is often considered to be the ultimate *bhāva* and is one that would come to Ramakrishna later on, as the crowning moment of his *sādhanā*. For most of his life, his predominant *bhāva* had been that of *dāsyabhāva* — the attitude of a servant towards their master or a child towards their parent. Now began a period of experimentation with the other four: *śāntabhāva*, the conventional attitude of creature towards their Creator or worshipper to Worshipped; *sakhyabhāva*, the attitude of a friend; *vātsalyabhāva*, the attitude of a mother towards her child; and most controversially in this case, *madhuryabhāva*, the attitude of a woman towards her lover. The *madhuryabhāva* is classically exemplified by Radha, the beloved of Krishna, and from her example we can see that as well as being Krishna's lover, she was also at turns, his worshipper, friend, servant, and motherly protector. For this reason, the *madhuryabhāva* has a special status amongst the dualistic devotional attitudes, as it contains within it all of the others. Ramakrishna, not one to do things half-heartedly, threw himself utterly into the role of lover, and not, as some might expect, in his role as a man. Ramakrishna instead *became* Radha. An assistant provided him with a sari, a gauze scarf, a skirt and a bodice, as well as a wig and some gold jewellery, and he began to imitate the speech and mannerisms of a woman down to the smallest gesture. He then began frequenting a house belonging to Rani Rasmani — the woman who had funded the temple complex at Dakshineswar — to spend time amongst the women of the family. His nephew Hriday tells us:

> When he remained thus surrounded by ladies it was hard for even his closest relatives to recognize him at once. One day at that time Mathur took me into the women's quarters and said, 'Can you tell me which of them is your uncle?' And although I'd been living with him so long and serving him daily, I couldn't, at first. Uncle used to collect flowers every morning, with a basket. We'd watch him and we'd notice that he always stepped out left foot first, as a woman does.[31]

Needless to say, this latest spiritual practice caused a good deal of scandal and gave new life to the accusations that Ramakrishna had gone mad. Nevertheless, just as soon as the inner work had been done and its fruits borne, he dropped his new identity as quickly as it had been assumed and returned to temple life.

Around this time a visitor came to Dakshineswar — a handsome, middle-aged Brahmin woman wearing the ochre robe of a nun. She was a *tantrika* of the Vaishnava sect, the devotees of Vishnu, and her meeting with Ramakrishna marked a turning point in his life. Upon seeing him for the first time she began to shed tears and exclaimed:

> Ah my child! Here you are at last! I knew you lived somewhere along the banks of the Ganges — but that was all; and I've been searching for so long![32]

Here was an adept that understood the elevated states that Ramakrishna was experiencing and could sympathise with him. She became his confidant and began teaching him a series of tantric practices which helped stabilise his erratic inner states by giving him a context within which he could better understand them. From their initial meeting, they connected like lifelong friends, as Ramakrishna described his visions and experiences in detail, as well as his own doubts as to his sanity. To all of this she listened intently before telling him:

> My son, everyone in this world is mad. Some are mad for money, some for creature comforts, some for name and fame; and you are mad for God.[33]

Thus began a new phase of practice and, as with his previous *sādhanās*, Ramakrishna made swift progress. As the days passed into weeks, the Brahmani not only became convinced of Ramakrishna's elevated spiritual status, but began openly declaring him to be nothing less than an *avatar* — that most rare example of God's wilful incarnation on earth so as to revitalise a waning spiritual current. To the Brahmani, Ramakrishna was no less than a living God, with the same historic import as Rama, Krishna or the Buddha. In time, this conviction led her to convene a conference of pundits, holy men and scholars to deliberate the matter. The meetings took place over several days and concluded with all those present agreeing with the Brahmani's assertion — Ramakrishna was indeed an *avatar* — a perfect incarnation of God on earth. As the devotees, temple attendants and others present stood dumbstruck by the verdict, Ramakrishna was heard to say, "Well I am glad to learn that after all it is not a disease".[34] All of a sudden, to those around him, Ramakrishna's "crazy" had become "wisdom". The method in his madness, though still incomprehensible to most, was now held in esteem rather than contempt, and devotees began to swarm to the temple complex at Dakshineswar.

Although his fame was now spreading rapidly and drawing seekers and pilgrims from afar, there was still one last *sādhanā* to perform, one last veil to rend before he could truly abide as the *avatar* that many now took him to be. Ramakrishna had plumbed the depths of dualistic worship and scaled the heights of *savikalpa samādhi* — the absorption of the self into Saguna Brahman, the Absolute with form — but he had yet to experience *nirvikalpa samādhi* — the dissolution of the self into Nirguna Brahman, the formless Absolute. The means the universe contrived for this to happen was the arrival at Dakshineswar of a new teacher, a wandering monk from a monastic order of the great Advaitic reformer Shankara — a naked Naga called Tota Puri. In Ramakrishna's own words:

After initiating me, the Naked One taught me many sayings expressing the philosophy of non-dualism. He told me to withdraw my mind from all creatures and objects, and plunge it into contemplation of the Atman. But when I sat down to meditate in this way, I found I couldn't make my mind go quite beyond name and form. I couldn't stop it working and make it still. My mind could stop being conscious of creatures and objects — that wasn't difficult; but whenever it did this, the Divine Mother appeared before me in that form I knew so well — that form which is made of pure consciousness. It was her own living form which stopped me from going any farther. Again and again, I listened to the instructions and sat down to meditate; and again and again it happened. I almost despaired. I opened my eyes and told the Naked One, 'No—it can't be done. I can't stop my mind from working. I can't make it plunge into the Atman'. The Naked One got excited. He scolded me severely. 'What do you mean — can't be done?' he cried. 'It must be done!' Then he looked around the hut till he found a bit of broken glass. And he stuck the point of it into my forehead, between the eyebrows. It was sharp as a needle! 'Fix the mind here', he told me. So I sat down to meditate again, firmly determined. And as soon as Mother's form appeared, I took my knowledge of non-duality as if it was a sword in my hand, and I cut Mother in two pieces with that sword of knowledge. As soon as I'd done that, there was nothing relative left in the mind. It entered the place where there is no second—only the One.[35]

Ramakrishna had finally achieved *nirvikalpa samādhi* — the complete obliteration of self and other, knower and known, seer and seen, in formless radiance — and on this first occasion he remained there for three whole days. Tota Puri was astonished. Ramakrishna had achieved in a single day what he had struggled for 40 years to attain.

Although his inner *sādhanā* was now complete, his outward practice, for the sake of understanding others, continued. In the true spirit of universality and in recognition of the essential authenticity of all paths to God, Ramakrishna immersed himself in both Christian as well as Muslim modes of worship. After having been read verses from the Bible by one of his devotees, his thoughts began to dwell upon the personality of Jesus Christ, known as Sri Isha by the Hindus. There then followed a period when all of his traditional worship of Vedic deities dropped away and his mind was filled with devotion to Sri Isha. This phase of his life culminated in a vision of Christ as he walked through the temple gardens, a vision in which Jesus embraced him and passed into his body, leaving Ramakrishna with the conviction that Jesus was a genuine *avatar*, and that in Christianity was a spiritual path that was just as authentic as any other. At another time, a Muslim that followed the practices of the Sufis came to Dakshineswar. His holiness and the way in which he spoke of God charmed Ramakrishna and he requested to be initiated into Islam. Of this period he tells us:

And then, I devoutly repeated the name of Allah, wore a cloth like the Arab Moslems, said their prayers five times daily and felt disinclined even to see images of the Hindu gods and goddesses, much less worship them — for the Hindu way of thinking had disappeared altogether from my mind. I spent three days in that mood, and I had the full realization of the sadhana of their faith.[36]

If the crazy-wisdom of the tantric *mahāsiddhas* and the divine madness of the *masts* and *bāuls* blurred the lines between religious divides, Ramakrishna completely obliterated them. His conscious attempt to understand and practice the *sādhanās* of all the religions he came into contact with was a genuine reflection of his having transcended the forms in favour of their essence. The perennial philosophy of a uniting principle behind all apparent religious differences, though so often denied by sane orthodoxy, is warmly embraced, and its truth realised, by the mad mystics of all persuasions. Whereas the narrow gaze of scholars tends towards seeing only the multiplicity of religious symbols, the panoramic command of the sage captures a vista broad enough to reveal the unity of their essence. To pundits and pedants, there is discord and debate; to adepts and masters, only concord and silent agreement. Some are called mad and others, sane. May you be the only judge as to which is which.

Sri Ramakrishna's transformation was now complete. By no means had he subdued his craziness but had rather raised up his wisdom to be its equal. As a result, he could be both sublime and absurd, Godlike and childlike, in one moment expounding the highest philosophy to his devotees and in the next, telling them a funny animal story as a parable. He could proffer stern advice to his disciples with all the mature wisdom of a protective father or be cared for by them like a helpless child. He could lose consciousness at the mere mention of God and would sing, dance and stagger in ecstasy like a drunkard, often losing his wearing-cloth to stand among them naked and without shame like a newborn babe. In reference to his divine madness, Ramakrishna was once asked by a visitor if it were a desirable state to which he replied:

> What absurdity are you suggesting? Is the magnificent, ecstatic madness of Radha, who is the very embodiment of Divine Love, to be compared with the insanity of unbalanced minds or with the ordinary madness that worldly people exhibit in their relentless pursuit of self-centered pleasure and power? The madness that you call being sensible is indeed an undesirable state. Have you never heard mention of the love-madness and knowledge-madness displayed by the saints?[37]

The Avadhūta

Avadhūta is the name given to a special kind of mystic saint, so beyond egoic consciousness, so utterly removed from worldly concerns and the interests of the average person, as to often appear mad. The root *avadhū* means "to cast off", "to shake out", or "frighten away" and refers to one who has cast off all bondage, desire, concern, ignorance and attachment, thus frightening away all enemies and evil spirits. Having achieved the ultimate state of non-dual, abiding awareness, they care little for the often petty rules of communal engagement and the niceties of social decorum. Although precedents can be found in the character of Shiva — whom one of his thousand names describes as being "the one concealed in the guise of madness"[38] — the original and consummate *avadhūta* was the mythological *avatar*, Dattātreya, a combined incarnation of the great trinity of Vedic gods, and mentioned in many of the ancient scriptures as one of the Lords of Yoga.

Some of the key scriptures of Advaita Vedanta are attributed to him, including the *Avadhūta-gītā (The Song of the Avadhūta)* and the *Tripurā Rahasya (The Mystery Beyond the Trinity)*, and a number of yogic and monastic traditions consider him their founder. Dattātreya himself gives the derivation of the term *avadhūta*, as an acronym composed of the four syllables *a, va, dhū, ta* that stand for *akṣara, varenya, dhūta-saṃsāra-bandhana,* and *tat-tvam-asyādi-lakṣya*. In the *Bṛhad-avadhūta Upaniṣad*, written as a dialogue between Dattātreya and his student Sāṃkṛti, this is the opening exchange:

1. Once Sāṃkṛti went up to the Blessed Avadhūta, Dattātreya, and asked: Lord, who is an Avadhūta? What is his state? What is his emblem? What is his conduct? The most compassionate Lord Dattātreya said to him:
2. Because he is imperishable [*akṣara*], because he is the most excellent [*varenya*], because he has shaken off the bonds of *saṃsāra* [*dhūta-saṃsāra-bandhana*], and because he is denoted by the phrase "You are that" [*tat-tvam-asyādi-lakṣya*], he is called "Avadhūta".[39]

One legend in the *Mārkaṇḍeya Purāṇa*, tells of Dattātreya's attempt to escape the distractions to his spiritual practice caused by his disciples. His plan was simple — he would immerse himself in a lake and wait for them to lose interest and leave. However, after the passing of "one hundred divine years", and seeing that time had not dulled their enthusiasm, he came up with a new idea and instead, emerged from the lake with a "beautiful and fortunate lady" who "possessed splendid buttocks and was attired in divine garments". If that was not enough to shock the "sons of sages" who had been sitting patiently on the shore awaiting his return, he "started to drink liquor with the woman" and indulged "in singing and musical instruments". His disciples were unfazed by these flagrant violations of social etiquette, and remained steadfast in their belief that Dattātreya was a true *avadhūta* — "a great-souled one, unaffected by such external tasks".[40]

On occasions portrayed as an ascetic and yogi, engaged in meditative practices and austerities, and on others, as a carefree sensualist, indulging in comfort and worldly pleasure, Dattātreya ranks as one of the great Transcenders as one who penetrated beyond the illusory battlefield of dualistic delusion with its warring dichotomy of Ascent and Descent. The *Nārada-parivrājaka Upaniṣad* says of him, "he has no visible emblem; he keeps his conduct concealed; he acts as if he were a fool, a lunatic, or a goblin; and, although he is sane, he behaves like a madman".[41] Like a true crazy-wisdom master, he stands with his head in the clouds and his feet on the ground, a bridge from this-world to the otherworld, with one hand beckoning, and the other, pointing the way.

One clear sign of the elevated vision of the *avadhūta* and the true crazy-wisdom master in general, is the ability to perform acts that seem shocking or transgressive, but turn out to have positive consequences that no one else could have imagined. Bhagawan Nityananda, an *avadhūta* born at the close of the nineteenth century, demonstrated this on many occasions throughout his life. Something of an eccentric holy man, and wearing only an ill-fitting loincloth, if anything at all, he was known to stand motionless for hours on end, up a tree in front of the local temple. Though he was known for his equanimity and indifference to pain, disgust, embarrassment and other negative emotions, no one, least of all his devotees, could have quite expected to find him one day, sat in front of a pile of excrement beside the local lavatories, with human faeces smeared all over his body. "Bombay halwa — very tasty — want to eat?"[42] he said to passers-by much to the utter embarrassment of his followers, who had not attained to the same equanimity in such matters, and who thought that their beloved master had finally gone utterly mad. There he sat all day, ignoring the pleas of his disciples, until evening when he finally relented and allowed them to scrub him down. The whole episode remained a mystery until a small group of his devotees admitted, that in a conversation about their master's equanimity, they had wondered if he would eat human faeces if offered to him. It seems they got their answer in a most memorable fashion and rather than a psychotic episode, Nityananda's behaviour was revealed to be a contrived crazy-wisdom teaching stunt for the benefit of his students.

On another occasion, he caused quite a scene by grabbing a woman's dress as she passed him by. Some onlookers gave chase but Nityananda ran away shouting "She's healed! She's healed!" Only afterwards was it revealed that the woman had been suffering from breast cancer and, from that moment, had indeed been healed.

A similar story tells of how, on a busy road, he stopped and began fondling the breasts of a pregnant woman. Although the woman showed no resistance and seemed unmoved by this strange violation of her intimacy, once again some outraged passers-by gave chase. As he ran away, Nityananda shouted back to the woman that this time her baby would survive. She called to the pursuers to stop and told them that her previous three children had died after their first breastfeeding. Shortly after this strange event, she delivered a healthy baby that, unlike its less fortunate siblings, survived, and a delegation from the village was sent to find the strange holy man and thank him.

A similar event involved Neem Karoli Baba, the crazy-wise guru made famous by the one-time Harvard-psychology-professor-turned-yogi, Richard Alpert, better known as Ram Dass.

One Indian widow who had no children came to Maharajji, worried about who would take care of her. Maharajji said, 'Ma, I'll be your child'. She started to treat him like a child and then he said, 'You know, Hariakhan Baba used to suck the breasts of women. I'll sit on your lap'. And he sat on her lap and he was so light and small, just like a child. He sucked on her breasts and milk poured out of them, although she was sixty-five. Enough milk came from her to have filled a glass. After that she never missed not having children.[43]

So just what are we to make of these stories? Are they genuine accounts of *siddhis*, demonstrated by true spiritual masters? Or psychodramas whose success is due to the placebo effect of people who believe their lives have been touched by a great master? Or, to be perfectly sceptical, are they perhaps the record of the perverse moments of imperfect men, whitewashed into miracles by their doting devotees after the fact? Maybe any attempt to wring the truth out of these strange events with the pitiful grasp of the intellect are doomed to failure in any case. If the *avadhūta* truly has shaken off all attachments and traces of egoic consciousness, then what common standard is there for a worldly man to judge by? And how can any standards apply to the one who has left all such standards behind him? The only true means of verification is to do the work and strive for the peaks of spiritual attainment and, in attaining them, attain the clarity that their heightened perspective provides. Beyond the intellect, beyond all reason, beyond the mind — this is the domain of the *avadhūta* and the crazy-wise, and ultimately it takes one to know one.

DRUNK ON THE WINE
OF THE BELOVED

Forgo safety and make a home in danger.
Sacrifice your reputation and become notorious.
I have tried caution and forethought;
from now on I will make myself mad.[1]

— RUMI

The Sufis

It should perhaps come as no surprise that if we wish to find a vein of crazy-wisdom within the teachings of Islam, we must turn away from the orthodox imams and teachers and towards the adepts and masters of their esoteric tradition. Here, as in the mystical currents of other Great Traditions, with little more than a cursory glance we begin to find the same motifs, ideas, and practices found elsewhere; the same crazy-wisdom essence with a uniquely Arabic flavour.

The Sufis — the mystics of Islam — like many of their crazy-wisdom compatriots, practiced poverty and self-abnegation and favoured direct knowledge of the Divine over dry scholarship or empty ritual. Abu Darda 'Uwaymar bin Zaid, one of the early companions of the Prophet Muhammad, used to say that "one hour of reflection was better than forty nights of prayer, and that one particle of righteousness, combined with godliness and assured faith, was preferable to unlimited ritual observance".[2]

He belonged to the *Ashab al-Suffa*, or Companions of the Bench, a select group of early Muslims who had given up everything in order to dedicate their lives exclusively to the spiritual life. Their name refers to the *suffa* — usually translated as "verandah", "porch" or "bench" — a sheltered, raised platform at the rear of the Prophet's Mosque in Medina where they lived, and *ashab* means "friends" or "companions". These were the proto-Sufis — the Sufis in deed before the name had been conceived as a label for them. Of the contending theories as to the etymology of the name "Sufi", one suggests that it is from *suffa*, the verandah where these holy men lived and practiced. Another suggests it is from the Arabic for "wool", or *ṣūf* — the word "Sufi" meaning "one who wears wool" — a practice associated with the ascetics and mystics of the time, and one that had come down to them from the Old Testament prophets and early Christian monks. As with other traditions, while the orthodox engaged in religious practices as an aside to their busy daily lives, the adepts and in this case, the *Ashab al-Suffa*, engaged in mundane matters as an aside to their busy spiritual lives. So while the first followers of this new religion of the Prophet would pray five times a day and fast during Ramadan, the *Ashab al-Suffa* would pray incessantly and fast frequently throughout the year. As well as the exoteric doctrine that was given to the people openly, they were also the guardians of the esoteric, mystical teachings that could only be given to those that had prepared themselves with inner work. When Jesus was asked by his disciples "Why do You speak to them in parables?" he told them, "Because it has been given to you to know the mysteries of the kingdom of heaven, but to them it has not been given... Therefore I speak to them in parables, because seeing they do not see, and hearing they do not hear, nor do they understand".[3] Like the twelve apostles of Christ, the *Ashab al-Suffa* were the intimate spiritual companions of the Prophet Muhammad — those that could see, hear and understand — and the ones who had been entrusted with the mystical teachings of Islam. They were the living proof of the great scholar Ja'far al-Sadiq's popular saying that many quoted but few lived up to: "Whoever knows God turns his back on everything else".[4] Though taken by many as an exhortation to reject materiality and worldly possessions, the Sufi knows this to be a reference to the ultimate sacrifice of the mystic — the one that few are prepared to make — the sacrifice of the self.

Fanā

As with other non-dual traditions, when the adept penetrates beyond those states that can be spoken of using positive affirmations such as "mystical union", "cosmic consciousness", "oneness with all things", "merging with the Divine", and so on, they come up against the inherent limitations of affirmative language and are at a loss to describe what lies beyond. From here on, the only things that make any sense at all are stated in negative terms.

Quite likely derived from the Buddhist term *nirvana* which means literally "blowing out" or "becoming extinguished", as one might the flame of a candle, the advanced Sufi speaks of *fanā*, "passing away" or "annihilation" — the complete death of the self, or at least the death of the sense that there was one in the first place. Here, there is no self to merge with anything — no one to be at one —only the realisation that what was considered to be a permanent abiding self is nothing more than a ceaseless and impersonal flux of sensation, feeling and thought with no personal, separate "I" and no more owned than the breeze or the clouds passing overhead. Sura 55:26 of the Quran states: "All on the earth shall pass away, But the face of thy Lord shall abide resplendent with majesty and glory" which, while taken conventionally as an affirmation of the eternal nature of God over and above the temporal nature of His creation, is understood by Sufis on a deeper level to be a reference to *fanā*. The self is "on the earth" and so "shall pass away", whether whilst alive, as is the goal of the Sufi, or in death, as is the fate of most. To those that achieve *fanā* then, all that remains after the annihilation of the self is "the face of thy Lord... resplendent with majesty and glory", or as one Sufi prayer has it: "May God empty my very self of all except His own presence".[5] In reference to this, Hasan

157

of Basra, considered to be one of the greatest Sufis, once said: "Not he who dies and is at rest is dead, He only is dead who is dead while yet alive".[6]

Fanā — the annihilation of the self and the crazy-wise proclamations of what remains from apparently human mouths, has been the cause of much grief and persecution suffered by the Sufis over the centuries.

The Mystical Persecution

As is so often the case, when spiritual teachings are taken up by the worldly-minded and used as tools to further their own interests, the true mystics and adepts are not only marginalised but even become threats to the religious status quo. As the teachings become systematised into doctrines and then dogmas, and infiltrate the domains of politics and jurisprudence so as to more effectively control and coerce the masses, those living the ultimate freedom, just by their mere existence, are seen as agitators and dissidents and so become easy targets for the powers-that-wish-to-be. Some traditions, like those in the East, have tolerated well their spiritual outliers, perhaps realising that the path to adeptship is only ever desired and assumed by a small minority that they can afford to lose. The three great Abrahamic faiths, however, have felt a far greater need to silence the voices that have outgrown their need for mediation between themselves and God. Perhaps fearing a conflagration of spiritual fervour fanned from the fire of just one of these wayward and solitary flames, they have done everything they can at times to stamp out even a spark of the mystic impulse, especially when it strays too far from accepted doctrine and the established dualism of creature and Creator. Realise of course, that to maintain one's position as the sole sanctioned mediator and interpreter of the Divine Will, it is essential to maintain this dualistic religious outlook. After all, if every creature realises its own direct hotline to its Creator, or God forbid even discovers the essential shared identity that transcends even this duality, then what becomes of the mediators? All of a sudden their whole power-play becomes a redundant affair. For this reason, when religion becomes institutionalised and finds an ally in the political powers, the mystics and awakeners become prime targets and their teachings and practices, the first to suffer. Such has been the fate of the Sufis within Islam.

The Three Martyrs

Accused of blasphemy and heresy, the cruel death of Mansour Al-Hallaj, a Persian poet from the ninth century, serves as a poignant reminder of just how far orthodoxy is prepared to go to protect its monopoly on "truth". Even among Sufis, Hallaj was something of an outsider. Rather than wear their traditional woollen cloak, he wore instead a soldier's uniform and gathered several hundred disciples after his time spent as an itinerant preacher. Like many of those who esteem substance over form, he wandered throughout India studying the religious traditions there, and in the secret meetings held in his home, he taught that Sufism represented the deepest truths shared by all religions. He also maintained that Jesus was a Sufi teacher, which led to allegations that he was a secret Christian. It was at this time that, speaking from the post-*fanā* state, he uttered his most famous declaration — "*Ana'l-Haqq*" ("I am the Truth!"[7]) which led to his imprisonment for heresy. After nine years, in which time he wrote several books while his supporters and detractors argued the case, he was finally sentenced to death. On Tuesday, March 26, 922, showing no fear, he was taken to his place of execution. Reminiscent of Christ's plea from the cross, "Father, forgive them; for they know not what they do",[8] his final prayer before those present at his execution, while he was still capable of speech, is said to have been:

O Lord, make me grateful for the blessing which I have been given in being allowed to know what others do not

159

know. Divine mysteries which are unlawful to others have become thus lawful to me. Forgive and have mercy upon these Thy servants assembled here for the purpose of killing me; for, had Thou revealed to them what Thou hast revealed to me, they would not act thus.[9]

Hallaj was then tortured and dismembered before being hanged from a gibbet as a chilling reminder for all those who might be tempted to follow in his footsteps.

For some, however, the love of God and the lure of Eternity overshadowed even this gruesome display. Suhrawardī, also known as al-Maqtul ("he who was killed") was one such defender of the Hallaj legacy, whose life and death followed a similar fate. He was a prolific writer whose works included mystical treatises and detailed expositions of the angelic realm, as well as commentaries on the works of Aristotle and Plato, but it was his magnum opus Ḥikmat al-ishrāq ("The Wisdom of Illumination") blending elements of Sufism, Zoroastrianism and Greek philosophy, that established him as the founder of a new school of Islamic philosophy known as Illuminism. As is so often the case, his brilliance as a religious figure on the fringes of orthodoxy aroused jealousy amongst the ranks of officialdom and he was imprisoned before being executed at the age of 38.

The same fate also took the life of Ayn al-Quzat Hamadānī, mystic, philosopher, poet and judge, at the Christly age of 33. After a formal complaint was brought against him, he was imprisoned in Baghdad to await trial for heresy. After some months in prison in which time he wrote his defence against the charges brought against him, he was taken for execution, which included flaying, crucifixion and being burnt alive, all by direct order of the sultan himself. There is little doubt that sometimes the craziness of wisdom is too much for the insanity of ignorance to bear.

Abu Bakr al-Shibli

To your mind, I am mad.
To my mind, you are all sane.
So I pray to increase my madness
And to increase your sanity.
My "madness" is from the power of Love;
Your sanity is from the strength of unawareness.[10]

— ABU BAKR AL-SHIBLI

Perhaps one of the most bizarre affirmations of the transcendent, non-dual perspective came from the lips of Abu Bakr al-Shibli, a contemporary and friend of al-Hallaj who was present at his execution:

O God, hand this world and the Otherworld over to me so that I may make a morsel from this world and throw it into a dog's mouth, and make a morsel of the Otherworld and put it into a Jew's mouth, for both are veils before the true goal.[11]

In his own peculiar way, Shibli reveals that ultimately both this-worldly and otherworldly orientations — Descent and Ascent — are merely "veils before the true goal" of non-dual realisation. It is no wonder that like many other of his radical Sufi compatriots, he spent his life in and out of prison and ended his days as an inmate of a lunatic asylum.

Although as a high government official in Baghdad, his early life held the promise of a long and successful career, a series of spontaneous spiritual experiences and the ensuing disillusionment with his worldly life, led him to resign his post and pursue a higher calling. He approached Junayd of Baghdad, the founder of the "sober" school of Sufi thought, and pleaded with him to become his student:

"You are recommended as an expert on pearls", he said.

"Either give me one, or sell one to me."

"If I sell you one, you will not have the price of it, and if I give you one, having so easily come by it you will not realize its value", Jonaid replied. "Do like me; plunge head first into this Sea, and if you wait patiently you will obtain your pearl."[12]

What then followed were many years of practice at the direction of his newfound master, most of it designed to undo the damage of his former life and undermine the pride, security and comfort he had become so dependent upon.

For a year he was sent to sell salt in the market, then for a year he was told to beg his sustenance in the very same neighbourhoods of Baghdad where previously he had been held in such high esteem. Four more years were spent seeking out all those he had wronged during his time as a government official so as to plead for forgiveness, and then another year was again spent begging. Finally, a year was spent as the lowliest of servants to Junayd's disciples. After his eight year ordeal, Junayd asked him: "Abu Bakr, what is your view of yourself now?" to which he replied, "I regard myself as the least of God's creatures". "Now", Junayd remarked, "your faith is whole."[13]

Shibli was a seeker on fire with the love of God who spent much of his life consumed by divine madness. When in the throes of self-mortification, he would rub salt in his eyes to stay awake and continue his prayers, beating himself with a stick when his mind wandered. On one occasion "overwhelmed by mystical tumult", he threw himself into the Tigris but was washed ashore. Next he jumped into a fire but escaped unhurt. Then he sought out a pride of hungry lions and offered himself to them but they ran away. Finally he hurled himself from a cliff but was deposited gently on the ground by a freak gust of wind.

"Woe to him", he cried, "whom neither water nor fire will
accept, neither the wild beasts nor the mountains!"
"He who is accepted of God", came a voice, "is accepted of
no other."[14]

Not surprisingly, this little escapade earned him another stretch
in the madhouse. Perhaps they didn't hear the voice.

Nevertheless, Shibli was a genuine seeker and at times it
would seem, a finder. Once, when reproached by Junayd for
crying out the name of God in public whilst lost in rapture,
Shibli responded:

I am speaking and I am listening. In both worlds who is
there but I? Nay rather, these are words proceeding from
God to God, and Shebli is not there at all.[15]

It is fair to say that few affirmations of non-duality have been so
direct and to the point.

Dhul-Nun "The Egyptian"

Another great Sufi, Dhul-Nun al-Misri "The Egyptian", was
arrested twice on charges of heresy. Like the three martyrs, he
went too far in affirming his shared identity with God, however,
unlike them, luckily his life was spared. Once when asked,
"What is the end of the mystic?" he replied (sounding very
much like a Zen master expounding upon the "original face"
koan) "When he is as he was where he was before he was".[16]

Such statements, although implicitly non-dual, were
ambiguous enough to be taken as mere mystic wordplay by the
religious inquisitors of the time. Other statements, however,
were more to the point and less open to interpretation:

When I love a devotee, I, the Lord, become his ear so
that he hears through Me, I become his eye so that he

sees through Me, I become his tongue so that he speaks through Me, and I become his hand so that he possesses through Me.[17]

It was comments like this that earned him a 40 day stretch in a Baghdad prison, however, his eloquent defense not only secured his freedom but also made a disciple of the caliph.

Abu Sa'id Abu'l-Khayr

People called me a lunatic, and I allowed them to give me that name, relying on the Tradition that a man's faith is not made perfect until he is supposed to be mad.[18]

—ABU SA'ID ABU'L-KHAYR

Abu Sa'id Abu'l-Khayr, the first Sufi to draw up a set of monastic rules for his disciples, was another to fall foul of the authorities, but for entirely different reasons. His early life was spent in religious study before retiring from the world and spending seven years as a hermit in an old ruin, practising intense asceticism. Thanks to a worried father who would spy on him from time to time to ensure his wellbeing, we have a rare eyewitness account of one of his more bizarre practices known as *ṣalāt maqlūba* — hanging by the feet into a dark well while reciting the Quran:

My son walked on until he reached the Old Cloister (*Ribát-i Kuhan*). He entered it and shut the gate behind him, while I went up on the roof. I saw him go into a chapel, which was in the *ribát*, and close the door. Looking through the chapel window, I waited to see what would happen. There was a stick lying on the floor, and it had a rope fastened to it. He took up the stick and tied the end of the rope to his foot. Then, laying the stick across the top of a pit that was at the corner of the chapel, he slung himself into the pit head downwards, and began to recite the Koran. He remained in that posture until daybreak, when, having recited the whole Koran, he raised himself from the pit, replaced the stick where he had found it, opened the door, came out of the chapel, and commenced to perform his ablution in the middle of the ribát. I descended from the roof, hastened home, and slept until he came in.[19]

At the age of 40, he reached a state of perfect illumination, ceased his harsh practices and returned to normal life. But not just any old normal. Instead he began entertaining his Sufi friends by holding opulent feasts with music and dancing and thousands of burning candles. Soon, the once emaciated ascetic had become plump. Although he had courted some controversy by stating, in the spirit of Hallaj, "There is none other than God in this robe",[20] and claiming that he had no need to make the pilgrimage to Mecca, as instead, the Kaaba would come to him several times a day to perform circumambulations above his head, his problems with the religious authorities only really began with his newfound self-indulgence. A formal letter of complaint was sent to the sultan claiming:

A certain man has come hither from Mayhana and pretends to be a Sufi. He preaches sermons but does not quote the Traditions of the Prophet. He holds sumptuous feasts and music is played by his orders, whilst the young men dance and eat sweetmeats and roasted fowls and all kinds of fruit. He declares that he is an ascetic, but this is neither asceticism nor Sufism. Multitudes have joined him and are being led astray. Unless measures be taken to repair it, the mischief will soon become universal.[21]

An official investigation began into his activities which it is said, Abu Sa'id discovered through his telepathic powers, but instead of toning down his extravagant behaviour, he duly ordered another sumptuous feast. His indifference to their authority coupled with his sheer presence and spiritual charisma, as well as his alleged supernatural powers, led the authorities to drop their investigation against him and no further action was taken.

Having now passed through phases of both self-mortification and self-indulgence, Abu Sa'id stabilised into a new state that was neither one nor the other and beyond both. Sometimes he would wear coarse woollen garments and sometimes he would wear silk, sometimes he would feast and at others he would fast. The ultimate aim of the Sufi, as he had finally found out, lay not in either possession or privation, neither asceticism nor hedonism, but rather in transcending them entirely. In his own words:

> The true saint goes in and out amongst the people and eats and sleeps with them and buys and sells in the market and marries and takes part in social intercourse and never forgets God for a single moment.[22]

After realisation, one must ultimately return to the "marketplace" and continue to chop wood and carry water — a phase known to the Sufis as *baqā*.

Baqā

Whereas it might be imagined that the state of *fanā* (the annihilation of the self) marks the end of the Sufic path, just as in other non-dual traditions, there remains one final step to be taken. Beyond *fanā* lies *baqā*, meaning "subsistence" or "permanence" in God. If *fanā* represents the death of the personal sense of self and the collapse of the subject/object duality that all people labour under, then *baqā* is the resurrection of a universal Self and a return to subject/object awareness. Only this time, rather than a binding reality, multiplicity is seen as merely a useful convention — its illusory nature now laid bare and transparent to the transcendent vision of the realised adept. Whereas prior to *fanā* the separation of things in space and time was indicative of an individual self-nature, in *baqā* lies the clear realisation that there exists nothing more than modifications of the one underlying Reality common to all, and that there is no abiding self-nature in anything but only relationship and mutual dependence — "dependent co-arising" as the Buddha called it. The pre-*fanā*, *fanā* and *post-fanā* stages are perhaps what Zen master Qingyuan Weixin was referring to when he said:

> Thirty years ago when I had not studied Zen, I saw that mountains are mountains and waters are waters. Later I intimately met my teacher and entered this place. I saw mountains are not mountains and waters are not waters. Now I have attained the place of resting. As before I simply see that mountains are mountains and waters are waters.[23]

Everyone sees that "mountains are mountains and waters are waters". This is the conventional viewpoint dominated by a sense of separation, inherent self-nature, multiplicity and finitude. With the annihilation of the self-sense, suddenly "mountains are not mountains and waters are not waters". There is only emptiness, the void, no-self, non-dual and infinite — to the Sufi, God in His formless absolute sense. The stage of *baqā* emerges from this to see once again that "mountains are mountains and waters are waters" but now separation is just a convenient convention; self-nature, a mere gossamer web of interrelations; and the world is now a finitude sustained by infinity — a multiplicity within the perfect embrace of unity — only God, here, there and everywhere. What else could it possibly be?

The Malamatiyya and the Path of Blame

A particularly interesting formalisation of the divine madness impulse amongst the Sufis, spoken of at times as an independent sect, and at others as merely a phase of practice, came in the form of the Malamatiyya, "those who draw blame (*malāmah*) upon themselves". Very much in tune with the Fools for Christ and mad saints of other traditions, they sought to intentionally undermine the very foundations of the ego — the lower self or *nafs* — at any cost. With foundations in such Quranic declarations as "do not fear the blame of a blaming person",[24] and developing out of a keener sense of the virtue known as *ikhlās* or "perfect sincerity", the Malamati was painfully aware of the subtle games played by the ego in order to foment a sense of pride in even the most seemingly innocent of acts. Demonstrations of asceticism, although performed for the purpose of subjugating one's baser tendencies and negating the ego's wants and desires, too often lead to the exact opposite, instead reinforcing one's sense of their own holiness and virtue. With this in mind, the Malamatis would conceal their spiritual attainments and perform any pious acts in private. Even their *dhikr* (the prayer in remembrance of God) was to be done silently so as to avoid others overhearing, or more importantly, to avoid the prayer being used by the ego as a means to reinforce its own sense of virtuousness. Further to this, and not content to leave to mere chance moments of humiliation or embarrassment, they would intentionally bring them upon themselves, often inciting the scorn, contempt and hostility of others by transgressing religious and societal norms. At other times, their shock tactics were simply practical means to safeguard their solitude and avoid disturbance by keeping potential admirers at bay. The fifteenth-century Sufi poet and scholar, Jāmī, recounts a classic example of this:

One of them was hailed by a large crowd when he entered a town; they tried to accompany the great saint; but on the road he publicly started urinating in an unlawful way so that all of them left him and no longer believed in his high spiritual rank.[25]

Bāyazīd Bistāmī, also known as Abū Yazīd, was a Sufi from the ninth century and the first proponent of the "drunken" or "ecstatic" school of Islamic mysticism as opposed to the "sober" school of Baghdad. Known for his ecstatic outbursts, his most famous being: "Glory be to Me! How great is My Majesty!"[26] he was also an early expositor of *fanā* as well as one of the earliest exemplars of the Path of Blame. In the *Tadhkirat al-Auliya'* or *Memorial of the Saints*, by Farid al-Din Attar from the twelfth century, we are told the following story about him:

> In one town he passed through on the way a great throng became his followers, and as he left a crowd went in his wake.
> "Who are those men?" he demanded, looking back.
> "They wish to keep you company", came the answer.
> "Lord God!" Abu Yazid cried, "I beg of Thee, veil not Thy creatures from Thee through me!" Then, desiring to expel the love of him from their hearts and to remove the obstacle of himself from their path, having performed the dawn prayer he looked at them and said, *"Verily I am God; there is no god but I; therefore serve Me"*.
> "The man has become mad!" they cried. And they left him and departed.[27]

On another occasion, to achieve the same ends and ward off a crowd of admirers, he took out a loaf of bread and began to eat it, even though it was Ramadan and Islamic law required all Muslims to fast.

The Qalandariyya

A curious offshoot from the Malamatiyya, and one that would later become a sect in its own right, was the Qalandariyya. Like many other religious heterodox sects, the ambiguity of even the earliest references to them makes an almost impossible task of ascertaining just who or what they were. No doubt there were charlatans among them, as well as criminal types whose unlawful activities could be more easily accomplished in the guise of a mad dervish, but to see nothing more, as some would assert, is to have sadly missed the point. Like a Rorschach inkblot, people's opinions of them are often more a reflection of their own unspoken fears and prejudices than anything else; the world of the Qalandar being so broad as to be able to reach whatever conclusion one wishes, depending on what is focused upon and what is left out.

To illustrate this, we have, on the one side, such scathing accounts as those of Ottoman commentators Geovani Menovino, a slave at the Ottoman court in Istanbul, or Vāḥidī, a Sufi critic of the same period, who have said of the Qalandariyya that they "prefer pleasure to work and live disordered lives given to gluttony, luxury, and sodomy", and that "the kalendar sinks deeper into sin and shame...living at the expense of others in flagrant violation of prophetic tradition and Islamic moral injunctions".[28] On the other side, we have such spiritual giants as Rumi, who in mentioning the Qalandars wrote:

Carousing and ruby-wine and ruins and unbelief,
These are the kingdom of the qalandar, but he is detached
    from it.
You say "I am a qalandar!" But the heart is displeased,
Since qalandardom is uncreated.[29]

or Aḥmad al-Ghazālī, the younger brother of the more famous Abū Ḥāmid al-Ghazālī who said:

> This is the lane of blame, the field of annihilation;
> This is the street where gamblers bet everything in one go.
> The courage of a qalandar, clothed in rags is needed
> To pass through in bold and fearless manner.[30]

Both of these mystic poets it seems, held the figure of the Qalandar in high regard; as a courageous renunciate striving for *fanā* and unattached to the world. It is interesting to note that the first two comments were made by worldly men, whilst the two poetic fragments were the opinions of men with deep spiritual insight and demonstrates once more the inability of the common man to understand the ways of the crazy-wise.

Unlike the Malamatis, who made no outward display of their status or affiliation, the Qalandars were shockingly conspicuous in their dress and appearance. Some went barefoot and naked, others immodestly covered with sacks, coarse felt or animal skins, but their most distinguishing characteristic was a lack of facial hair, especially considering the almost obligatory nature of the beard amongst Muslims. This strange measure, known as the *chahar zarb*, or "four blows", included the shaving of the head, the beard, the moustache and even, most bizarrely, the eyebrows. According to the great fourteenth-century Arabic explorer, Ibn Battuta, the practice began due to an incident involving the sect's founder, Jamal al-Din Savi, and a rather persistent woman who was not prepared to take "no" for an answer. Having coaxed him into her house under the pretext of helping to read a letter, she locked him inside, whereupon her slaves surrounded him. Ibn Battuta, in his *Travels* continues:

They then took him into an inner apartment, and the mistress began to take liberties with him. When the Sheikh saw that there was no escaping, he said, I will do what you like: shew me a sleeping room. This she did: he then took in with him some water and a razor which he had, and shaved off his beard and both his eyebrows. He then presented himself to the woman, who, detesting both his person and his deed, ordered him to be driven out of the house. Thus, by divine providence, was his chastity preserved. This appearance he retained ever after; and every one who embraced his opinions also submitted to the shaving off of his beard and both his eyebrows.[31]

Showing a complete disregard for the local laws and customs, the Qalandars were nomadic wanderers, travelling in groups and usually staying on the outskirts of towns. As enthusiastic users of cannabis and known to frequent cemeteries, their penchant for baldness notwithstanding, it is hard not to notice a strong connection with the tantric *sadhus* or *bāuls* of India, and early accounts of the Qalandars often assert that many were foreigners with only a rudimentary grasp of Arabic. Like the first Indian *tantrikas* who rejected outright the religious orthodoxy of their time, the Qalandars would both feast and fast, pray serenely or dance and sing wildly, demonstrating both piety and sacrilegiousness, restraint and abandon, forever attempting to maintain their detachment from both and constantly frustrating the ego's attempts to build an identity out of them. So to the question, "What is a Qalandar?" the Qalandar himself has a simpler answer:

I am the vagabond whom they call qalandar.
I have no provision, no refuge, no harbor.
During the day I travel round
At night, I sleep with my head on the ground.[32]

Rabia al-Adawiyya

One of the most celebrated Sufis, and all the more so for being a woman in a world dominated by men, is Rabia al-Adawiyya. Her earliest biographer, the great Iranian poet Farid al-Din Attar, called her:

> That one set apart in the seclusion of holiness, that woman veiled with the veil of religious sincerity, that one on fire with love and longing, that one enamoured of the desire to approach her Lord and be consumed in His glory, that woman who lost herself in union with the Divine, that one accepted by men as a second spotless Mary.[33]

Born into a poor family in the slums of Basra in the eighth century, her life story reads like an ode to suffering, as much through misfortune and circumstance as her own divine madness and ascetic contrivances. Orphaned as a child, then kidnapped and sold into slavery, she was later freed by her master, who saw in her the signs of a saint. Now a free woman, she would never again serve another earthly master. From now on she would serve only God.

Malik Dinar, a Muslim scholar of the time and one of the most important disciples of Hasan of Basra, relates the time he "went to visit Rabe'a, and saw her with a broken pitcher out of which she drank and made her ritual ablutions, an old reed-mat, and a brick which she occasionally used as a pillow". He was much saddened by what looked to him to be a sorry state and offered to approach one of his many rich friends on her behalf. From her state of absolute surrender to God's will that looks nothing less than madness to the worldly-minded, Malik recounts her saying to him:

> "Is not my Provider and theirs one and the same?"
> "Yes", I replied.

"And has the Provider of the poor forgotten the poor on account of their poverty? And does He remember the rich because of their riches?" she asked.

"No", I replied.

"Then", she went on, "since He knows my estate, how should I remind Him? Such is His will, and I too wish as He wills."[34]

On another occasion, when asked why she did not simply pray to God for sustenance, she replied: "If God knows of my poverty, then what need have I to remind Him of it?"[35]

It is difficult, as with other historical personages of her spiritual stature, to discern myth from reality, as even the earliest accounts of Rabia are hagiographical rather than biographical, replete with miracles and events of a dubious nature. What does seem to be clear, however, is her one-pointed dedication to the annihilation of the self in God, through the absolute denial of creature comforts and bodily desires. She denied herself what most would consider basic necessities and remained a virgin throughout her life, rejecting several proposals of marriage from well-respected suitors held in esteem by most other women. After receiving one such proposal from the great Hasan of Basra she replied:

"The tie of marriage applies to those who have being... Here being has disappeared, for I have become naughted to self and exist only through Him. I belong wholly to Him. I live in the shadow of His control. You must ask my hand of Him, not of me."

"How did you find this secret, Rabe'a?" Hasan asked.

"I lost all 'found' things in Him", Rabe'a answered.

"How do you know Him?" Hasan enquired.

"You know the 'how'; I know the 'howless'", Rabe'a said.[36]

Rabia could be quick to dismiss the comments of others, no matter who they might be, and correct them or even chastise them for their lack of sincerity, calling them out for any pretence or self-deception. She was a woman, so on fire with the love of God, as to possess a spiritual authority that even the religious giants of her time showed deference to. This, coupled with a paradoxical personality that combined both extreme humility with a self-assuredness that at times bordered on arrogance, made her a force to be reckoned with, and allowed her to get away with things that for others would seem presumptuous and disrespectful. An absolute faith in God; an unswerving allegiance to Truth at all costs; a cleaving to the Eternal over the temporal — the power of these things can at times appear miraculous. When ordered by one of Alexander the Great's henchmen to come or else be beheaded, the naked Indian monk, Dandamis, merely laughed and told him, "If you need Dandamis, you must come to him".[37] Not only did he keep his head but Alexander came to him and sat at his feet on the forest floor for an hour in order to speak with him. Who but the wise-fool, St Basil the Blessed, had the gall to confront Ivan the Terrible? Likewise, who but Rabia could chastise so respected a man as Hasan of Basra and others like him and get away with it — and of all people a poor, lowly, unmarried woman. On one occasion Rabia is said to have sent Hasan a lump of wax, a needle and a hair with the advice to:

> Be like wax ... Illumine the world, and yourself burn. Be like a needle, always be working naked. When you have done these two things, a thousand years will be for you as a hair.[38]

There are many such incidents in her life, like crazy-wisdom performances, designed to challenge one's comfortable assumptions about Truth, holiness and what it means to live a life in God. Much like Diogenes' stunt of wandering the streets of Athens in broad daylight with a lighted torch looking for an "honest man", another story told of Rabia has her hurrying through the streets of Basra with a flaming torch in one hand and a bucket of water in the other. When stopped and asked what she was doing she replied:

> I am going to quench the fires of Hell and burn Heaven, so that both these barriers to understanding shall vanish from the eyes of pilgrims, so that they may seek Truth without hope or fear.[39]

Just what exactly motivates these contrived teaching demonstrations one can only guess, nevertheless they are clearly universal methods used by masters and adepts from all Traditions. Many of these practical demonstrations of crazy-wisdom have developed into stories that are passed down from master to disciple, and over the centuries, the Sufis have developed an entire corpus of these teaching tales, designed, like *koans*, to derail the practitioner's habitual train of thought in an epiphany of insight. As the protagonist of these stories, one name stands out above all others: the archetypal crazy-wisdom Sufi master *par excellence* — Mulla Nasruddin.

Mulla Nasruddin

Mulla Nasruddin, Chief of the Dervishes and
    Master of a hidden treasure, a perfected man...
Many say: I wanted to learn, but here I have found
    only madness.
Yet, should they seek deep wisdom elsewhere, they
    may not find it.[40]
— *Teachings of Nasrudin*, Bokharan MS. of 1617, by
    ABLAHI MUTLAQ, "THE UTTER IDIOT"

DRUNK ON THE WINE OF THE BELOVED

The character of Mulla Nasruddin is as complex and varied as the cultures who consider him their own. Among these are the Persians, Greeks, Afghans and Uzbeks but perhaps none have taken this more seriously than the Turks who claim that he was born there, in Hortu Village in Sivrihisar, just over 100 kilometres south-west of Ankara, and died in Konya, 200 kilometres to the south, at the end of the thirteenth century. They even have his alleged tomb in Akşehir, where he was said to have lived most of his life. Every summer, the International Nasreddin Hodja Festival is held there in his honour, in which devotees dress up and re-enact the Mulla's stories in celebration of this elusive character.

According to another version, Nasruddin was born in the city of Khoy in the West Azerbaijan Province of present-day Iran. He was educated in Khorasan and became a *kadi* (Islamic judge) in Kayseri, a role that he often assumes throughout his stories.

The Uyghurs claim instead that he was from Xinjiang in China, while the Uzbeks believe he was from Bukhara in Uzbekistan, leading us to the more probable conclusion that nobody really knows. In Arabic-speaking countries he is often called Juha or Djoha, with other variations of the spelling, however, Juha was an earlier folk character from the ninth century who became fused with the character of Nasruddin in the nineteenth century due to the cross proliferation of translations from Arabic, Turkish and Persian, and the similarity of the stories about them.

Ultimately though, few solid historical facts can be established. At best, we have the speculations of scholars, and at worst, the machinations of the tourist industry in sleepy, out-of-the-way towns and villages, looking for a way to boost their revenue. Nasruddin would certainly be amused at these attempts to bring back from oblivion the details of his earthly life; details which would have been inconsequential even to him whilst he were alive.

Whether Nasruddin was an actual historical figure, a composite of several different historical characters or a folk myth really has little bearing on his stories and the teachings they contain. What he has become a reflection of, beyond any passing concerns with the details of his earthly life, is an archetype — a representation of certain universal aspects of the human condition and experience and a psychological mirror that one can use to peer ever more deeply into their own nature, for those who are so inclined. To others, he is a mere fool, a joker and a trickster.

Whatever the case may be, what we do know is that the figure of Mulla Nasruddin and the stories about him have been used as a teaching tool amongst the Sufis for many hundreds of years. To them, the stories represent a rich repository of esoteric knowledge that within the context of genuine spiritual practice, can be used to catalyse intuitive insight and deepen one's understanding of the divine.

No one has done more than Idries Shah in introducing the figure of Mulla Nasruddin to Western audiences. He was the first to publish popular compilations of his stories in English and in his book *The Sufis*, he tells us:

The Nasruddin stories, known throughout the Middle East, constitute one of the strangest achievements in the history of metaphysics. Superficially, most of the Nasruddin stories may be used as jokes. They are told and retold endlessly in the teahouses and caravanserais, in the homes and on the radio waves, of Asia. But it is inherent in the Nasruddin story that it may be understood at any of many depths. There is the joke, the moral — and the little extra which brings the consciousness of the potential mystic a little further on the way to realization.[41]

Far from being mere jokes or entertaining stories, to the dervishes the tales of Mulla Nasruddin are treated in much the same way as the *koan* in the tradition of Zen Buddhism, something to be meditated upon and turned over and over in one's mind. If diligent in this practice, often one arrives at sudden clarity or a flash of insight and illumination. Either this, or the momentary but complete cessation of all cognitive activity to give a glimpse of the pure and radiant consciousness that lies behind, beyond and beneath. For centuries they have been employed for this purpose; to bring about or further the mystical intuition and awareness of the practitioner and as a tool amongst others to deepen their spiritual insight and bring them closer to God.

The Tales of Nasruddin

Some people say that, whilst uttering what seemed
    madness,
he was, in reality, divinely inspired,
and that it was not madness but wisdom that he
    uttered.[42]

— *The Turkish Jester or The Pleasantries of
Cogia Nasr Eddin Effendi*, 1884

The tales of Nasruddin are as eclectic and broad in scope as the people who tell them, embodying sentiments both high and low, from the crude and obscene to the sophisticated and sublime, as well as everything in between. Over the years, as the Mulla Nasruddin corpus has been added to, they have become simply whatever people want them to be: sleazy jokes, mediocre wisecracks, entertaining stories, amusing anecdotes, social critiques, rallying cries of the oppressed, illuminating parables and even, on rarer occasions, the means by which eternal truths are preserved and transmitted. All of them have vied for people's attention, their only common factor being the name of their protagonist: the archetypal wise-fool, Mulla Nasruddin.

Some of the tales can be traced to earlier sources such as the ancient Greek *Philogelos* or *The Laughter-Lover*, widely considered to be the world's first joke book and written in the late fourth or early fifth century. Another even earlier Greek source text is the *Aesopica*, commonly known as *Aesop's Fables*, a collection of fables attributed to Aesop, a slave and storyteller thought to have lived around the sixth century BC.

From their genesis in the Middle East, the Nasruddin stories have found their way into the works of Baldakiev in Russia, *Don Quixote* in Spain, and the twelfth-century *Fables* of Marie de France. They crossed the Atlantic to the New World when Benjamin Franklin published a Nasruddin story in a newspaper he owned — *The Pennsylvania Gazette*. Perhaps to make it less exotic and more agreeable to his audience, he replaced the protagonist's name with "Old Man", although its provenance remains undeniable. Mark Twain also published a Nasruddin story that he had come across on one of his journeys in his collection of humorous tales *Mark Twain's Library of Humor*.

The tales have been told, retold, adapted, redacted, translated, misheard, misunderstood and twisted to purposes for which they were never intended. Like Chinese whispers, at times they have ended up as something unrecognisable from their original form. Along the way, substandard jokes and stories have acquired his name in their telling, like a stamp of approval or a gold star, beguiling the less discerning into holding them in higher esteem than they deserve and lending a certain credibility to things that in their substance, show a marked lack thereof. Of the elusive Mulla, Idries Shah tell us:

Nobody really knows who Nasruddin was, where he lived, or when. This is truly in character, for the whole intention is to provide a figure who cannot really be characterized, and who is timeless. It is the message, not the man, which is important to the Sufis.[43]

Who and what Mulla Nasruddin is then, no one can say. He has become too many things for us to pin down and comfortably evaluate. Just when we think we have him in our sights, like a pleomorphic chameleon, he changes colour and form and scuttles away to escape our intellectual grasp. He is too broad to measure, too grand to grasp and too elaborate to assess. In his entirety, he is an amalgamation of so many different and diverse personality traits as to be no one in particular. And in being no one in particular, he becomes anything we want him to be depending on where our prejudices lie. We construct his personality by what we care to see and what we care to leave out. The rascal guru Osho had this to say about him:

> Mulla Nasruddin is not a person; he is the whole humanity. He is you; he is you, all together. Whatsoever you can do, Mulla can do more stupidly. He is perfect! Whatsoever any human being can do, he can do more perfectly. He is your stupidity. And if you can understand it you will laugh and you will weep also. You will laugh at the ridiculousness of it and you will weep that that ridiculousness is yours. When you laugh at Mulla Nasruddin, remember, you are laughing at yourself. He just brings you face to face with whatsoever you are, so that it can be encountered.[44]

I shall refrain then from any attempt to define definitively just who or what Mulla Nasruddin was but shall instead explain as best I can just who and what he is to me.

Although not averse to dirty jokes or silly stories, I do not care to write about them. Although sympathetic to social critique or the plight of the downtrodden, I see a deeper issue that each of us must face alone, and that enables us in doing so, to step out of the arena in which these things take place. I acknowledge worldly problems and struggles and yet at the same time recognise that they only affect those who are "of the world" and not those that are merely "in it". Those great souls who speak to us across the ages, who see Truth and abide in It single-mindedly, dwell in a realm free from the troubles that affront the common man and woman. This is my only carrot that I, the humble donkey, lumber towards, urged on by the adepts and masters such as Mulla Nasruddin who have eaten theirs and speak of its flavour. And even this analogy fails me, for I have tasted the carrot, but I am a forgetful and stubborn donkey, plagued by old habits that die hard.

My Nasruddin then, is not the simpleton, the butt of the joke, nor the clown to be laughed at in order to lighten the load of our own failures and deficiencies. My Nasruddin is the mystic, the crazy-wisdom master, the wise-fool, the Perfected Man, the awakened Sufi teacher, whose exploits highlight the existential predicament of selfhood and point to an entirely different plane of being — the ground, game and goal of existence that any of us in our right minds would be wise to pursue wholeheartedly. This is what moves me as I believe it once moved the one we call Mulla Nasruddin, and this is what I am compelled to communicate and why the great Mulla figures so prominently in Part II of this book.

Mulla Nasruddin's tales have been recounted and received, written and read, considered and contemplated in countless languages for hundreds of years all over the world. The good ones can make people laugh or cry. They can give a flash of critical insight or a glimmer of hope in times of despair. They can uplift us momentarily from the mire of the mundane or serve as timely and tender advice for facing the vicissitudes of life. They can hold our hand, kiss us on the cheek or slap us across the face. They can do all of this, and the best ones can do even more.

Teaching-Tales as Legominisms

The conventional transmission of spiritual insight from teacher to student in an unbroken lineage suffers from one fatal flaw: there is no guarantee that every link in the chain will be forged with equal force. At times, the chain can only be as strong as its weakest link, or at least until such a one arises to regenerate the potency of its original transmission. One weak link — a student who has not rightly grasped the knowledge of his forebear — and the chain has at times been broken and lost forever. There does seem to be, however, a strategy to overcome this; to preserve and perpetuate a teaching without the need for perfect students every step of the way.

In his magnum opus, *All and Everything*, in which Mulla Nasruddin is mentioned no fewer than 110 times, George Ivanovitch Gurdjieff introduces to us the idea of the "legominism". In it we are told by his protagonist Beelzebub:

> This word Legominism, is given to one of the means existing there of transmitting from generation to generation information about certain events of long-past ages, through just those three-centered beings who are thought worthy to be and who are called initiates.[45]

Gurdjieff, himself something of a wise-fool, surmised that there are methods by which authentic teachings can be transmitted to successive generations beneath a form ostensibly intended for quite a different purpose. One of his examples of this was the Egyptian pyramids, whose architectural features encoded esoteric truths that would only be apparent to initiates but aesthetically appreciated by one and all. In this same way, the Sufis have used the stories of Nasruddin as a means of transmitting spiritual wisdom across time, disguised as simple tales and jokes so as to ensure their endurance and propagation far and wide. What better way to ensure the longevity of a teaching than to embed it into a joke or humorous story that even an unlearned illiterate would be able and willing to commit to memory and pass on, even though oblivious to its deeper meanings. By doing this, even simple folk and those unacquainted with the themes concerned would serve as the transmitters of transcendent wisdom through the ages.

In this sense, much of what we call "mythology" is in effect a legominism, in which profound insight into the nature of reality and the human condition can be embedded, preserved and transmitted — passed from generation to generation in the form of captivating tales and epic events wherein eternal truths and the collective wisdom of our ancestors can live on long after they are gone. Perhaps this can help explain their ability to fascinate and captivate across the millennia. Perhaps it is why they become so entwined with human affairs and penetrate all aspects of our lives, as even those who cannot understand the depths they reach, can nevertheless unconsciously intuit them. Scriptural stories, the Indian epics, the Greek triumphs and tragedies, the parables of Christ and the teaching-tales collected and told herein — they are all far more than they appear to be — far greater than just interesting stories well told. They plumb the depths of reality itself, inching us towards Truth. In the right hands, with the right frame of mind and with one's heart in the right place, they can even bring us face to face with who we are. And then beyond...

PART II

It's Not Where You're from; It's Where You're At

Mulla Nasruddin was sitting on a bench at one of the entrances to his village when a traveller approached him.

"Sir, are you from this village?" the man asked him.

"Yes", the Mulla replied.

"And what are the people like here?" the traveller continued.

"Where are you from?" Nasruddin asked him.

"From a town over the mountain there."

"And what are the people like there?" the Mulla continued.

"They are narrow-minded, selfish and miserly", the traveller replied.

"Yes, here they are very much the same", Nasruddin told him.

The traveller thanked him and continued on the path away from the village.

A short while later, another traveller approached Nasruddin.

"Are you from this village, Sir?" the man asked him.

"Yes", the Mulla replied.

"And what are the people like?" the traveller continued.

"Where are you from?" Nasruddin asked him.

"From a town far away by a river."

"And what are the people like there?" the Mulla continued.

"They are open-minded, generous and kind", the traveller replied.

"Yes, here they are very much the same", Nasruddin told him.

The man thanked him and entered the village.

Is That So?

The Zen master Hakuin was well-known throughout the land not only for his deep wisdom but also for his moral purity. Not far from where he lived was the home of a beautiful girl whose parents ran a small grocery store. One day, the parents found out that the girl was pregnant and they pressed her to discover who the father was. After continued pressure the girl relented and named Hakuin as the father. When confronted by the angry parents with the accusation, Hakuin's only response was, "Is that so?"

Once the child had been born it was brought to Hakuin to look after. By this time, the once respected Zen master's reputation was in tatters. Even so, he cared for the infant impeccably, taking care of the baby's every need.

After more than a year had passed the girl's conscience began to weigh heavy on her until she could stand it no longer. Finally she told her parents the truth — that the real father of her child was a man who worked in the local market.

Full of shame and remorse the parents rushed to visit Hakuin and beg his forgiveness. As they fell to their knees before him, apologising profusely for their mistake and the indiscretions of their daughter, whilst explaining the situation and the identity of the real father, all Hakuin had to say as they took the child back from him was, "Is that so?"

Bend or Break

A hunter in the desert saw Abba Anthony enjoying himself with some of his brethren and was appalled, thinking their behaviour inappropriate for monks. He approached the old man to tell him so in no uncertain terms. Anthony stood in silence and took the scolding without saying a word.

"Put an arrow in your bow and shoot it", Anthony said to him when the hunter had finally finished. Although puzzled the hunter did as he asked.

"Now shoot another", Anthony continued, and once again the hunter did so.

"Shoot one more", the old man continued, but this time the hunter refused and said:

"If I continue to shoot arrows and bend my bow, it will break."

"It is much the same with the work of God", Anthony said to him. "If I stretch the brethren beyond their capacity, they will break. Like your bow, they also need some time to rest."

At these words the hunter was filled with remorse at having questioned the monks' behaviour. He apologised profusely and left them, greatly edified by the encounter.

Innocent as Charged

A royal pardon was granted to free one of the prisoners at the local jail and Nasruddin was there talking to the inmates and listening to their complaints in order to choose one to be freed.

"I am innocent!" pleaded the first. "I only wanted to give the man a fright but accidently killed him."

"I too am innocent!" said the second. "They said it was a bribe when it was just a harmless gift."

"I have done nothing wrong either!" said the third man. "They accused me of stealing but I was only borrowing the donkey and was planning on giving it back."

Nasruddin came to the fourth prisoner.

"I am guilty", he said. "I lost my temper and wounded my brother in a fight. I deserve to be punished for what I have done."

"Remove this criminal at once!" the Mulla cried to the guards. "If not, he will surely corrupt all these innocent men!"

I'd Give You the Moon

Zen master Ryōkan lived a simple life in a small hut at the foot of a mountain. One evening, a thief burst into his house, only to discover that there was nothing of any value in it to steal. As the man was leaving empty-handed he came face to face with Ryōkan who had returned from a walk.

"You must have come a long way to visit me and I never let my guests leave empty-handed", he told the thief. "The only thing I have are these clothes — please take them as a gift."

The thief was bewildered but took the clothes from Ryōkan and disappeared into the night. Now naked, he sat down and looked up at the full moon hanging in the black sky.

"Poor fellow!" he said to himself, "if only I could have given him this beautiful moon."

The encounter inspired him to write the following *haiku*:

The thief left it behind —
The moon
At the window.[1]

To Know or Not to Know...

One day Abba Joseph and a group of seasoned monks came to visit Abba Anthony. The old man quoted a verse from scripture and, starting with the youngest, asked them what it meant. After each explanation was given in turn, Abba Anthony shook his head and said, "No — you have not understood".

Last of all was Abba Joseph's turn but all he could say when asked was, "I do not know".

At this Abba Anthony said to them, "At last! Abba Joseph has found the true way for he says quite rightly 'I do not know'".

The Worth of a Man

One day a small group of visiting princes came across Mulla Nasruddin strolling among the trees in the royal garden and decided to test his wisdom.

"Please tell us, wise Master", one of them said to him sarcastically, "just how many stars are there up in the vast heavens?"

"I have no idea my dear fellow", came Nasruddin's reply. "Far too many for me to count." "Then tell us, good Mulla", said another, "why is the sky blue and not another colour?"

"Good question", Nasruddin replied, "but for the answer you would have to ask its Creator and not a humble man who can only marvel at His creation."

"Then, good Master, indulge us", said a third, "and tell us what happens to us when we die?"

"That we will all find out in good time for sure", Nasruddin replied.

"Then surely you can tell us", said the first prince snickering, "just why it is that the sultan feeds you the finest foods and dresses you in the softest silk as if you were the wisest in the land when you have not been able to answer even one of our questions?"

"Now that is quite simple, good prince", Nasruddin said with a smile. "I am fed with the finest foods and dressed in the softest silk as a reward for the little that I do know. Were I to be rewarded for everything that I do not know, then all the treasures of the world together would not suffice."

Holy Frog Song

Shortly after the maggid's death, his disciples were gathered together reminiscing on his life. At one point Rabbi Zalman asked them:

"Do any of you know why our master went down to the pond every day at dawn?"

The others shook their heads so the Rabbi continued:

"Our master went down every day in order to learn the song with which the frogs praise God — and that song takes a long time for a man to learn."

A Secret Is a Secret

Nasruddin had retreated to a cave in the mountains in order to seek respite from the many visitors who came to him in pursuit of advice and blessings. However, even in his remote hermit's abode, he was still assailed by the more determined pilgrims and devotees, desperately seeking his counsel.

One afternoon, a young man arrived, threw himself down in the dust at the Mulla's feet, and began to prostrate before him.

"O wise Master", the man began. "Please initiate me into the secret wisdom! I beg of you!"

Nasruddin looked around in a shifty manner and then beckoned the young man to follow him inside the cave.

"You are still young", the Mulla whispered to him. "Are you truly capable of keeping a secret?"

"Of course!" the young man replied. "I shall breathe not a word of it to anyone — I swear — with God as my witness!"

"Very good", Nasruddin continued in a whisper. "So you understand the importance and magnitude of faithfully keeping a secret?"

"Yes Master!" nodded the young man enthusiastically. "I most certainly do!"

"Then", Nasruddin continued, raising his voice to a normal tone, "just what makes you think that at my age and with my reputation, I do not?"

Almost a Buddha

Zen master Gasan once received a visit from a university student who asked him if he had ever read the Christian Bible.

"No", the master responded, "why don't you read it to me."

The student opened his copy and began reading from the Gospel of Matthew:

"And why take ye thought for raiment? Consider the lilies of the field, how they grow; they toil not, neither do they spin: And yet I say unto you, That even Solomon in all his glory was not arrayed like one of these... Take therefore no thought for the morrow: for the morrow shall take thought for the things of itself."

"Whoever spoke those words I consider to be an enlightened man", Gasan replied as the student continued reading.

"Ask, and it shall be given to you; seek, and you shall find; knock, and it shall be opened unto you. For everyone who asks receives, and he who seeks finds, and to him who knocks it shall be opened."

"Most excellent!" Gasan exclaimed. "Whoever said that is almost a Buddha."

The Evil Urge

On one occasion when Rabbi Pinhas entered the House of Study, his disciples, who had been busy talking, suddenly stopped upon seeing him.

"What were you all talking about?" the Rabbi asked them.

"We were just speaking of the Evil Urge", they replied, "and our fears that it will pursue us."

"There is no need for you to worry about that", the Rabbi told them. "You have not gone far enough for it to pursue you yet. For the time being, you are all still pursuing it."

The I of the Beholder

The sultan was not a handsome man to put it mildly — he was lame in one leg, had only one eye and his general features fared little better. However, in a moment of capriciousness and for the benefit of future generations, or so he explained, he was seized by the desire to immortalise his image in a huge painting, to be displayed in a prominent place in the palace. To this end, he announced a reward to all the painters across the land, of one thousand pieces of gold, to anyone who could undertake this great task to his satisfaction.

Although it was well-known throughout the land that the sultan was a hard man to please, still, with the lure of generous recompense, two of the most famous painters of the time came forward to offer their services. At the great unveiling ceremony, the two men stood nervously next to their paintings. The sultan approached the first man and pulled the cord to reveal the painting. Slowly his face grew red with anger.

"It is true but ugly!" he screamed. "Take him away! And his abomination too! I wish to look on neither of them again for as long as I live!"

The guards dragged the poor man away. Then came the turn of the second painter. This time, upon revealing the work, the sultan at first smiled, before once again turning red with rage.

"It is beautiful but false! How dare you attempt to flatter me with this fakery! Take him away and let me no longer set eyes upon him and his fawning fabrication!"

Once again the guards dragged the poor man away.

Just when the sultan had thought that his hopes for a painting had been dashed, Nasruddin stepped forward with a huge, veiled canvas of his own.

"Perhaps I can be of some assistance", he said as he bowed his head.

"You!" the sultan laughed. "Since when can you paint?"

"Do not be surprised", Nasruddin replied calmly. "There are many talents that I have yet to reveal to Your Majesty."

"Go ahead then!" the sultan said nonchalantly. "I have nothing else to lose."

Upon revealing the painting, the sultan at first stood motionless. He then went up close and then moved further away, then to the left and then to the right, before returning to the middle, whereupon a smile spread across his face.

"Well, well, well", he said in disbelief. "I believe you've done it. Although I'm not handsome, I look majestic and noble. The horse hides my lame leg and the profile captures only my good eye. This is the real sultan that I wish to immortalise for all the generations to come! Congratulations Nasruddin! The painting is both true and beautiful!"

Just Three More Days

Suiwo, one of the main disciples of Hakuin, was renowned as a good teacher. During one of his summer retreats, a student came to him from one of the southern islands of Japan.

Suiwo gave him the *koan*: "What is the sound of one hand clapping?"

The young man worked on his *koan* for weeks and months and remained struggling with it for three years with no success. One night he came to Suiwo with tears in his eyes:

"Master, please give me leave. I cannot solve the *koan* and must return in shame to my village."

"Try for just one more week", Suiwo advised him, "and meditate upon it constantly."

After a week had passed the student returned even more desperate than before.

"Just one more week", Suiwo advised and continued to convince him to stay week after week in the same way until the young man could take it no more. In utter despair, the student threw himself at his master's feet and begged to be released but Suiwo managed to bargain a further five days of meditation. At the conclusion of the five days with still no success, Suiwo told him:

"Meditate for just three more days. If you fail to attain enlightenment, then it would be best for you to kill yourself."

On the second day, the student resolved the *koan* and attained enlightenment.

Prior Priority

Some brothers proposed to travel to Thebaid in order to buy some flax. As their journey would take them past the cell of Abba Arsenius, they also decided to pay the old man a visit. On arriving, they met with Abba Alexander, who went to notify the old man of the visitors.

"Some brothers have come from Alexandria to see you", he told him.

"Ask them why they have come", the old man replied.

Upon learning that they were on their way to Thebaid for flax, he informed the old man who said:

"In that case they will certainly not see the face of Arsenius. They have not come on my account but because of their work. Send them away in peace and tell them the old man cannot receive them."

Just Say When

Nasruddin paid a visit to his local tailor to have himself measured for a new shirt.

"So when will it be ready?" he asked the tailor when he had finished.

"God willing — in a week's time", the tailor replied.

Seven days later, the Mulla returned to his tailor but is disappointed to find that his shirt is not ready.

"God willing it will be ready the day after tomorrow", the tailor tells him this time.

Two days pass and Nasruddin returns again for his new shirt.

"God willing Mulla — tomorrow it will be ready", he is told this time.

The following day, and, by now, somewhat disillusioned with his tailor, Nasruddin returned.

"God willing...", his tailor begins but Nasruddin cuts him off.

"Now look here", Mulla said to him, "I am paying *you* for the shirt, so just leave God out of it and tell me: when will it be ready?"

No Water, No Moon

For many years the nun Chiyono studied Zen under master Bukko of Engaku but to little avail. Finally, one moonlit night when she was carrying water in an old pail, the bamboo gave way and the bottom fell out of the bucket. At that moment Chiyono attained enlightenment.

To commemorate the special moment she wrote the following poem:

In this way and that I tried to save the old pail
Since the bamboo strip was weakening and about to break
Until at last the bottom fell out.
No more water in the pail!
No more moon in the water![2]

Question Everything

A young boy was pestering his father with a barrage of questions that his father was unable to answer. Finally, his father said to him in frustration:

"So many questions! Do you know what would have happened to me if I would have asked so many questions when I was your age?"

"Perhaps", Nasruddin said, interrupting them, "you would now be able to answer some of his."

Only the Will of God

One day a magistrate came to Abba Arsenius to present him with the will of a wealthy senator; a relation of his who had left him a substantial inheritance. The old man took the document and was about to tear it up when the magistrate fell to his knees.

"Please Abba! I beg you. Do not destroy it otherwise they will have my head!"

"I was dead long before this senator", Abba Arsenius replied and handed him the will without accepting a single thing.

In the No

It was Nasruddin's duty to give the Friday sermon at the mosque and so he asked the congregation:

"Do you know anything about the subject of the sermon I am about to give?"

"No", they responded collectively.

"Then I refuse to preach to such an ignorant bunch!" the Mulla said before leaving.

The following week, he turned up again and asked them the same question:

"Do you know anything about the subject of the sermon I am about to give?"

With some hesitation and not wishing to have a repeat of the previous week, they replied tentatively:

"Yes."

"In that case", the Mulla told them, "there is no point in me telling you what you already know."

Once again he turned and left.

The following week he returned once again and asked them all the same question but this time, not knowing quite what to say, some of them say "yes" while others said "no".

"In that case", Nasruddin said to them before leaving, "those that know can tell those that don't."

See Through

Rabbi Mikhal once visited a city he had never been to before. As the more prominent members of the congregation came to see him, he fixed his gaze upon their foreheads before telling each of them the essential flaws in their characters and what could be done to remedy them. As word began to spread of his amazing ability, more people flocked to see him, however, these people arrived with their hats pulled down tightly over their foreheads.

"What do you think you are doing?" the Rabbi said to them and laughed. "Do you honestly think that the eye that can see through your thick skulls cannot see through a hat?!"

No Place for Monsters

Nasruddin passed a friend on the street. The man looked worried, so Nasruddin asked what was troubling him.

"Well", the man began, "I have this recurring nightmare that there is a monster under my bed. I wake up and get out of bed to check and there is nothing there but I cannot sleep for the rest of the night. I am on my way to see the doctor — he says he can cure me for five silver pieces."

"Five!" the Mulla exclaimed. "I can do it for one!"

Without hesitation, the man took a silver piece from his pouch and gave it to Nasruddin.

"Please Mulla", he said, "tell me what to do!"

"That's easy", Nasruddin said, pocketing the silver. "Cut the legs off your bed."

The Scholar and the Lama

Drukpa Kunley was staying in the house of the governor of Jayul enjoying the lavish hospitality in the company of scholars, monks and priests. One day as they were drinking *chung* and conversing, an elderly scholar said to him:

"You claim to be a Lama but do not wear the clothes of a Lama. Nor do you wear the dress of a monk or a sage. You do whatever you please and set a bad example to the common folk. Why do you not find yourself a home and settle down instead of aimlessly wandering around seducing women like a wild dog? You are giving all us religious people a bad name. Why do you do it?"

The Lama emptied his glass of *chung* in a single gulp and responded:

"If I became a proper Lama I would then be the slave of my attendant disciples and lose my freedom. If I became an ordained monk I would be obliged to keep the precepts, and who can keep their vows unbroken constantly? If I became a sage I should have to engage myself in discovering the Nature of Mind — something that to me is already self-evident! The desire for a permanent home or the fixation upon any object or possession only deflects one from the Path by strengthening the idea of 'I' and 'mine'. And the question as to whether or not I am a bad example depends entirely upon the intelligence of the individual in question and is something that is beyond my power to change. Furthermore, if a man is destined to spend his life in hell, then imitating a Buddha will not save him. And if a man is destined to become a Buddha, then the kind of clothes he wears is irrelevant, and his activity, whatever that may be, is naturally and spontaneously pure."

The scholars were all impressed with his reply and thanked him. They then inquired further as to his views and the goal to which he was committed and he sang them a song in reply:

Although I cannot pray with constant sincerity
To the Three Jewels, in which people put their trust,
I vow to maintain the Threefold Commitment —
Keep this vow in your hearts, my friends!
Although I am unable to practise recitation and visualisation
To the Deity who grants realisation and power,
I vow to desist from cursing and malediction —
Keep this vow in your hearts my friends!
Although I cannot rejoice in sacramental and symbolic offerings
To the Reality Protectors who keep enemies at bay,
I vow not to invite disaster upon my adversaries —
Keep this vow in your hearts, my friends!
Although I cannot meditate without fancy or bias
With a perspective that is always originally pure,
I vow to see through the illusory nature of concrete Name and Form —
Keep this vow in your hearts, my friends!
Although I am unable to keep my behaviour
In harmony with the regimen and conventions of the day,
I vow to avoid a hypocritical front and self-deception —
Keep this vow in your hearts, my friends!
Although what I am is not thoroughly comprehended
As the consummate goal — with inexpediency abandoned and
    reality realised,
I vow to abandon hope of future attainment —
Keep this vow in your hearts, my friends!
Although I cannot seal an inactive mind
In an experience that is inexpressible and inconceivable,
I vow never to put faith in my mind's conceptions —
Keep this vow in your hearts, my friends!

Passing Worries

One evening, Nasruddin's wife noticed him pacing up and down the verandah.

"What's the matter, dear?" she asked him.

"I borrowed three gold coins from the neighbour last month and tomorrow is the deadline to return the loan", Nasruddin explained in a worried tone. "I don't have the money and I don't know what to do."

He continued his pacing up and down the verandah.

"Well, what is there to do?" his wife said to him. "Go and tell him that you cannot pay."

Nasruddin took heed of her advice and went over to his neighbour's house to tell him. A short while later he returned, this time looking relaxed and happy.

"So?" his wife asked him. "How did he take it?"

"I'm not sure", Nasruddin tells her, "but I left him pacing up and down his verandah."

Dreamland

"Our schoolmaster would always take a nap every afternoon after lunch" related a disciple of Zen master Soyen Shaku.

"When we would ask him why he always slept in the afternoon, he replied that it was so that he could visit dreamland and question the great sages there just as Confucius once did. One day, on a very hot afternoon, some of us took a nap. When we were scolded by the school master, we told him 'We only went to visit the ancient sages of dreamland just as Confucius did!' 'And what did they tell you then?' he demanded angrily. One of the boys replied: 'Well, we asked about your daily visits to them in the afternoon and they told us that they'd never seen you before'."

Let He Who Is Without Sin...

Abba Ammonas came to visit some brothers where there lived a monk of ill repute. As it happened, whilst he was there, a woman was spotted entering the cell of the brother in question. The other monks gathered and planned to chase him from his cell and asked Abba Ammonas to join them. As they marched to his cell, the brother inside heard the commotion and hid the woman in a large wooden trunk. Upon entering, Abba Ammonas saw quite clearly the situation and went and sat on the wooden trunk as the man's cell was searched by the other brethren. When they had searched high and low without finding the woman, Abba Ammonas began to pray and then sent the others out. When they had gone, he took the man by the hand and said to him: "Brother, be on your guard!" and then left.

i and I

Nasruddin was out searching for his donkey who seemed to have gone, once again, for a walkabout.

"Please God!" the Mulla said with hands clasped, looking towards the sky. "If you help me find my donkey, I will pass the whole night in prayer!"

After a short while, Nasruddin found the donkey.

"It's okay God", he said once more looking towards the sky. "You can stop searching now. Thank you, but I've found him myself."

The Voice of the Voiceless

The wife of Rabbi Wolf once had a quarrel with her servant. She accused the young girl of having broken one of her favourite dishes and insisted that she pay the damages. The girl, however, was adamant and maintained that she had not broken anything and so refused to pay the damages for something she had not done. The argument became more and more heated until finally, the Rabbi's wife decided to take the matter to the rav and the local court of the Torah. She went to change her clothes and on seeing this, the Rabbi began changing too. When his wife asked why he was getting changed, he replied that he intended to accompany her.

"It's not appropriate for you to accompany me", she told him, "and besides — I know exactly what to say."

"I'm sure you know only too well", the Rabbi replied. "Unfortunately, that poor orphan — the servant girl whom you are accusing, doesn't. Who is there but me to defend her case?"

Outrageous Fortune

Nasruddin was accompanying the king as he reviewed his archers practising. As they watched, Nasruddin, who had never shot an arrow in his life, began to coach them:

"Your bow arm is too tense", he said to one. "Relax your shoulders and straighten your back", he said to another. "Pluck, not grasp the arrow", he said to a third.

Surprised, the king turned to him with a smile, and said, "I never knew your expertise extended to archery. Perhaps you could give us a demonstration of your skills".

The king promptly summoned one of his soldiers and before he knew it, Nasruddin was handed a bow and a quiver of arrows. Never one to turn down a challenge, Nasruddin slung the quiver over his shoulder and walked over to the shooting mark as the soldiers lined up on either side. He drew back the first arrow and with a loud twang it sailed into the ground just a few metres away, just missing a soldier's foot. They all erupted in laughter but Nasruddin, unfazed, said to them: "That, you see, is what happens when you grasp instead of pluck the arrow."

He took another arrow and this time it flew halfway to the target, veering off sharply to the left. Some of the soldiers laughed while others remained silent.

"And that is what happens when one's back is not straight and their shoulders too tight", he said, calmly loading the bow with another arrow.

The third arrow looked hopeful but fell at the base of the standing target. A few of the soldiers were heard to chuckle but most were silent.

"And that is what happens when one's bow arm is too tense", he said and proceeded to load the bow with another arrow.

This time, the arrow flew straight and true, hitting the bulls-eye dead centre. The assembled crowd watched on in astonished silence.

"And that, my dear fellows", Nasruddin said as he turned and handed back the bow and quiver. "That is the correct way to shoot an arrow."

Thief or Disciple?

One evening, as Zen master Shichiri Kojun was reciting sutras, a thief burst in, sword in hand, and demanded the master's money or his life.

"Do not disturb me", the master responded calmly. "There is money in that drawer but don't take it all as I need to pay some taxes tomorrow."

He then proceeded with his recitation as the thief fumbled around in the drawer. As the man was about to leave, master Shichiri added:

"It is good to thank the person that gives you a gift."

At this, the man thanked him and was gone.

A few days later the man was caught and confessed to several crimes, including the offence against master Shichiri. When the master was summonsed to court as a witness he told the judge:

"This man is no thief. I gave him the money and he thanked me for it."

After serving time for his other crimes the man sought out master Shichiri and became his disciple.

A Bird in the Hand

As Nasruddin's fame as a wise man grew, so too did the numbers of sceptics and doubters wishing to expose him as a mere fool. To get away from it all, he had retreated to a remote hermitage — a cave, high in the mountains. Even so, two young princes had gone out of their way to follow him up there with the intention of mocking him.

"Let us catch a sparrow", said one to the other, "I will hide it behind my back and we will ask that fool to tell us what I have in my hand. If he gets it right, then we will ask him, 'Is it dead or alive?' Now we have him trapped for if he says 'alive', I will wring its neck and if he says 'dead', then I will bring it out alive."

The two of them chuckled at their ingenuity before making their way to the entrance of the cave to confront the Mulla.

"My dear princes", Nasruddin said to them in greeting. "Do you bring me the sparrow for company?"

The two men blushed angrily before one of them stammered, "Ah yes — but is it dead or alive?"

"Now that", Nasruddin replied as he gave them a stern look, "that is up to you."

A Purpose for All Things

On one occasion, some young men came to Rabbi Wolf to complain about a group of their peers who were spending the nights gambling and playing cards.

"Very good!" the Rabbi exclaimed, much to their surprise. "Like all people, they wish to serve God but have yet to learn how", he continued. "For now, they are learning how to stay awake all night and persevere in doing something. All they need to do now is to turn towards God — then just imagine how great will be their service to Him!"

To Each, What Is Needed

One day, three old men, one of whom had a bad reputation, came to visit Abba Achilles.

"Father, will you make me a fishing-net?" the first man asked him.

"No", Abba Achilles replied, "I will not make you one."

"From your charity make us one Father, so that we may have something to remind us of you in the monastery", the second man insisted.

"I do not have the time", the old man answered.

Then the third man who had a bad reputation asked him: "Make me a fishing-net so that I may have something from your hands, Father."

"For you, I will make one", Abba Achilles replied without hesitation.

Later on the other two men asked him privately: "Father, please tell us — why when we asked, you refused, yet you accepted the same request from him without question?"

"When I refused your request, you were not upset", the old man said to them. "However, if I had refused him the same request, he would have thought it due to his reputation as a sinner, which would have caused him grief and our relationship would have suffered. Instead I have cheered his soul, which is something that he lacked but you both possess."

He Who Laughs Last

A wealthy merchant would often make fun of Nasruddin, thinking him to be an idiot. He would try to humiliate the Mulla by offering him a large gold coin in one hand and a small gold coin in the other and would laugh at him when he took the smaller one as he always did. On one such occasion, after the merchant had left, a concerned man approached the Mulla and said to him:

"Why do you not take the big coin Mulla? Don't you know it's worth more? He laughs at you for being foolish enough to not know."

"Oh I know", Nasruddin replied, "and I appreciate your concern. But do you think if I had taken the bigger coin, he would still be offering them to me? I see him every week — you work it out."

God Knows

One day, Abba Agathon was questioning Abba Alonius: "How can I control my tongue so as to no longer tell lies?" he asked him.

"If you tell no lies, you will sin often", Abba Alonius replied.

"How is that?" Abba Agathon asked with surprise.

"Suppose a man had committed a murder and fled to your cell seeking refuge. The magistrate then comes and asks if you have seen the man. If you do not lie you will have delivered that man to his death. It is better to abandon him to God for only He knows all things."

What's Mine Is Yours

Late one night, thieves broke into Rabbi Wolf's house. The noise aroused the Rabbi, who remained in his room, calmly watching them. As they gathered up his possessions, he noticed that they had taken a jug that a sick man had taken a drink from that very day. He burst out of his room.

"My good people!" he said to them. "Whatever goods you have found here, consider them gifts from me, but I must warn you about that jug to which the breath of a sick man still clings!"

It is said that from that day on, he would say before retiring to bed:

"Anything that is mine belongs to all."

In this way he ensured that should thieves come again, they would not be guilty of theft.

Credit to the Debtor

One evening, Nasruddin turned up on the doorstep of one of his neighbours.

"Sorry to bother you", he said to him on opening the door. "I'm just collecting funds for a poor man who is in debt and cannot meet his obligations."

"How much does he owe and when must he pay by?" the neighbour asked him.

"The situation is dire. He owes three gold coins and only has until tomorrow to pay", Nasruddin said.

"Well it's good of you to be looking out for him", his neighbour said, handing him three gold coins. "Just who is the poor fellow?"

"Me", the Mulla replied as he turned and swiftly left.

Sometime later, Nasruddin was back, knocking on his neighbour's door.

"I suppose you're here to help a poor man to pay his debt?" his neighbour said to him. "How much is it this time?"

"Four gold coins", Nasruddin replied.

"And I suppose that the poor man in debt is you", his neighbour continued.

"Why, no!" Nasruddin replied, feigning shock. "I promise you — I am not the one in debt this time."

"Well, in that case", his neighbour said, handing over the money, "take this to him."

"Oh, I don't need to", replied Nasruddin casually, as he turned to leave.

"And just why not?" his neighbour called after him.

"Because he owes it to me!" Nasruddin called back.

The Weight of the World

A monk was doing some weeding in the monastery's vegetable garden when he came to a particularly large and resistant weed. After a short struggle, he managed to pull it up. A fellow brother who had been watching him from over the wall remarked:

"Well done! You must be very strong to pull up such a big weed!"

"Not really", the monk replied. "I had the whole world pulling from the other side."

It Takes One to Know One

Rabbi Levi Yitzhak was once asked: "Concerning the passage of scripture that states that King Solomon was wiser than all other men, it has been written: 'Even wiser than fools'. What is meant by this? Surely anyone who is not a fool himself is wiser than a fool".

The Rabbi explained as follows: "The fool's greatest folly is to consider himself wiser than others and no matter what is said to him, nothing can convince him of his own foolishness. King Solomon's wisdom, however, was so great that he could assume many roles, even that of the fool. Only in this way could he converse with fools on their level to reach to their hearts and reveal their folly to them."

He's No Poet but He Don't Know It

The sultan had written a poem and read it to Nasruddin.

"Well?" he said expectantly. "Do you like it?"

"Not really", Mulla replied. "It is overly sentimental, shallow, full of clichés, and its cadence is jarring to the ear."

The sultan became enraged and threw Nasruddin in jail for three days.

The following week, the sultan summoned Nasruddin to read him his latest poem.

"Well?" he asked him again. "What do you think of this one?"

Without saying a word, the Mulla turned to leave.

"And just where do you think you're going?" the sultan called after him.

"Back to jail", said Nasruddin.

Who Needs Me Most?

When Zen master Bankei held his meditation retreats, students would come from all over Japan to attend. During one such gathering, an attendee was caught stealing. When the matter was brought before Bankei for some sort of disciplinary action to be taken, Bankei ignored the whole affair and did nothing. Some time after this, the same young man was caught stealing a second time and once again, Bankei decided to do nothing.

This complete lack of punishment angered the other students, who presented their complaint to Bankei and insisted on the culprit being expelled from the retreat. If their demands were not met, they threatened to all leave in protest. When Bankei had considered their petition, he said to them:

"You are wise brothers for it is clear that you all know right from wrong. You may go somewhere else to study if you wish. However, this poor fellow does not even know what is right from wrong. It would seem that he needs me the most. Who will teach him if I do not?"

The young man who had been caught stealing burst into tears and was filled with remorse for what he had done. In a moment, every desire to steal had vanished.

A Donkey's Tale

A villager visited Nasruddin to report the theft of his sandals in the hope that he could solve the crime and have them returned.

"I was invited to a friend's house", the man told him, "and I left them with the other shoes when I entered but when I went to leave, they were gone."

"And how many others were there?" Nasruddin enquired.

"There were seven of us including the host", the man replied.

"This is a simple matter", Nasruddin told him. "Have them all come around to my house for tea tomorrow afternoon."

The man left in a better state than he had arrived and returned the following afternoon with the six other men as Nasruddin was pottering around in his vegetable garden. Nasruddin first welcomed them all and then said:

"I understand that one of you has the sandals of my friend here. Before we have tea I would like to resolve this issue. Would anyone here like to make this easier than it has to be and step forward?"

The men all looked incredulously at one another and no one said a word.

"Alright then!" Nasruddin continued. "We shall do this the hard way!"

He began leading them to his donkey's stable and stopped short just outside.

"I, gentlemen, have a psychic donkey", he continued. "And my psychic donkey will tell us which of you is the sandal thief. One by one, please enter into the stable, close the door, and gently tug the tail of the donkey. He will recognise the thief and bray."

Giving each other looks of disbelief they went, one by one, into the barn to tug the donkey's tail.

After they had all finished, the man whose slippers had been stolen, said to Nasruddin:

"Well that was no good. They have all been in and your donkey has not made a sound."

"Hmm", said Nasruddin stroking his beard. "Well then — now I need you to all file past me and touch my nose."

The men, looking even more perplexed, assented and filed past the Mulla touching his nose as they passed. When they had finished, Nasruddin pointed at one of them and said to him:

"It is you. You are the sandal thief. Give this man back his sandals before it's too late."

The man was visibly flustered and it was clear to everyone, especially himself, that he had somehow been found out.

"I'm sorry. I shall give them back", he said after an uncomfortable pause. "But please, Mulla — how did you know?"

"Smell your hands", Nasruddin told him.

"They smell of nothing", the man replied, puzzled.

"Exactly. Now everyone else smell your hands", the Mulla continued.

"Why — they smell of mint", they all concluded unanimously, looking even more perplexed than before.

Nasruddin let them wallow in their confusion for a while before telling them:

"I rubbed my donkey's tail with mint, knowing that one of you would not risk tugging it. So the smell of mint is the smell of innocence!" Nasruddin laughed.

They all laughed with him and applauded, even the petty thief, who went to get the sandals, before sitting down to have tea.

God Is

One day, Abba Doulas was walking beside the sea with his teacher, Abba Bessarion, when he was overcome by thirst.

"Father, I cannot continue much further without something to drink", he said to the old man, whereupon Abba Bessarion said a short prayer and then urged his disciple to drink some of the sea water. The water to his surprise was sweet, so he drank his fill and then poured some more into a small bottle to take with him. Seeing this, the old man asked what he was doing.

"Forgive me Father, it is for fear of being thirsty later and again having nothing to drink."

"God is here and God is everywhere", the old man said to him, "what need would you have of carrying Him around with you?"

Mistakes Are High

Nasruddin was on a pilgrimage in India and was walking down a dusty road under a blazing sun. He was hot and thirsty and began to feel the need to cool off and quench his thirst. Just then, he came across a street vendor selling shiny bright red fruits and so he stopped to rest and try a few. After paying the man, he sat down in the shade to enjoy his refreshing fruits.

After a few moments of chomping, tears began streaming down his face and he began to sweat profusely as the stall owner looked on aghast.

"What on earth have you given me?!" Nasruddin blurted out to him as he continued to eat.

"These juicy looking fruits you have sold me are burning me up and not cooling me down!"

"They are chillies", the stall owner replied, "and they are used to give flavour when cooking food, not to be eaten as you are doing!"

"I see", said Nasruddin as he continued to munch them down.

"So stop!" the vendor said to him. "Why do you continue to eat them?"

"Well", Nasruddin replied, "if we are committed to accepting the full consequence of our mistakes, we are sure to make fewer of them."

Black-Nosed Buddha

A nun, in her search for enlightenment, made a statue of the Buddha and gilded it with gold leaf. Wherever she would go, she would take the beautiful golden statue with her, no matter what.

Many years later she came to live in a small temple in a country that had a different Buddha for every occasion, each with its own special shrine. The nun, wishing to burn incense before her Buddha without the perfumed smoke straying to any of the others, devised a funnel to direct the smoke towards just her own statue and none other. Before long her invention had blackened the nose of her golden Buddha making it the ugliest of them all.

Walking Each Other Home

After a visit to a nearby town, Rabbi Elimelekh boarded his carriage and began the journey home. The hasidim of that town, to show their devotion, followed behind him and continued even after leaving the gates of the city limits. The Rabbi signalled for the coachman to stop, whereupon he got out before again signalling for him to continue, as he walked behind the carriage in the midst of the crowd. The hasidim were astonished and asked him what he was doing.

"When I saw your great devotion and the good work of accompanying me", he told them, "I couldn't bear to be excluded from it any longer!"

Double or Bust

Nasruddin decided to visit his two sons to see how they were. The first son was a farmer who worked the land and had an orchard.

"This year", his son said to him, "I am holding nothing back. I have spent all my savings and have planted everything my land will allow. If it rains, I'll hit the jackpot. If not, then I'm sure that Mother will be shedding tears for me."

Nasruddin bid him farewell and continued on to his second son who was a potter.

"This year", the young man said to him, "I am holding nothing back. I have spent all my savings on the best quality clay and will make as many pots and pitchers as my time will allow. If it doesn't rain, I'll hit the jackpot. If not, then I'm sure that Mother will be shedding tears for me."

Nasruddin bid him farewell and returned home to his wife who asked him how their boys were doing.

"Well, I don't know about the boys", Nasruddin told her, "but I do know that whatever happens this year, one way or the other, you'll be shedding tears for one of them."

Beauty Is a Beast

In 1797, the Buddhist nun Ryonen was born. As a young girl she was known for her poetic genius, as well as her striking beauty, and at the age of seventeen was already serving as a lady-in-waiting in the court of the empress. When the empress died unexpectedly, Ryonen's dreams were shattered. The event was a turning point for her; it was her first real confrontation with suffering and impermanence and gave rise to a strong desire to study Zen. Her family, however, disagreed with her new-found interest and instead forced her into marriage. With their guarantee that she could become a nun after having borne three children, Ryonen agreed and settled into married life and motherhood. By the age of twenty-five, she had fulfilled her part of the bargain and there was little that her family could now do to dissuade her further. Having shaved her head and taking the name Ryonen, meaning "to realise clearly" she began her pilgrimage.

When she arrived at the city of Edo she visited the Zen master Tetsugyu in the hope of becoming his disciple but was rejected by him for being too beautiful. She then sought out another master, Hakuo, but was refused for the same reason.

Putting an end to the blessing that to her had now become a curse, she took a hot iron to her face and in just a moment, her beauty vanished forever. On returning to Hakuo, she was then accepted as a disciple. To commemorate the occasion, Ryonen wrote a poem on the back of a small mirror:

In the service of my Empress I burned incense to perfume my exquisite clothes,

Now as a homeless mendicant I burn my face to enter a Zen temple.[4]

The World to Come

Rabbi Elimelekh once said: "I am certain to have a share in the world to come. When I stand before my final judgement and I am asked, 'Have you studied all that you could have studied?' I will answer, 'No'. And when I am asked, 'And have you prayed all that you could have prayed?' I will answer, 'No'. And when I am asked, 'And have you done all the good works that you could have done?' I will answer for the third time, 'No'. Then will come the verdict: 'Rabbi Elimelekh — you have told the truth and for the sake of truth you shall have your share of the world to come'."

Suffering Desire

Nasruddin had a buffalo with horns spread wide apart. He had often imagined himself riding the buffalo into town, and wondered what it would feel like, perched on its head between the horns like a throne.

One day, the buffalo was grazing with its head lowered to the ground, and Nasruddin's curiosity got the better of him. He ran over to the buffalo and sat down on its head, grasping its horns. At this the buffalo reared its head and shook it violently, tossing the Mulla to the ground. His wife, hearing the commotion, ran outside to find Nasruddin lying on the ground, stunned, and on seeing him injured, began to cry.

"Do not cry my dear!" Nasruddin said to her.

"Although my head may hurt for a day or two, my curiosity has been extinguished for a lifetime! Now I know, and my mind is at rest."

Don't Even Think About It

Abba Zeno was walking in Palestine, and feeling tired, he sat down to rest. Next to him grew a cucumber plant and he thought to himself, "Why don't you take a cucumber and eat it. It will be refreshing and is only a small thing to take".

He then answered his thought with another, "Thieves are punished for stealing. Examine yourself then to see if you can bear punishment".

He then got up and stood in the hot sun for five consecutive days. When he was burnt and utterly exhausted, he said to himself, "It seems you cannot bear punishment. That being the case, do not steal nor even think of stealing".

The Fate of Free Will

"What is fate?" Nasruddin was asked one day by a scholar.

"It is an endless succession of interconnected and interdependent arisings", came Nasruddin's elegant reply.

"And what of free will? Where is the individual's will to choose in all of this?" the scholar asked him.

"It is buried", the Mulla replied.

"Buried?" the man remarked, puzzled. "Buried under what?"

"Well, take that for example — that man there", the Mulla said, pointing to a passing procession with a prisoner, on his way from the courthouse to the jail.

"Why is he there? Is it because someone gave him the money to buy a knife? Or because he was slighted? Or because he used it to exact revenge? Or because he was caught? Or because the judge sentenced him to prison? Or because he experienced a lack of maternal love that led him to become an aggressive man in the first place? I could go on all day, could I not?"

The scholar nodded.

"So there is your answer — there is your free will. It is buried under all of that."

No Coming, No Going

Shortly before Ninakawa passed away, Zen master Ikkyu paid him a visit.

"Shall I lead you on?" Ikkyu asked him.

"I came here alone and shall go alone too", Ninakawa replied. "What help could you be to me?"

"If you truly are deluded to think that you come and go", Ikkyu told him, "then allow me to show you the true path on which there is no coming and no going."

With these simple words Ikkyu revealed the true Buddhist way with such clarity that Ninakawa smiled and peacefully passed away.

The Faster

In a small village, there lived a man who fasted so frequently that he was known to the villagers as "The Faster". When word of him had reached Abba Zeno, he was sent for and came gladly. Having prayed together they sat down and the old man proceeded to go about his work once more in silence. With no more conversation, The Faster soon became bored and said to the old man, "Pray for me Father, it is time for me to go".

"Why?" the old man enquired.

"Because my heart is on fire and I don't know what the matter is. When I am in the village and fast until the evening, nothing like this happens to me."

"In the village you feed yourself through the ears", Abba Zeno said to him. "So go now if you must but from now on, eat at the ninth hour and whatever you do for God, do it secretly."

The Faster returned to the village and began to act on the advice of Abba Zeno but now found it hard to keep his fast until even the ninth hour. After struggling for some time like this, he returned to the old man and told him of his troubles.

The old man smiled. "This is the way according to God", he said.

Everybody's a Nobody

Mulla Nasruddin was in the mosque praying, when suddenly he was overwhelmed by the presence of the Divine and the immensity and splendour of the universe. Enraptured in this beatific vision of wonder and adoration, he cried out awestruck, "I am nothing! Truly — nobody!"

Just then, a local merchant entered the mosque — an affluent man who wished to be thought of by others as being very devout. Kneeling beside the Mulla and with a quick glance around him to see who might be watching, he closed his eyes and began to cry out in feigned humility, "I am nothing! O Lord! I am nobody!"

As this was going on, the caretaker of the mosque, who until now had been quietly sweeping the floor, moved by the emotional outpouring of the Mulla, dropped his broom and fell to his knees in a quiet corner and began repeating softly to himself, "I am nothing. I am nobody".

At this, the merchant opened one eye and gave Nasruddin a nudge.

"Well, well, well", he said to him out of the corner of his mouth. "Just look who thinks he's nobody!"

The Cape Caper

A woman once came to Rabbi Israel, the maggid of Koznitz, with tears in her eyes, as she had been married for twelve years but still had not borne a child.

"What are you willing to do about it?" he asked her, however, the woman remained silent as she had no idea what to say.

"My mother", the maggid continued, "was getting on in years and still was without child. After hearing that the holy Baal Shem was stopping over nearby from his journey, she hurried to his inn and begged him to bless her with a child. 'What are you willing to do about it?' he asked her. 'My husband is just a poor book-binder', she replied, 'although I do have one thing of value that I can bring to you as a gift to show my sincerity.' She hurried home to fetch her best cape — a family heirloom that was safely stowed away in a wooden chest. But by the time she made it back to the inn, the Baal Shem had already left to continue his journey. As my mother had no money for a carriage or a horse, she set out on foot, from town to town, for several days until she finally caught up with him. She presented him with the cape which he took and hung on the wall. All he said was, 'very well', and that was that. My mother then retraced her steps and after a few more days she was back home. A year later I was born."

"Please stay right here!" the woman cried. "I too have a beautiful cape. I shall bring it to you right now so that I may bear a son!"

"That won't work", the Rabbi said. "You heard the story. My mother had no story to go by."

Pray for Me

One evening, as Nasruddin was sitting at the village tea-house relaxing after a long day, a dervish happened to come by, wailing and moaning his prayers to God:

"O Lord! Praise be unto You the All Powerful, All-Merciful! Grant me faith so I may trust in Your Will at all times!"

He wandered amongst the men drinking their tea.

"O Lord, grant me humility so I may see that I am nothing before You!"

He passed by the Mulla's table and fell to his knees.

"O Lord! Grant me forbearance so that I may confront both joy and suffering with indifference! Grant me moderation and protect me from greed! Bless me with tolerance of those who sin!"

Nasruddin waited for a pause in the man's wailing before standing up and shouting at the top of his voice:

"O dear God! Praise be unto You above all else! May you in your goodly grace grant me gold so that I may never see poverty, give me a beautiful woman so that I may be forever satisfied, bless me with obedient children and protect me from the envious who would take these from me!"

He sat down again as the dervish brought himself to his feet, a look of horror on his face. "How dare you!" he said to Nasruddin. "How dare you ask the Lord for such selfish things! Shame on you!"

Nasruddin turned to him and smiled.

"Why, my good man — don't we, each of us, pray for what we do not yet have?"

The Way of the Monk

One day, Abba Moses said to brother Zacharias, "Tell me what I ought to do".

Zacharias threw himself on the ground at the old man's feet and said, "Surely you cannot be asking me, Father?"

"Believe me Zacharias my son, I have seen the Holy Spirit descending upon you and since that moment I have been compelled to ask", the old man said.

Zacharias took the hood from his head, threw it in the dust and trampled it underfoot saying, "The man who will not let himself be treated like this cannot become a monk".

The Smug Smuggler

Nasruddin arrived at the border with a donkey loaded with straw bundles. The inspector stopped him and began to search through the straw bundles looking for contraband. After finding nothing he allowed Nasruddin to pass.

The next day, Nasruddin was there again with a donkey loaded with bundles of straw. The inspector, now a little suspicious, checked him more thoroughly but once again found nothing and had to let him pass.

This went on every day for several years and as time went by, Nasruddin passed the checkpoint in ever more expensive clothing and jewellery. The inspector always checked him thoroughly but never once found anything on him.

Many years later after the inspector had retired, he spotted Nasruddin in a crowd and went up to him.

"I remember you", the inspector said to him. "You would pass the border every day with your donkey loaded with straw. I know you were smuggling something but could never figure out where you were hiding it. I'm long retired now so please — you must put me out of my misery — it will be our secret, I promise — tell me, just what were you smuggling?" Nasruddin smiled and replied, "Donkeys".

Playing in the Mud

Chuang Tzu sat fishing by the Pu River with an old bamboo pole when two officials of the prince approached and said:

"Master Chuang Tzu, the prince hereby appoints you as the prime minister."

Without so much as turning towards them Chuang Tzu replied:

"I have heard that three thousand years ago a tortoise with special markings on its shell was killed and is now kept in the king's private shrine, wrapped in silk and displayed in a ivory box, hand-crafted by the greatest artisans in the land. Now tell me", he continued, "do you think the turtle would prefer to be dead with its remains honoured like this or alive and playing in the mud?"

"No doubt it would prefer to be alive and playing in the mud", one of the officials replied.

"Then go away", Chuang Tzu said to them, "and leave me in peace to play in the mud."

The Will of God

Mulla Nasruddin had retired to a small hut on a hill on the outskirts of the village in order to intensify his spiritual practice and deepen his relationship with God. One day the villagers sought him out in distress:

"All our chickens have died!" they told him. "What shall we do?! How shall we awake in the morning on time and how can we raise more chicks?!"

"Not so much as a leaf is overturned that is not overturned by the will of God", the Mulla told them in an attempt to placate their worry.

The crowd returned to the village, very dissatisfied with the Mulla's response.

A short while later they returned, even more agitated than the first. This time they tell him:

"Now all our fires have gone out! There isn't a live coal in the whole village! How will we cook dinner and keep ourselves warm tonight?!"

"I cannot solve your problem", the Mulla told them, "but I do know that not so much as a leaf is overturned that is not overturned by the will of God. Find consolation in that and have faith that all will be well."

Once again, the villagers returned home, even more frustrated than when they had arrived.

Before the sun had disappeared beyond the horizon, they were all back again.

"What is it this time?!" the Mulla asked them as they arrived at his hut.

"Now it is the dogs! They have all died! What sort of a malevolent curse has been cast upon us?! First the chickens, then the fires, and now the dogs! They have all died — just like that!"

The Mulla shook his head and attempted to sympathise with their plight.

"Now what will we do?! Who will scare away the wild animals?! Who will warn off the thieves?!"

"Well now, this is all very puzzling", Nasruddin told them, "however, I really only have one thing to say to you."

"Yes — we know", they all responded as they turned to leave. "Not so much as a leaf is overturned that is not overturned by the will of God. That's the last time we come to you looking for advice!"

That night, just before the break of dawn, Nasruddin was woken by the sound of a large group of men approaching the village. They stopped behind the bushes next to his hut:

"Well men, I think we've had a good run — burning down villages and pillaging whatever takes our fancy", he heard one of them say. "I think we should call it a day. The village down there is obviously abandoned. There's no smoke from the chimneys, no dogs barking and no cocks crowing, even at this time in the morning. Let's move on."

On hearing them disappear, Nasruddin smiled — the puzzle of the previous day now clear to him.

Gudo and the Emperor

The emperor Goyozei was studying under Zen master Gudo and on one occasion enquired:

"Would it be correct to say that according to Zen, this very mind is Buddha?"

"If I say 'yes', you may think that you understand without really understanding", Gudo replied. "And if I say 'no', I would be contradicting a fact which many have correctly understood."

On another occasion the emperor asked: "Where does an enlightened man go when he dies?"

To this Gudo responded simply "I don't know".

"Why don't you know?" the emperor pressed him.

"Because I haven't died yet", Gudo replied.

Gudo then beat the floor with his hand as if to awaken him and the emperor was enlightened.

The Work of the Soul

A brother questioned Abba Theodore of Pherme saying, "What is the work of the soul and what is that which is subordinate?"

"Everything that is done as a commandment of God, for the sake of God, is the work of the soul", the old man replied, "and to work and gather goods and everything else that is of a personal motive is subordinate."

"Explain this matter to me", the brother urged.

"Suppose it is time for prayer", Abba Theodore continued, "but you say to yourself 'I had better finish my work and then go', or again, another brother comes and says to you, 'Lend me a hand brother', and you say to yourself, 'Shall I leave my own work to go and help him?' If you do not go, you are disregarding the commandment of God which is the work of the soul, and instead doing the work of your hands, which is subordinate. God must come before all else."

You Can't Please Everyone

Nasruddin was riding his donkey to the market as his son walked beside them, when a passerby was heard saying:

"Look at that poor boy having to walk while that lazy man rides the donkey!"

The Mulla stopped the donkey, dismounted, and told his son to ride for a while.

A little further on, another passerby was heard to say:

"Look at that poor old man made to walk while that fit young lad just sits there. What's the world coming to!"

At this, the Mulla mounted the donkey with his son and the two of them continued to ride. Still further on another traveller was heard saying to his companion:

"For God's sake! That poor donkey! How cruel for those two men to both be riding it!" When Nasruddin heard this, he got down from the donkey and told his son to do the same.

As they neared the market, walking along beside the donkey, some villagers started making fun of them:

"Look at those silly fools", they said. "They have a donkey and yet they are both walking!" As they heard this last comment, Nasruddin turned to his son and said:

"My son — there will always be people who find fault in whatever you do. So walk your own path as you see fit and never let the opinions of others cause you to stray from it."

The Funeral of Chuang Tzu

When Chuang Tzu was approaching the end of his earthly life, his disciples began planning a grand funeral. When he found out their plans, he told them:

"I shall have heaven and earth for my coffin, the sun and moon hanging by my side. Planets and stars will shine like gems all around me and all beings will be as mourners at the wake. What more is needed? Everything is already taken care of."

"We fear the crows and buzzards will eat our dear master", the disciples replied.

"Above the ground are crows and buzzards and below the ground are ants and worms", Chuang Tzu said to them. "In either case I am to be eaten — why do you favour the ants and worms?"

The Cost of a Slap

Nasruddin was having a heated debate with another man about non-violence when suddenly, in anger, the man slapped Nasruddin across the face.

The Mulla took the man to court but when they arrived there, the judge greeted the man warmly and it was clear that they knew each other well. After an overly brief trial, the judge handed down an extremely lenient sentence.

"I deem the fine for a slap to be one silver coin", the judge proclaimed. "If you don't have it then go home and get one and bring it here."

The man left the courthouse and the Mulla sat down to wait for his return.

After several hours of waiting and with no sign of the man, Nasruddin jumped to his feet,

"When he finally gets back", the Mulla said to him as he turned to leave, "you have the coin."

The Hand of Destiny

When the great Japanese warrior, Nobunaga, decided to launch an attack on his enemy, he knew he was outnumbered ten to one. Though convinced of a win, his men were showing signs of doubt. On the way into battle he stopped at a shrine and told his men:

"After offering my prayers I will toss a coin — if it is heads, we will win and if it is tails, we will lose. Destiny holds us in her hand."

He entered the shrine and offered his prayers in silence before returning to the men and tossing a coin before them. The coin fell on heads and such confidence was aroused in his men that they won the battle easily. As the men began celebrating their win, Nobunaga's attendant said to him:

"No one can change the hand of destiny."

"Indeed — no one", Nobunaga replied, as he showed him the coin with heads on both sides.

Only the Paths Are Many

Nasruddin was sitting with some companions when a man approached them and asked the Mulla:

"Does God exist?"

"He most certainly does", Nasruddin replied.

Some while later, another man approached them and asked the Mulla the same question:

"Does God exist?" he asked.

"Of course not", Nasruddin told him.

Later still, another man approached and asked the same question:

"Does God exist?"

"Only you can decide", the Mulla replied this time.

After the man left, his companions turned to him and said:

"Three men have asked you the same question and yet you have given each of them a different answer. How can this be so?"

"Well you see", Nasruddin replied, "a man can only reach God by his own path. The first man was open to what I would tell him, whilst the second will do anything he can to prove me wrong. The third man will believe nothing anyone else tells him and will only follow his own conclusions. They all got what they needed — it's just that their needs were different."

Usefulnessless

Hui Tzu said to Chuang Tzu: "Why is it that you are always talking about what is of no use?"

"If you cannot appreciate what has no use", Chuang Tzu replied, "you cannot begin to talk about what can be used. The earth, for example, is broad and vast but of all its space, a man uses a space just the size of his feet — the piece upon which he happens to be standing. Now suppose that all the land he was not using was suddenly taken away so that all around him was now a great empty void — everything a yawning abyss except the ground under each foot. How long would he be able to use what is now of use to him?"

"It would no longer be of any use to him whatsoever", Hui Tzu replied.

"Then the usefulness of what is of no use is clear", Chuang Tzu concluded.

Silence Is Golden

One day Abba Theophilus, the archbishop, came to Scetis. The brethren who were assembled there said to Abba Pambo, "Say something to the archbishop so that he may be edified".

"If he is not edified by my silence", the old man said to them, "then he will not be edified by my speech."

Only the Pot Dies, Never the Space Contained

Nasruddin had borrowed a large cooking pot from his neighbour. When it was time to return it, he put a small cooking pot inside and gave it back saying:

"It seems your pot was pregnant and had a baby."

The neighbour said nothing and happily took the two pots.

Some time later, Nasruddin asked to borrow his neighbour's large pot again but this time did not give it back until finally his neighbour confronted him and asked for it to be returned.

"Ah yes", the Mulla said. "My condolences — your pot is dead."

"Don't be ridiculous!" his neighbour replied. "A pot cannot die!"

"What do you mean?" Nasruddin said with surprise. "Surely a pot that can give birth is a pot that can die?!"

True Prosperity

On one occasion, Zen master Sengai was asked by a wealthy man to compose something to help ensure the continued prosperity of his family. Sengai agreed and took a large piece of paper upon which he wrote in beautiful calligraphy:

"Father dies, son dies, grandson dies."

The man became angry and said to Sengai:

"I asked for something to ensure the happiness of my family and you write this? Is this supposed to be a joke? If it is, it is not funny."

"It is certainly not a joke", Sengai explained. "Would it not be a terrible tragedy for your family were your son to die before you, or your grandson before your son? However, if your family were to pass away in the manner I have described, it would not be a tragedy at all but rather the normal course of life. To me this is true prosperity."

Casting Stones

One of the brothers at Scetis had been accused of a petty crime. A council was called and Abba Moses was summoned by them to pass judgment on the man. At first he refused but after further pressure he decided to attend. Before leaving, he took a leaky jug, filled it with water, and set off for the trial. As he walked he left a trail of water behind him and as he arrived, the final drops of water fell from the jug.

"What is this Father?" the others asked him as they came out to meet him. Abba Moses held up the empty jug:

"In this jug are my sins", he told them. "And if you don't look back, you will never see them. Now that it is empty, do you deem me fit to judge my brother?"

At this, the other brothers gathered together and decided to drop all charges.

Just Passing

When a visiting scholar called in on the Mulla at his humble home, he was surprised to see just a table, a small bench, and some books on a shelf.

"But Mulla", the man asked him, "where is all your furniture?"

"And where is yours?" Nasruddin asked.

"Yes — but I am just passing through", the scholar explained.

"Indeed", Nasruddin replied. "And so am I."

The Foolish Monkey

As soon as the King of Wu and his entourage arrived on Monkey Mountain, the monkeys fled in panic and hid in the treetops — all of them, except one bold monkey, who remained, swinging from branch to branch and utterly unconcerned by the men moving around beneath him. The king shot an arrow at him, which to everyone's surprise, the monkey caught in mid-flight. Taken as a provocation and insult, the king ordered all of his men to shoot down the monkey. In an instant, the poor monkey was shot full of arrows and fell from the tree, dead. The king turned to his companion, Yen Pui, and said:

"Did you see? This foolish animal made a display of his cleverness and agility and trusted too much in his own skill. His arrogance sealed his fate. Remember this well. Do not rely on distinction and talent when dealing with men."

When they had returned home, Yen Pui became the disciple of Tung Wu and gave himself to the teaching. He renounced what had once given him pleasure and rooted out all that had led to pride and distinction. After three years, no one in the kingdom knew what to make of him, and so held him in awe and admiration.

Greed Will Get You Nowhere

A dispute between two merchants was brought before Mulla Nasruddin as the presiding judge.

"Your Honour", began the plaintiff. "Before embarking on a long and perilous journey, I entrusted all my money — one hundred gold coins — to my friend here for safekeeping. I agreed with him that were I not to return after a year had passed, then he would be free to do with the money what he wished. Were I to return before then, then he would only have to give me back what he wanted and keep the rest. Having been away for only six months, I have now returned and when asked about the money, all I have been given is ten gold coins! I therefore bring the case before you, Your Honour, as it is my conviction that this is anything but fair."

At this the defendant chimed in:

"Your Honour, I was only being faithful to the terms of our contract, and that was to give him what I want."

Nasruddin was silent a while in thought and then summoned the two to the bench.

"The defendant is right in that a contract must be honoured to the last letter", he told them. "In that case, the agreement was for you, the defendant, to give back what you want and to keep the rest. Seeing as what you want is ninety of the hundred gold coins, in accordance with the agreement you must give back the ninety coins and keep ten, which is the rest. Case dismissed!"

A Time to Die

Zen master Ikkyu was very clever even as a young boy. His teacher had an antique teacup that he treasured and one day, Ikkyu accidentally broke it into pieces. On hearing the approaching footsteps of his teacher he held the pieces behind his back and when he had appeared Ikkyu asked him: "Why do people have to die?"

"Everything has an allotted time", his master explained to him. "Everything has its day and this is the natural way. There is nothing to fear in it."

"That's good then", Ikkyu said as he produced the broken teacup from behind his back, "I guess it was just time for your teacup to die."

Where Is the Tao?

Master Tung Kwo asked Chuang Tzu: "Where is what you call the Tao to be found?"

"There is nowhere it is not to be found", Chuang Tzu replied.

"Show me then some definite place", Tung Kwo insisted.

"It is here in this ant", said Chuang Tzu pointing to the ground.

"Is it in a lesser being than the ant?" Tung Kwo asked.

"It is in those weeds", Chuang Tzu continued.

"And lower?" said Tung Kwo.

"It is in this earthenware tile too", said Chuang Tzu.

"Surely that is the lowest?"

"It it even in that turd."

To this, Tung Kwo gave no reply.

Chuang Tzu continued: "None of your questions are to the point. They remind me of the inspectors in the market, prodding the pigs in an attempt to ascertain their value. Why would you look for the Tao by singling out any one thing? Do you think the lowest or the least has less of it? The Tao is great in all things. There are three terms — 'Complete', 'All-embracing' and 'Whole'. Although the names are different, the reality is One and the same. Only in the palace of No-where might we speak of what has no limitation and no end. Only in the land of Non-action would it make sense to speak of simplicity, stillness, indifference, purity, harmony and ease. My will would be aimless there. If the Tao went nowhere, I would not know where it had got to. If it went and returned, I would not know where it had gone. And if it kept on coming and going, I would not know when the process would end. In the great Void, the mind remains undetermined. What is even the highest knowledge, when here, knowledge is unbounded? That which makes things what they are, has not the limits of the things. So when we speak of limits, we remain confined to limited things.

The Tao is the limitlessness of the limited and the limit of the limitless. It is the source of both fullness and emptiness but is itself neither of these things. It produces renewal and decay but is neither renewal nor decay. It causes being and non-being but is neither being nor non-being. It creates and destroys but is itself neither created nor destroyed."

A Little Give and Take

Nasruddin and some friends were sitting on the edge of a lake having a picnic, when suddenly a man fell into the water and began shouting for help. Some of the Mulla's friends ran to his aid.

"Give me your hand!" they called to him, but the man continued to thrash around helplessly in the water.

Nasruddin stood up and walked calmly over to the edge of the lake and said to the drowning man:

"Take my hand", at which point the man grabbed his hand and pulled himself out of the water.

The others were curious. "Why did he refuse our help but accept yours?" they asked the Mulla.

"Well you see", Nasruddin explained to them, "the man is a money-lender so when you said 'Give me your hand!' it made no sense to him. It was only when I said 'Take my hand' that he understood it to be a worthwhile offer."

Blow Out the Candle

Tokusan was a great scholar who had written a long and elaborate commentary on the Diamond Sutra. Having heard of a Zen school in the south where the Sutra was being discussed he travelled there to debate with the master, Ryutan.

Having met, the two men discussed the Diamond Sutra late into the night. Finally taking leave of the master, Tokusan bowed and opened the screen door to step outside:

"It is very dark outside", he commented.

Ryutan offered him a lighted candle to find his way but just as Tokusan took it, Ryutan proceeded to blow it out. At that moment, Tokusan attained enlightenment.

The following day, Tokusan brought his commentary on the Diamond Sutra before all the monks assembled in the hall and said to them:

"Having mastered the esoteric doctrines is like a single hair compared to the great sky of this realisation. Having learned all the secrets of the world is like a drop of water compared to the great ocean of this enlightenment."

He then burnt his commentary to ashes and left the monastery.

To Each His Own

Abba Poemen travelled to Thebes from Scetis to ask a question of Abba Joseph.

"What should I do when passions assail me?" he asked him. "Should I resist them or let them enter?"

"Let them enter", the old man told him, "and wage war against them."

Now satisfied, Abba Poemen returned to Scetis.

Some time afterwards, a brother who had just returned from Thebes was heard by him saying:

"I asked Abba Joseph if I should resist passions when they arise or allow them in to struggle with them and he told me that I should not allow them even the smallest entry but cut them off immediately."

To clarify his doubts, Abba Poemen made the journey to see Abba Joseph once more and said to him:

"Father, I consulted you about my passions and you gave me counsel but also gave contrary counsel to another brother on the same question. Now I am confused."

"Do you not know that I love you?" the old man replied.

"Yes Father. I do believe so", Abba Poemen said.

"And did you not say to me: 'Speak to me as you speak to yourself?'" the old man continued.

"I did indeed", the brother responded.

"In truth, if the passions enter and you fight them, you become stronger. In this I spoke to you as I do to myself. But there are others who cannot profit in this way and must not allow the passions to enter", the old man explained. "Instead, they must cut them off immediately."

The Almond Vine and the Watermelon Tree

Nasruddin was resting under a large almond tree pondering to himself. As he looked around him, he noticed a huge watermelon growing on a thin vine. He looked at it for a moment and then looked up at the almonds hanging in the tree before saying out loud: "Please God — tell me why it is that these little almonds grow on this huge tree while these huge watermelons grow on a thin, feeble little vine? Surely it should be the other way around?"

Just as he finished speaking, an almond fell from the tree and hit him on the top of the head.

"Aha!" he exclaimed. "Thank you — now I understand."

Unwanted Gifts

The Buddha was sitting quietly with his disciples under a tree when a man approached and began to insult and mock him in an aggressive manner. The disciples became more and more agitated as the man continued his tirade but the Buddha remained silent, smiling peacefully. When the man eventually left them, the disciples asked the Buddha why he had not defended himself from all of the malicious accusations.

"If you bring me a gift and I do not accept it", the Buddha said to them, "whose gift is it?"

"Well, if you will not accept it, then it would still be mine", one of the disciples offered.

"Indeed", the Buddha replied, "and that is just what happened."

The Fruits of Monkhood

In the monastery at Heracliopolis stood a huge mulberry tree with abundant, sweet fruit. One day at dawn, Abba Joseph of Panephysis said to one of the younger brothers:

"Go and eat your fill from the tree."

As it was Friday, a day of fasting, the brother was tormented by the instruction of his elder. By the end of the day, having still not eaten from the tree, he could take it no more and went to see Abba Joseph.

"Father, please explain to me", he said. "Although you told me to eat from the tree, I have not done so, as it is a day of fasting. Now I feel guilty for having disobeyed you."

"At the beginning the Fathers do not speak to the novices in a straightforward manner", the old man explained, "but rather in a manner so as to see if what they do is right. Afterwards, we tell them solely the truth, but only after they have shown their submission to God's will."

The Gift of Absence

A friend of Nasruddin was moving to a village far away and paid a visit to the Mulla to say goodbye.

"Perhaps you can give me your gold ring so I can remember you every time I see it", he said to the Mulla.

"No — that's no good", Nasruddin replied, "because if you lose it, you'll forget about me. How about I don't give you the ring so that every time you see your finger and notice that my lovely gold ring is not on it — you'll think of me. I'm sure your finger is harder to lose."

Not the Flag, nor the Wind

Two monks stood arguing about a temple flag waving in the wind. One said:

"The flag is moving."

The other said:

"No, it is the wind that is moving."

At that moment the sixth patriarch, master Hui-Neng passed by and said:

"Not the flag, nor the wind — only the mind is moving."

For Whom Do You Pray?

Nasruddin went to the mosque one evening but was in a rush to get back home. The Iman saw him hurriedly saying his prayers and said to him angrily:

"It is not right to offer God such hurried prayers — start over again!"

Nasruddin complied and repeated his prayers, at which point the Imam returned and said to him:

"Now, is that not better? Do you not think that God appreciated the second prayers more than the first that were hurried?"

"Why would that be?" Nasruddin replied. "Although the first prayers were hurried, at least they were said for God. The second prayers were said for you."

Duke Hwan and the Wheelwright

Duke Hwan of Khi was sitting under a canopy reading, when Phien the wheelwright set his tools aside, climbed the steps and said to him:

"May I ask you Lord, what it is you are reading?"

"The masters. The experts. The authorities", the duke replied.

"A long time dead", said the duke.

"Then all you are reading is the dirt they left behind", the wheelwright said to him.

"What do you know of it?" the duke responded angrily. "You are just a wheelwright. You better have a good explanation or you will pay a high price for this insolence."

"When I make wheels", he continued unmoved, "if I am too gentle, they fall apart and if I am too rough, they don't fit. However, if I am neither rough nor gentle, not too soft nor too violent, then a good wheel is the result and my work is what I want it to be. I cannot put it into words nor can I even explain to my own son how it is to be correctly done and so here I am — seventy years old and still making wheels! Those masters, experts and authorities you read took all they really knew with them to the grave. And so I say, Lord, that what you are reading there is only the dirt they left behind."

Bread and But...er

Some of the sultan's scholars had accused Nasruddin of heresy and he was brought before them to answer these accusations in the royal court. Having heard them expound their charges, Nasruddin finally got his turn to speak:

"Oh wise scholars!" he began. "Tell me — what is bread?"

They turned to each other with confused looks.

"Bread is a food — it is our main sustenance", said one of them finally.

"Bread is a combination of flour and water that has been cooked in an oven", said another.

"Bread is a gift from the Almighty", said a third.

Nasruddin turned to the judge.

"Your honour, how can you trust these men?" he said. "How can they possibly be unanimous when it comes to a charge of heresy when they cannot even agree on the nature of bread?"

What's in a Name?

Two brothers met in the desert on their way to visit Abba Joseph. One said to the other: "Tell your disciple to saddle the mule."

"Call him and he will do as you ask", the other replied.

"What is his name?" the first enquired.

"I do not know", said the other.

"How long has he been with you for you to still not know his name?" said the first.

"Two years", came the reply.

"If in two years you have not had reason to learn your own disciple's name", said the first, "then do I need to know it for a single day?"

What Goes Around...

Nasruddin had always had problems with the royal barber and had suffered his petty jealousies on many occasions due to the Mulla's closeness to the sultan.

One day, as the barber was seeing to the sultan's hair and beard, he began to relate an amazing dream of the previous night:

"Your Majesty", he said, feigning sincerity, "last night I dreamt that I was spirited away to heaven. I beheld the holy faces of saints and martyrs of the past in a land where the rivers ran with milk and honey and dancing girls tended to my every whim."

The sultan's eyes lit up.

"And did you perhaps come across my saintly father?" he enquired with intrigue.

"I did indeed!" came the barber's reply. "And he gave me a message to pass on to you." The barber gave a dramatic pause for effect.

"Well? Go on! Go on!" the sultan urged him, now enthralled.

"He told me to tell you that he is in great health and brimming with a joy rarely glimpsed in life. Everything in heaven is just perfect except for one thing."

He paused once again for effect.

"Well?" the sultan urged him impatiently. "What is it?"

"Well", the barber continued with a sly smile, "he said that the only thing missing is the presence of a competent storyteller — a man who can entertain him with jokes and stories — someone to lighten the mood and make him laugh."

The barber stopped with his fiddling and turned to look sternly at the sultan.

"Your Majesty — your father wishes you to send him Nasruddin."

After a moment's thought the sultan called for Nasruddin and related to him the wonderful dream.

"So, my good man", the sultan continued, "I am sending you to Paradise. Your worries are over. Rejoice and prepare to meet your Maker!"

"Of course Your Majesty", Nasruddin replied calmly, "but please, allow me a month to cleanse myself of all sinful thoughts, as well as choose the manner of my demise."

"Why of course", the sultan replied. "I knew I could rely on you. I will ensure your legacy lives on in the hearts and minds of men forever."

Nasruddin returned home and began digging a tunnel from the bottom of his well to the basement of his house and then stocked up the basement with everything one could possibly need. At the passing of a month, he returned to the palace.

"Your Majesty", he said to the sultan. "I am ready and I have chosen my end. I shall jump into the depths of my well with you as my witness. Please seal the well with a rock so it may never be used again."

Six months later, having spent his time snacking on delicious foods and entertaining himself quietly in the basement of his house, Nasruddin returned to the palace with a matted beard and long unkempt hair. The sultan and his court were in shock at seeing him.

"Do not fear!" Nasruddin said to them holding up his hand. "It is I, Nasruddin. Your father, the saintly man, has sent me back to live out my final years on earth. He was much pleased by my storytelling but asked me to return to make one final request to his dear son."

"Of course!" the sultan replied, still in shock. "Anything for my dearest father in heaven!" "As you can see", Nasruddin continued, "there are no barbers in heaven. Your father wishes for you to send him yours."

Not Enough Time

A young student of Zen approached his master in silent meditation.

"Please Master", the man begged. "You must accept me as your student. How long will it take to become an illumined one like yourself?"

"Hmm", the master pondered with eyes half open. "About twenty years."

"Twenty years!" the young man exclaimed. "I don't have that sort of time. I need it faster than that. If I study and work every day for twelve hours straight then how long will it take?"

"Hmm", the master said to himself, pondering again. "About forty years. If you have one eye on the goal, it must mean that you have only one eye on the Path."

The Saintly Deceiver

As the saintly reputation of Abba Longinus spread, a woman who was suffering from an incurable disease heard of his holiness and sought him out in the hope of being cured. Told only that he lived at the ninth milestone from Alexandria, the woman travelled there and began looking for him. She met an old man collecting firewood by the sea and asked him:

"Please Sir, where does Abba Longinus, the servant of God live?"

"What do you want with that old impostor?" the man said to her. "Stay away from him. He is a deceiver. What is the matter with you?"

The woman showed him her sores and the old man made the sign of the cross and sent her away saying:

"Go in peace. God will heal you. There is nothing that Longinus can do to help."

The woman left, confident in his words and was healed from her affliction.

Only much later, when telling her story to others and mentioning the distinctive marks of the old man, did she find out it was Abba Longinus himself.

To the Point

A cousin of Nasruddin had moved to a distant village and left some of his possessions, as well as his cat, with the Mulla for safe keeping.

One day, the cat died and Nasruddin sent his cousin the simple message:

"Your cat is dead."

His cousin responded:

"Do you not understand tact? Where I'm from, you'd perhaps first say 'I think your cat has a fur ball, he seems to be coughing a lot', then perhaps later, 'he seems quite ill', before finally saying, 'I'm sorry to say, he has passed away'."

Several months later his cousin received a letter from Nasruddin saying:

"I think your mother has a fur ball."

Drop Everything

On a pilgrimage to a holy site, two Zen monks, Tanzan and Ekido, were walking down a muddy road. They came to a river and, sitting beside the rushing water, was a beautiful young woman in a silk kimono and sash, too scared to cross.

"Please help me to cross", she implored as they came closer.

With no hesitation Tanzan picked the woman up and strode through the river with her before placing her gently on the other side and continuing on his way. The two men walked on in silence.

After much time has passed and upon reaching their destination, Ekido finally spoke:

"I am sorry, I can bear it no longer. We are on a sacred pilgrimage. We are not to so much as look at a woman, let alone touch one. How could you have done such a thing?"

Tanzan stopped and turned to the young man with a gentle smile and said:

"I left that woman way back at the river — are you still carrying her?"

Either Him or He

A respected holy man was out walking with some disciples one day, when a ferocious dog approached as if to attack. It leapt up at the old man but with a blow from his walking stick he caught it across the back and it ran away.

After the incident, one of the disciples asked him:

"If God is equally present in all things, why did you just hit Him with your stick?"

"No, no — nothing of the sort", the old man replied. "God hit Himself with His stick, so as to avoid biting Himself on His leg."

That Sinking Feeling

Nasruddin was out in his boat making a little extra money as a ferryman. A learned scholar with books under his arm climbed aboard and rudely gestured for Nasruddin to take him to the other side.

"How deep is the river?" the scholar asked after a while.

"I don't know", Nasruddin replied.

After another period of silence the scholar spoke again:

"How wide is the river?"

"I don't know that either", replied Nasruddin for the second time.

"Then you are a fool and have wasted half your life", the scholar said with a shrug before opening one of his books.

As they neared the middle of the river, Nasruddin noticed water flooding in through a crack in the boat.

"Do you know how to swim?" Nasruddin asked the man.

"No", he replied without lifting his face from the book.

"Then you are a fool and have wasted your whole life", Nasruddin said to him. "We are sinking!"

Everything Everything?

One day, Abba Macarius the Egyptian, travelled from Scetis to the mountain of Nitria. The brethren there said to him: "Father, please say a word to us about the life of a monk."

"I have not yet become a monk myself", he replied to them, "but I have seen monks. One day when sitting in my cell, my thoughts were troubling me — urging me to go to the desert. For five years I remained, struggling against this thought, worried that it was the work of demons. Since the thought resisted all my attempts to banish it, I left for the desert. There I found a watering hole with an island in the middle where the animals would come to drink. In the midst of the animals were two naked men and I was filled with fright, thinking them to be spirits. 'Do not be afraid' they said to me, 'we are men.' 'Where have you come from and what are you doing here?' I asked them. 'I am an Egyptian and he is from Libya', one of them said. 'We came to a monastery here forty years ago.' Then I asked them, 'How can I become a monk?' and they said to me, 'You can only become a monk if you are ready to give up everything'. 'But my flesh is weak' I said, 'and I fear I cannot do as you do.' 'Then sit in your cell' they said, 'and weep for your sins.' Curious to know more, I asked them, 'When winter comes do you not freeze? And in the summer, do you not burn?' 'No', they replied, 'the changing seasons do us no harm. God has made this way of life for us. Now it is all we know.' That is why, my brothers, I say that I have not yet become a monk myself, but I have seen monks."

The Sheepish Rebel

Master Bankei's talks were attended not only by Zen monks but also by laymen and students of other sects. During one such talk, a priest from the Nichiren sect, angered that all his adherents had left to listen to Bankei, stood up, determined to debate with him.

"Hey! Zen master!" he shouted. "What is this? A fool, fooling the people and foolish enough to think that they will heed his advice? I, for certain, will not obey a single one of your foolish instructions!"

"Is that so?" Bankei responded. "In that case why don't you come up here and show me where I am wrong?"

The man made his way up to the front of the crowd ready to engage in debate.

"Come here and stand on my right", Bankei continued as the man positioned himself on the right of the Zen master.

"No, no, that's no good, sorry. Please — come here and stand on my left. That will be much better." The man then moved to his left.

"Well, for someone who was not willing to obey even one of my instructions", Bankei said to the man as he raised three fingers, "you have now obeyed three!"

As the crowd started to laugh, the man began to blush and fidget nervously on the stage.

"You seem like a gentle person", Bankei continued, "now go and sit down and listen."

The man slunk off the stage in embarrassment to the laughter of the crowd. As he sat down Bankei held up four fingers and said, "Four!"

The Lion's Share

A famous scholar was visiting and arranged to have a meeting with the wisest man in the town. The Mulla of course volunteered, which received mixed reactions from the villagers. The meeting was held over lunch, where they ordered the special of the day and were presented with two stuffed roasted aubergines. With no hesitation the Mulla took the larger of the two and put it on his plate. After a brief look of disbelief, the scholar proceeded to school Nasruddin on etiquette, right action, social morals and generosity, whilst the Mulla listened patiently.

"So tell me sir", Nasruddin said to him when he had finally finished, "what would you have done?"

"Being a gracious and generous man", the scholar replied, "I would have taken the smaller aubergine for myself."

"Just as I thought then", the Mulla said and served him the smaller aubergine that was left.

Full of It

A university professor was once received as a guest in Zen master Nan-in's home. He was welcomed cordially and served tea but when Nan-in poured his visitor's cup, he first filled it to the brim and then continued to pour, making it overflow onto the tray and table.

The professor watched until he could hold back no longer. "Stop!" he exclaimed. "It is full — no more will go in!"

"And like this cup, you sir, are full of your own opinions and speculations", Nan-in said to him as he put the tea down. "How can I possibly give you anything unless you first empty your cup?"

The Burden of Proof

A seeker sat with a sage admiring the sunrise, the clouds and the landscape.

"Where did it all come from?" he asked after a while.

The sage, as if posed to speak, sat silent. Hours passed. Sunset came and went and soon it was pitch dark.

"I'll tell you where it came from" he said finally, "if you tell me where it went."

Where God Lives

As Nasruddin sat in the teahouse a man came up to him and said jokingly:

"Mulla — I'll give you a gold coin if you tell me one place where God lives."

"I'll give you two", Nasruddin replied, "if you can tell me one place where he doesn't live."

The Living Stupa

Drukpa Kunley had arrived at the Palkhor Stupa where he found some scholars engaged in debate and others circling the *stupa* performing prostrations. He watched them for a while and noticed a beautiful woman sitting on the edge of the *stupa*. At the head of a line of monks there was an old monk who said to him:

"You know, your magical powers and signs of accomplishment may be remarkable but your refusal to bow before the *stupa* and to the monks is wrongheaded and goes against the Buddha's own laws."

"I am an experienced *naljorpa* who has completed his prostrations and confessions long ago", the Lama replied, "but if it will make you happy, I will perform them again for you." At that, Drukpa Kunley made his way towards the beautiful woman and began prostrating before her as he recited the following prayer:

> *I bow to this body of beautiful clay,*
> *Not counted amongst the Eight Sugata Stupas;*
> *I bow to this marvellous creation,*
> *Not fashioned by the hand of the god of craftsmen;*
> *I bow to these Thirteen Wheels,*
> *Unsurpassed in the Thirteen Worlds;*
> *I bow to the cheeks of the Gyangtse maiden,*
> *Not regarded in the body of the Saviouress.*[5]

"How vulgar!" the old monk exclaimed. "This Drukpa Kunley is truly crazy!"

"Crazy is to prostrate to a pile of dead stones!" the Lama retorted. "This woman is a living *stupa*! She is the way that all good and evil enter the world. She is the source of man's deepest pleasure — the object and objective of his love. You and I are only here thanks to her! What has your *stupa* to say about any of that?"

When the Grass Is Greener

A neighbour woke Nasruddin one morning complaining that his donkey was in his field again and was eating the grass. Mulla tried to bargain with the man:

"I'll tell you what", he told him, "send me over your donkey and he can eat my grass."

"But your land is dry and bare — you have no grass!" the neighbour protested.

"Then", Nasruddin replied, "perhaps now you can understand my donkey."

The Open Secret

Ramanuja, a Hindu Vedantin, once visited a local spiritual teacher having heard that he possessed a particularly potent esoteric teaching that only he knew. Before instructing Ramanuja, the teacher told him that the secret he was about to disclose was so powerful that to hear it just once would guarantee eternal salvation, however, should he reveal it to another, he would be damned to eternal hell. Having received the secret teaching, Ramanuja bowed and hurried outside to the town square where he proceeded to call everyone's attention before shouting out the secret teaching to them at the top of his voice. Hearing the commotion, the teacher came running in a panic.

"What on earth are you doing?! You will be damned to eternal hell you fool!" he shouted.

"Yes!" cried Ramanuja with excitement. "How wonderful for so many to be saved at the expense of just one!"

Heaven and Hell

Zen master Hakuin was sitting in quiet contemplation when a soldier approached him.

"Tell me — do heaven and hell really exist?" he asked.

Hakuin looked the man up and down with a scornful expression on his face and replied:

"What makes you think a dumb brute like yourself can grasp such refined things? You are just a foolish soldier. There is nothing that I could teach you that you would understand."

He shooed him away like a dirty dog. "Be gone with you and stop wasting my precious time."

The soldier stood there momentarily dumbfounded before his body began to shake and his face became red with rage. He reached for his sword and let out a bloodcurdling cry as he raised it up above his head about to cleave the Zen master in two.

"That", Hakuin said to him calmly, "is hell."

The soldier was taken aback as he realised that the words were not what they had at first appeared to be. His face softened, his sword fell from his hand and he dropped to his knees at Hakuin's feet, now weeping with gratitude.

"And that", continued Hakuin with a smile, "that is heaven."

Shoot!

Nasruddin had been invited out hunting with a visiting dignitary and only conceded to go with great hesitation. On spotting a wild turkey, the man took a shot and missed.

"Well done!" the Mulla cried.

"Please sir", the man said to him. "Do not make fun of me."

"You are mistaken sir", Nasruddin replied. "I was talking to the turkey."

Appearances

Once, a rich merchant invited a number of abbots and well-known priests to a banquet. Among the attendees was Zen master Ikkyu, who arrived in a shabby robe and a tattered straw hat. Mistaken for a simple beggar, he was given a copper coin and turned away at the door.

After having gone home to change into his finest robes, he returned again, this time to be welcomed in and given the best seat in the house. When the soup was served he began to dip the cuffs and hem of his robe into it saying, "Go ahead — eat, robe — eat".

The guests all watched him in amazement until finally someone questioned his strange behaviour. Ikkyu replied, "It was the robe that got me in so the robe should eat first".

Tip for Tat

Once, Nasruddin went to a bathhouse in ragged clothes. The bath attendant threw him a towel rudely, and for the most part, ignored him for the rest of his stay. On the way out, however, Nasruddin gave the man a huge tip.

The following week, the Mulla returned and instead was given the royal treatment and pampered exquisitely. This time, however, on the way out, Nasruddin left him just a measly tip. The bath attendant looked at him, puzzled.

"Last week's tip was for this week", the Mulla said to him, "and this is for last week."

The Lord Taketh Away

While he was in Egypt, Abba Macarius came upon a man with a beast of burden engaged in stealing the old man's possessions from his cell. Approaching the thief as if he were a stranger, he helped him to load the animal with all his own belongings and then saw him off saying, "For we brought nothing into the world and we can take nothing out of it. The Lord giveth and the Lord taketh away; blessed be the name of the Lord".

Sitting Ducks

Rabia al-Adawiyya was sitting amongst a group of contemplators when Hasan al-Basri approached and said to her:

"I have the ability to walk on water. Come — let us sit on the lake and speak of spiritual things."

"If we are to leave this holy company here, why not let us fly up into the air and speak there?" Rabia replied.

"Would that I could, I would join you in the air", Hasan said to her, "but I possess no such power."

"Your power to sit upon the water is possessed by ducks", Rabia said to him, "as is the ability to fly. These things have nothing whatsoever to do with Truth. In that case, instead of sitting on the water or flying through the air and talking of spiritual things, let us sit right here and be silent."

Don't Be a Donkey

Nasruddin was on his way to the market with his faithful donkey, who was carrying a large sack of salt on its back. As they crossed the river, the donkey stumbled and the sack of salt was dunked into the water and dissolved. Although the Mulla was fuming, his donkey seemed relieved by his lightened load and began bucking and jumping with joy.

The following week they headed back to the market, this time loaded with a large bag of wool. As they crossed the river the donkey stumbled in the same place and the wool was dunked into the water and soaked. This time the donkey left the stream struggling with the increased load.

"You thought you'd get off lightly again didn't you?" Nasruddin cried to the donkey. "Oh how wrong it is to think that the exact same actions will bring the exact same results!"

You Cannot Run Away from God

A holy man had spent some weeks deep in the forest with a group of disciples, teaching them to see God in all things. One day, their quiet meditation was interrupted by an elephant rampaging through the trees with its mahout chasing behind, shouting for people to get out of the way. Everyone scattered except for one of the younger devotees who sat there, unmoved by the approaching chaos.

"Run away!" the mahout screamed to him in desperation but the disciple remained calmly seated. Before anything else could be done, the stampeding elephant collided with the young man, leaving him lying unconscious on the ground. His teacher and the others returned as soon as the elephant was at a safe distance and soon revived the young man.

"What on earth were you doing?" they asked him dumbfounded. "Why didn't you run?"

"But Master, you have taught us yourself that it is only God Himself who has taken all these forms. Thinking that it was only God-as-an-elephant coming towards me, I thought it safe to stay."

"You are not wrong my dear boy", the Master replied tenderly. "It was indeed God-as-an-elephant that came charging. But God-as-a-mahout was screaming to you to 'Run!' Why did you not listen to God-as-a-mahout?!"

A Lesson from the Dead

One day, a brother came to see Abba Macarius the Egyptian.

"Father, give me a word that I may be saved", he asked him.

"Go to the cemetery", the old man said to him, "and insult and abuse the dead."

The brother did what he was told and hurled both stones and insults at them before returning to tell Abba Macarius.

"And did they not complain?" the old man asked him.

"No", the brother replied. "They said nothing."

"Now go back and give them praise and compliments", Abba Macarius told him.

This he did and once more returned to the old man.

"Did they delight in your praise?" the old man asked him.

"No", the brother replied, "again they said nothing."

"So do you see that having suffered insults, they did not reply and on receiving praise, again they remained silent?" Abba Macarius continued: "Likewise, you must become a dead man to both triumph and disaster, praise and blame and the scorn and approval of men. Only then can you be saved".

Busy Doing Nothing

One day, a man came to Nasruddin to lament his poverty and seek the Mulla's advice.

"I don't know what to do — I am at my wits' end", he said. "I live cramped together with my wife and six children in a small hut with only one room and with nothing but milk from my goat and eggs from my three chickens to feed all of us. Something must be done to improve my situation but I do not know what."

Nasruddin listened quietly to the man's emotional plea before responding:

"Your situation is indeed dire my friend. But fear not — there is always something that can be done for the better. Now listen carefully and don't question my advice. Go home and bring your goat into the house and care for it there and then come back and see me next week."

The man gave a puzzled look before thanking the Mulla and turning to make his way home.

The following week the same man returned, even more distressed than the previous week. He fell to his knees at Nasruddin's feet, tugging on his robe.

"Oh great Mulla!" he wailed. "Things have gone from bad to worse! We can hardly move in the house now! The place is a mess and smells to high heaven and we haven't slept in days because the goat keeps waking us up! Your solution has only made things worse!"

"Not to worry", Nasruddin said as he helped the man to his feet. "I've been giving it some thought and I'm sure that this time I can help your situation. Listen carefully and don't question my advice. Go home and bring your three chickens into the house to live with you as well and then come back to me next week."

The man looked even more confused than the previous week but in desperation, went home to follow the Mulla's advice.

The following week he was back, looking more dishevelled than ever, with a dirty robe, unkempt hair and red eyes. This time he collapsed before Nasruddin without even the strength to tug on his robe.

"My life is hell!" he gasped. "There is no room in the house to turn, the stench is unbearable, the chickens fight with the goat all day and my family and I haven't slept a wink all week. I cannot go on like this."

"In that case", the Mulla responded, "I am sure that this time I have the final solution to your problem."

With a look of utter defeat, the poor man looked up at the Mulla in disbelief.

"Now listen carefully and don't question my advice", Nasruddin continued. "Go home and take the goat and the chickens out of the house and put them back where you kept them before and then return to me again in a week. I am sure by then, your problem will be resolved."

With the last ounce of energy and hope left in him, the man pulled himself to his feet and stumbled away.

The following week he returned again, this time looking refreshed, with a clean robe, well groomed hair and beard, and a smile on his face.

"Greetings Mulla!" he said cheerfully and embraced Nasruddin. "God bless you good man! I followed your advice. My lovely house now seems twice the size it was since I moved the chickens and the goat out. It is clean and smells like home once again and my family and I have slept better then we have in many moons. I truly feel blessed by the hand of Almighty God!"

"Aah, think nothing of it", Nasruddin replied with feigned humility. "I did nothing."

Them Apples

A monk was in an orchard collecting apples, but instead of taking them from the tree, every so often, he would stoop down to pick one up from the ground. After a while, a neighbour who was watching couldn't contain his curiosity and called out to him:

"Why not pick the apples from the tree?"

"I only take what has been given", the monk called back to him.

"But the ones on the ground have worms!" the man continued.

"Yes!" the monk cried back to him with a big smile on his face.

"They too, understand!"

Bad Examples, Good Lessons

Some of Rabbi Mikhal's disciples were puzzling over a passage they were struggling to understand and so asked him:

"In the Sayings of the Fathers, it says: 'Who is wise?' He who learns from all men, as it is said, 'From all my teachers I have gotten understanding'. Why then does it say 'he who learns from all men' and not 'he who learns from all teachers'?"

"It is quite clear that the master who spoke these words wishes for us to understand that we are to learn from all men, not just all teachers", the Rabbi explained. "After all, from even one who is wicked or ignorant we can learn how not to conduct ourselves."

The Sound of Justice

Mulla Nasruddin was the judge presiding over a case brought before him by a falafel stall owner against a local beggar.

"This man", the plaintiff began, raising a pointed finger towards the defendant, "came to my stall and stood in the delicious wafting aromas of my falafels, eating some bread that he had brought with him. There is no doubt that the bread tasted better thanks to the smell of my falafels, so he must pay."

"It is indeed true that goods enjoyed must be paid for", Nasruddin said. "Tell me, how much is one of your falafels?"

"Three coins", the man replied.

Nasruddin summoned the defendant to his bench. "Now give me your purse and we shall settle this matter right here."

The man, with tears in his eyes, handed over his tattered purse with the few coins that he had left, whereupon the Mulla proceeded to take out three coins and shake them in his fist.

"Do you hear that?" he said to the stall owner. "The money is good. Are you happy?"

"Yes Your Honour", the man said as he held out his hand expectantly.

"Good", Nasruddin continued, handing the money back to the defendant. "Then you are paid in full — for the smell of food, he has paid the sound of money. Case dismissed!"

The Richest Pauper

Although in his early life, Rabbi Yehiel Mikhal lived in abject poverty, not for a moment did happiness desert him and still, every day he would pray:

"Blessed be Thou...who has supplied my every want."

One day a disciple asked him, "Rabbi, how can you continue to pray in that manner? Surely you lack almost everything a man could want!"

"You are wrong", the Rabbi replied. "My only want is poverty and that is exactly what I have been given."

Good God!

One day, Mulla Nasruddin came across a dervish stealing figs from his garden.

"What are you doing, thief?!" he said as he confronted the man.

"Why, nothing!" the dervish told him. "I am merely God's servant feasting on God's fruit from God's tree in God's garden."

At this Nasruddin struck the man with his stick.

The dervish cried out: "Stop I tell you! What are you doing?!"

"Why, nothing my good man", Nasruddin said to him. "I am just a servant of God too, striking God's servant with God's stick to protect God's fruits in God's garden!"

Upon hearing this, the dervish became enlightened.

How Much Do You Want It?

A hermit was sitting quietly on a riverbank when a young man interrupted his silence:

"Master, I wish to become your disciple", the young man said to him.

"Why?" the hermit asked.

"I need to find God", the young man explained.

Suddenly, the hermit jumped up and grabbed the youth. He pushed him into the river and held his head under the water until he kicked and struggled to be free. The hermit released the young man and pushed him back to the riverbank, choking and gasping.

"Tell me", the hermit asked him, "what did you want most of all under the water there?"

"Air!" the man cried, still gasping.

"So go home", the hermit said to him, "and come back when your need for God is as strong as your need for air."

Who Knows?

One day, the beautiful white horse belonging to an old Taoist farmer escaped from its field and ran away. After hearing the news, the villagers came to him and said:

"How unlucky you are! Such bad news!"

"Who knows?" the old man said to them. "Could be bad, could be good."

The following day, the white horse returned to the field with seven wild horses. Once again the villagers came, having heard the news:

"How lucky you are! Such good news!" they said to him this time.

"Who knows?" the old man said again. "Could be good, could be bad."

While attempting to break in one of the wild horses the following day, the farmer's son broke his leg and it was not long before the villagers came to lament the situation:

"How unlucky you are! Such bad news!"

"Who knows?" the farmer said as before. "Could be bad, could be good."

Several days later the king's army passed through the village looking for young men to take into battle with them. On seeing the farmer's son with a lame leg and unable to walk they passed his house by. Once again the villagers returned to tell the farmer:

"How lucky you are! Such good news!" to which the old Taoist farmer replied:

"Who knows? Could be good, could be bad."

Execute This

The sultan had heard from a wise teacher that to lie is one of the greatest of all sins and so decided to take action. He stationed his executioner at the gates to the city and told him to ask everyone who entered, why they were visiting, and if they were found to be lying, then they were to be executed.

On the very first day, Nasruddin strolled up to the gates on his way to the market.

"On pain of death", the executioner said to him, "tell me — why are you entering the city?"

"I am going to be executed", the Mulla replied.

Food for Thought

The philosopher, Diogenes, had been subsisting for some time on a poor man's diet of bread and lentils, whilst Aristippus, who also thought of himself as something of wise man, was living in a large house and feasting on sumptuous meals provided by the king himself. One day Aristippus said to him:

"If only you would learn how to flatter the king and be obedient to his every whim as I do, you would not have to live on bread and lentils every day. You would certainly have a healthier body. As it is, it is weak and frail."

Without hesitation, Diogenes replied:

"And if only you would learn how to live on bread and lentils as I do, you would not have to flatter the king and be obedient to his every whim. You would certainly have a healthier soul. As it is, it is weak and frail."

The King's Sweeper

On one occasion, just before the New Year, the Baal Shem arrived in a town and asked the gathered hasidim who was to read the prayers during the Days of Awe. Their reply was that this was traditionally done by the rav.

"And what is the manner of his praying?" he asked them.

"On the Day of Atonement", they answered, "he recites the confessions of sin in a most cheerful manner."

The Baal Shem then sought out the rav so as to question him on his strange method of prayer. In his defence the rav replied:

"He who is least among the servants of the king, the one whose task is to sweep the dirt from the forecourt, sings a merry song while he works, for his service helps in a small way to gladden the king."

"In that case", the Baal Shem told him, "may my blessings be with you."

Rude Awakening

Nasruddin was having a nap on a lush spot of grass in the royal gardens when the sultan himself, out strolling with his companions, stumbled over him lying there.

"You stupid oaf — what do you think you are doing?! Why don't you watch where you're going?!" Nasruddin said without even opening his eyes or turning to look at them.

"Your rudeness is equalled only by your stupidity", one of the sultan's companions said to him. "You should see who you're speaking to before you unleash such a foul tongue!" he continued.

"Do you think it is less of a thing to be kicked by a sultan than by any other man?" Nasruddin replied.

The sultan was impressed that Nasruddin had known it was him without even looking to see who he was talking to and said to him:

"Why should a sultan have to listen to such insults from you, old man?"

"Because", said Nasruddin, "all men require appropriate criticism, sultans and kings the most — it is what softens the heart and strengthens the character. The burnished metal shines the brightest — the knife struck with a whetstone cuts the best."

Open Windows

There was once a brother who wished to renounce the world and flee to the desert, and so he gave his belongings to the poor and kept just enough to cover his own meagre expenses. He first went to see Abba Anthony to tell him what he had done and of his wishes to become a desert monk.

"If you really want to become a monk", the old man told him, "then go to the village and buy some meat. Then cover your naked body with it and return to me here."

The brother obeyed but on his way back to the desert he was attacked by wild dogs and birds who tore at his flesh. When he finally made it back, Abba Anthony asked if he had followed his instructions, whereupon the poor brother showed him the wounds all over his body.

Saint Anthony said to him:

"In the same way, those who renounce the world but keep something for themselves are set upon and assailed by demons just as an open window tempts the thief."

Blink and You'll Miss It

Word had spread far and wide of a holy man who lived at the top of a distant mountain.

Upon hearing the marvellous stories told of him, a prince from a neighbouring province decided to go and find the holy man for himself. After a long and arduous journey, he finally arrived at the house indicated and knocked on the door.

"Take me to your master", he said as the door opened to him. "I have heard that he is the wisest man in the land and I wish to confirm the fact for myself."

He was led inside and through the house, looking around expectantly in anticipation of his encounter with the great sage but before he knew it he had passed through the house and was led back outside again through the back door.

"What is this?" he said as he turned in bewilderment. "I have come to see the great holy man!"

"And you just have", the old man replied as he closed the door.

He Blew It

A famous scholar had sought out Nasruddin from afar, having heard rumours of his special wisdom. As he approached the house, he saw the Mulla through the window, blowing on his hands.

"Why were you blowing on your hands?" the scholar asked him after they had greeted one another.

"I was blowing to warm them up", Nasruddin replied.

Just then, the Mulla's wife brought them two bowls of soup and Nasruddin proceeded to gently blow onto his.

"Why are you blowing on your soup?" the scholar asked him.

"I am blowing to cool it down", Nasruddin replied.

"Blowing to warm up — blowing to cool down?" the scholar thought to himself. "This man is surely a fool."

The King of Selfistan

A wandering monk was leaving a busy marketplace when he accidentally bumped into another man. The man flew into a rage and began to shout and curse.

"Do you know who I am?" he screamed. "I am the king's advisor!"

"That's very nice", the monk replied calmly. "I myself am a king."

"A king?!" the man scoffed. "And over which country do you rule?"

"No country", the monk replied. "I am the king of myself — the sovereign of my soul. I am the master of my passions and I rule over them even when others do not rule over their own."

At this the man became silent and apologised for his behaviour.

A Buddha or a Dung-Fly

Zen master Ikkyu was born in 1394, the son of emperor Go-Komatsu and a noblewoman of his court. When he was still very young, his mother left the palace in order to become a nun and study Zen. Shortly afterwards, Ikkyu too was sent to a Rinzai Zen temple in Kyoto. Some years later, when his mother passed away, Ikkyu was given the final letter she had written to him:

To Ikkyu,

I have now finished my work in this life and the time has come for me to return to Eternity. My greatest wish for you is to become a good student and realise your Buddha-nature. This way you will know if I am in hell or whether I am always with you or not.

If you attain to the realisation that the Buddha and his follower, Bodhidharma, are your own servants, then you may cease all study and instead work for humanity. The Buddha taught for forty-nine years and in all that time, found no reason to speak a single word. You ought to know why. However, if you don't but wish to — avoid vain thought.

Your Mother,

Not born, not dead

September 1st

P.S. Buddha's teaching was mainly for the purpose of enlightening others but if you concern yourself only with its methods then you are no better than a dung-fly. Even if you know the 80,000 holy teachings by heart, unless you open your eyes to your own Buddha-nature, then you will not even understand what I have written in this letter. This is my final will and testament.

Who's the Fool?

One evening, over a sumptuous court feast, the sultan was bragging about his ability to trick other people. After recounting a highly embellished version of one of his escapades, he concluded:

"It is true! I can fool anyone and yet no one can fool me!"

Above the polite murmur of approval Nasruddin was heard to say:

"Perhaps I could try, if it would please Your Majesty."

"You would dare? No one lies to me without serious consequence. You of all people should know that, Nasruddin!"

"And if perhaps I fool you", Nasruddin smiled, "without lying?"

The sultan laughed.

"Fool me without lying? Now I'm intrigued."

"Then sir, if it is your will, allow me to fool you, without lying and I shall do so before sunrise tomorrow."

The sultan let out a hearty belly laugh before accepting the challenge.

That night the sultan placed four guards on duty instead of the usual two and spent the night in and out of sleep, impatiently waiting to catch Nasruddin out. After an uneventful night and morning and with the sun now high in the sky, the sultan had Nasruddin brought before him.

"So?" he shrugged and laughed. "It seems you have been unable to fool me — as I thought." "I did indeed promise to fool you sir", Nasruddin replied.

"You did."

"And I didn't fool you. Did I?"

"Of course not!"

"And yet Your Highness waited all night and morning to be fooled — is that correct?"

"Well yes, of course — like you said."

"And yet instead, nothing happened — correct?"

"Yes", the sultan replied as the penny began to drop.

"Then sir, you have been fooled", Nasruddin said with a smile before bowing and taking leave of the sultan.

Metanoia

Abba Gelasius had a very valuable and beautifully bound Bible that he left in church for any of his fellow brethren to borrow and read. One day, a stranger came in to the church, and seeing the valuable item, stole it as he was leaving. He then took it to the city to sell and having found an interested buyer, offered to sell it to him for thirteen pieces of silver.

"Lend it to me first", the purchaser said "so that I may examine it in detail."

The thief consented and the man brought the book to Abba Gelasius in order to ask his opinion.

"It is most certainly a beautiful book", the old man said to him, "and definitely worth the price he is asking for it."

The interested buyer then returned to the thief in the city and told him something quite different from what the old man had told him.

"I have shown it to Abba Gelasius", he said to him, "and he told me that it was not worth the price you are asking for it."

"Did he not say anything else about the book?" the thief enquired.

"No, nothing more", the purchaser replied.

Filled with remorse, the thief took the book and returned to Abba Gelasius to return what he had stolen but the old man had no interest in taking it back.

"If you do not take it back, I shall have no peace", the thief begged him.

"If that is the case then I will take it back", the old man replied and took the book back to the church.

Having repented for his wrongdoing, the man went on to became a disciple of Abba Gelasius and stayed with him until his death.

No Problem

A man came to Nasruddin one day, lamenting his problems and hoping that the Mulla would be able to solve them for him. He described the first problem that was weighing on his mind and Nasruddin replied:

"Sorry, I can't help with that."

The desperate man began to recount to the Mulla his next problem but he responded in the same way:

"Sorry, I can't help with that."

This went on for a while — problem after problem — until the man lost his temper.

"You call yourself a learned man — a Mulla? And yet you cannot even solve a simple man's problems?" he said to Nasruddin.

"Let us say that you now have eleven problems in your life. There is only one I can help you rid yourself of", the Mulla told him.

The man listened expectantly.

"Yes?" he said. "Well? Which problem can you help me with?"

"The one about wanting to get rid of the other ten", Nasruddin replied.

The Question of God

Once a certain Rabbi asked a disciple who had just entered his room:

"Tell me, what do we mean when we say 'God'?"

The disciple remained silent and so the Rabbi asked a second time and then a third.

"Why are you silent?" the Rabbi asked him.

"Because I do not know", the disciple replied meekly.

"And do you think I know?" the Rabbi said. "But of course I must say it because it is so. He is definitely there, and except for Him, nothing is definitely there — and this is He. That is all I know. And that is enough to know."

Shivambu

As Drukpa Kunley was returning to his homeland, he encountered an old man carrying a painted scroll.

"Where are you going?" the Lama asked him.

"I am on my way to Ralung to ask Ngawong Chogyal to bless this *thanka* I have painted." "Let me see", the Lama ordered.

The old man handed it to him and asked his opinion of the work.

"Not bad", the Lama told him, "but I can improve it like this."

Drukpa Kunley then proceeded to take out his penis and urinate all over the old man's precious painting.

Upon seeing his work ruined the old man began to cry.

"What have you done you madman?" he said as he wept.

The Lama rolled up the scroll and calmly handed it back to the old man.

"Now you can take it to Ngawong for his blessing", he said.

When the old man reached Ralung and was finally granted an audience with Ngawong Chogyal, he said to him:

"Your Holiness, I spent many weeks painting a *thanka* of the Kagyu lineage and wanted to bring it to you for your blessing, however, on my way here a madman took it from me and urinated on it and now it is ruined."

Ngawong Chogyal asked to see the scroll anyway and upon opening it, saw that the splashes of urine had turned to shining gold.

"It seems there is no need for my blessing", he said to the old man. "It has been blessed in the best possible way."

At this the old man's faith was restored and he rejoiced at the miracle he had witnessed.

Nobody's Higher

A formal reception area had been set up in Mulla Nasruddin's village square to welcome a visiting dignitary. Nasruddin walked up and sat down in the most elegant chair at the head table. A Chief of the Guard approached him and said:

"I am sorry sir — these seats are reserved for the guests of honour."

"Oh I am more than just a normal guest", the Mulla told him confidently.

"So you are a diplomat?" the guard asked.

"More than that", Nasruddin replied.

"A minister perhaps?" the guard continued.

"Higher, higher", the Mulla said.

"Then you must be the king himself", the guard said sarcastically.

"Even higher still", Nasruddin replied.

"Higher than the king?" the guard laughed. "Nobody is higher than the king!"

"You are absolutely correct!" the Mulla told him. "And I am nobody!"

Original Face

The great Zen master, Keichu, was the head of the Tofuku temple in Kyoto. One day, the governor of Kyoto paid him a visit for the first time. On being received at the temple gates, the governor's attendant presented the monk with a calling card that read: *Kitagaki, Governor of Kyoto*.

"I have no business with such a fellow", Keichu replied to his attendant on being handed the card. "Tell him to get out of here."

The monk returned to the governor who was waiting at the gate and relayed the message with apologies.

"Of course", the governor replied as he took the card, "my mistake."

He then took out a pencil and scratched out the words *Governor of Kyoto* before handing it back to the monk and politely asking him to return to his master with the card once more.

Upon seeing the card master Keichu exclaimed, "Oh you mean Kitagaki — yes, I would like to see that man. Please tell him to come in".

Give and Take

One day, the local Imam paid a visit to the Mulla, looking for advice on a certain matter.

"May God bless you dear Mulla", he said. "You are wise in the ways of the world and a fountain of sagely advice to many. Perhaps you can help me in my dilemma. The more I advance in years, the more I wish to dedicate my time to those things that are closest to my heart — quiet prayer and meditation. However, I am constantly assailed by worldly people seeking advice on mundane matters that have nothing to do with a man of my inclinations and expertise. One wants this, another wants that, a third wants this and that — I do not wish to turn them away harshly but there is no end to it! Please, tell me — what would you do?"

Nasruddin took a moment to ponder his dilemma before responding:

"It is really quite simple", he told him. "If they are poor, lend them a little money. If they are rich, ask them to donate a little money. In both cases you are not likely to see them again."

Not That

Having heard of his great equanimity, some mischievous monks came to visit Abba Agathon to see if they could rouse him to anger.

"Are you not the Abba Agathon who is said to be a fornicator and full of pride?" they said to him.

"Yes, it is true", he replied.

"The same Agathon who is always talking nonsense?" they continued.

"The very same", the old man replied, unmoved.

"Agathon the heretic?" they continued.

"No", he answered, "there you are mistaken."

"Why did you accept the first insults but not this last?" they asked him, puzzled.

"The first I take for myself as they are good for my soul", the old man replied, "but heresy is separation from God and I have no wish to be separated from God."

At this the monks were humbled and respectfully took their leave of the old man.

A Fateful Day

Mulla Nasruddin had foolishly been bragging that he possessed the gift of prophecy and could see the future. The sultan, hearing of this blasphemy, confronted the Mulla with his sword drawn and raised.

"Tell me then, O prophet!" the sultan said to him, chiding. "Tell me quickly — when will you die? You never know, I may be something of a seer myself in these matters."

Nasruddin, knowing that the sultan was inclined to determine his own fate but never to tempt it, replied:

"Your Majesty, although I am hesitant to disclose to you the will of the Almighty, I can only say that I was blessed with a vision that showed me dying the very same day as you."

Lost in Translation

There is a long-standing tradition within Zen that if a wandering monk, arriving at any temple or monastery, defeats the resident monks in a debate on the Buddha's teachings, then he earns the right to stay. If he is defeated, he must move on.

In a temple in northern Japan there lived two brothers. The elder brother was learned and wise but the younger was a fool and had just one eye.

One day, a wandering monk came looking for a place to stay, and so, as was their custom, he challenged the monks there to a debate. The elder of the two brothers was not feeling his best that day, and so, sent his younger brother in his stead.

"Good luck", the elder brother said to him, "and request the dialogue in silence", he continued, knowing full well his younger brother's shortcomings.

The monk led the stranger to the shrine and they both sat down. A short while later, the debate had finished and the wandering monk stood up and made his way to leave. At the entrance to the temple he came across the elder brother.

"Your younger brother is an astute man", he said to him. "He defeated me fair and square."

Intrigued by this, the elder brother asked him to elaborate.

"Well", the traveller explained, "first I held up one finger to represent the Buddha, to which he held up two fingers to signify the Buddha and the Dharma. I then held up three to represent the Buddha, the Dharma and the Sangha. Your brother then closed his hand into a clenched fist to indicate that all three become just one through realisation. With that I had nothing more to add. I consider him the worthy victor and so have no right to remain here any longer."

With that the wandering monk bid farewell and left. Just at that moment the younger brother appeared shaking his clenched fist.

"Where is he?" he demanded angrily.

"I understand you won the debate", his elder brother said to him.

"Won?" the younger brother replied in surprise. "I won nothing. Where is he? He deserves a good beating!"

"A beating?" his brother said with equal surprise, "Why, what happened?"

"As soon as we sat down, he held up one finger as if insulting the fact that I have just one eye. I took a deep breath and, trying to be polite, I held up two fingers to congratulate him on having two. Then, to add insult to injury, he held up three fingers as if to say that between us, we only have three eyes — insulting me once again! At that I made my hand into a fist to show him that a beating was coming should he continue to insult me. He then got up and left before I could give him the beating he deserved."

What Goes Up

On one of his many travels, the sultan and his entourage came across a half-naked dervish on the outskirts of a small town. He was sitting cross-legged on the dusty ground inside a circle that had been drawn around him in chalk.

"What on earth are you doing here?" the sultan asked him. "And what is the meaning of this circle?"

"I am praising the glory of God", the man replied, "and this circle is for my alms. Whatever I am given, I throw in the air — what falls outside of the circle is God's share and what falls inside is for me."

The sultan turned to Nasruddin. "Look here. Now this is true humility", he said chiding him. "You speak much of modesty and humility but just what do you give to God?"

"What am I to give to the One who has all?" the Mulla said to him. "Everything is His", he continued. "Nevertheless, whatever I am given by your generosity, I throw in the air so that God may keep whatever he wishes. I only take for myself what falls back down."

The Spiritual Marketplace

A Sufi was visiting a mosque to pray. He settled himself down but could not help overhear the prayers of the man to his right.

"Dear God!" the man said, "if you grant me heaven I will worship you with all my heart."

At the same moment he heard the man on his left saying:

"Dear God! If you deliver me from hell I will worship you with all my heart."

The Sufi bowed his head and began his own prayer:

"Dear God! If I worship you through hopes of heaven, deny me heaven and if I worship you through fear of hell, cast me into hell. And please forgive these two men on either side of me."

Innocently Guilty

One night, Nasruddin's house was broken into and a number of items were stolen. As they stood outside, his wife scolded him for not locking the door properly. Another neighbour remarked that the locks were faulty and that he should have had changed them.

"You didn't close the window", said another.

"How could you sleep whilst your house was being robbed!" said yet another.

Just then, Nasruddin turned and began to leave.

"Where do you think you're going?" they all asked after him.

"To turn myself in", he replied. "After all — it seems that I am more to blame than the thieves."

Arresting the Stone Buddha

A merchant who had been carrying fifty rolls of cotton on his shoulders stopped beneath a shelter where a large statue of the Buddha stood, to rest from the heat of the day. As he lay in the shade, he dozed off and when he finally awoke, he found that all his goods had been stolen. Immediately he went to the authorities to report the matter.

A judge name O-oka was called to investigate.

"That stone Buddha must have stolen the goods", he concluded. "And in any case, his duty is to protect the welfare of the people and in this he has failed. Arrest him!"

Police were sent and the stone Buddha was carried to the courthouse, followed by a large noisy crowd of curious onlookers. When O-oka appeared on the bench, he scolded the boisterous crowd:

"What sort of a behaviour is this for a courthouse, laughing and joking and causing all manner of mayhem?" he said to them. "I find you all in contempt of court and subject to a fine and possibly, imprisonment!" he continued.

Those assembled quickly began to quieten down and apologise.

"I shall impose a fine", continued the judge, "that will be pardoned provided that each and every one of you bring a roll of cotton to this courthouse within three days. Anyone failing to do this will be arrested!"

The people hurried away and began bringing their cotton goods to the courthouse. One of them was recognised by the merchant as his own and the thief was discovered. His goods were recovered, the other rolls were returned to their rightful owners and the stone Buddha returned to its place. Although it had not stopped the theft, it had instead found the thief.

Two Rights Don't Make a Wrong

Judge Nasruddin was presiding over a case. After hearing the declaration of the plaintiff and being impressed by his eloquence and argument, Nasruddin, somewhat prematurely declared to him:

"I believe you are right."

"Objection your honour!" came a voice from the defence. "You have yet to even hear the other side of the story!"

"Of course", said Nasruddin composing himself. "Sorry — please go ahead."

After hearing another compelling speech from the defence, the Mulla said to him:

"I believe you are right."

At this point the clerk of the court interjected and said to Nasruddin:

"Your Honour — they cannot both be right!"

At which point Nasruddin responded once again:

"I believe you are right. Case dismissed!"

A Reasonable Prayer

A monk was sitting with some of his brethren talking about prayer.

"When I was young, I was full of fire", he said to them. "I wanted to awaken everyone. I would pray to God to give me the strength to change the whole world. Later in life", he continued, "it was enough for me to pray to God to give me the strength to change those closest to me."

The other monks murmured their approval.

"Now I am older and wiser still, my prayer is even simpler: 'God', I say to Him — 'just give me the strength and courage to change myself'."

Suffering Fear

Nasruddin was walking down a deserted country road one night, when he heard a strange noise. As he turned to run, he tripped and fell into a cell that had been partially dug into the ground by a dervish.

"Who are you?" Nasruddin cried out in fright, as he bumped against a dark figure.

"I am a dervish and this is my place of meditation and prayer", the voice replied.

"Well I'm afraid that tonight you'll have to share it with me", Nasruddin told him. "You scared me half to death and now I cannot continue any further until daybreak."

"Well, alright", the dervish said unenthusiastically. "Grab the other end of this blanket and lie down there. And please be quiet, I am in the middle of my practices."

Nasruddin lay quiet for some time and then said to the dervish:

"I'm thirsty. Do you have any water please?"

"Go down the road a little — there is a stream", the dervish mumbled to him.

"But I'm still afraid", Nasruddin whispered.

"Alright", the dervish said after a short silence. "I shall go."

"No — don't go!" Nasruddin implored him. "I'll be scared here all by myself!"

"Well, then take this knife to defend yourself", the irritated dervish said to him as he left the cell.

While the dervish was away, Nasruddin began to imagine all the dangers that could possibly await him in the darkness and by the time the dervish returned, he had worked himself up into quite a state.

"Who goes there?" he cried out upon hearing footsteps approach. "Stay away or I'll kill you — I have a knife!"

"It's me you fool!" the dervish hissed. "Put the knife down and let me in!"

"How do I know it's really you — and just who are you anyway?" Nasruddin cried out, the knife in his hand, shaking.

"I have brought you water — you were thirsty, remember?"

"Don't try to bribe me you fiend!" Nasruddin continued.

"But this is my cell!" the dervish shouted in desperation.

"Well you'll just have to find another one", Nasruddin told him.

"Well, really", the dervish said in despair. "I just don't know what to make of all this!"

"Well I can tell you one thing", Nasruddin said. "Fear is stronger than thirst, reason and even property rights. And you don't even need to be the one feeling it in order to suffer!"

Back to Front and Upside Down

A sage was sitting with his disciples one day. After several of them had come to him to lament their problems, out of the blue, he told them a joke to which everyone present laughed. After a few minutes had passed the sage repeated the joke and those gathered around him chuckled. A while later he told them the same joke for a third time, but this time, nobody laughed.

"Why is it", he said to them, "that you can cry over the same problem time and time again but you cannot laugh at the same joke? You are all back to front and upside down!"

Already There

A Zen master was sitting on the bank of a river when he heard a man call to him from the other side.

"Good sir!" the man cried. "Please tell me — how do I get to the other side?"

"You already are on the other side!" the master shouted back.

References

CHAPTER 1: CRAZY-WISDOM
1. Nisker, Wes. *Crazy Wisdom*. California: Ten Speed Press, 1990, p. 11.
2. Guy Claxton. *Wholly Human: Eastern & Western Visions of the Self and its Perfection*. London, Boston and Henley: Routledge & Kegan Paul, 1981, p. 31.
3. Chögyam Trungpa. *Journey Without Goal: The Tantric Wisdom of the Buddha*. Boston & London: Shambhala, 1985, p. 139.
4. Wei Wu Wei. *Why Lazarus Laughed: The Essential Doctrine, Zen-Advaita-Tantra*. Boulder, CO: Sentient Publications, 2003, p. 46
5. Sandra Bell. 'Scandals in Emerging Western Buddhism' from *Westward Dharma: Buddhism Beyond Asia*. Berkeley: University of California Press, 2002, p. 233.
6. Chögyam Trungpa. *Journey Without Goal: The Tantric Wisdom of the Buddha*. Boston & London: Shambhala, 1985, p. 140.
7. Chögyam Trungpa. *Crazy Wisdom*. Boston & London: Shambhala, 1991, p. 112.
8. Ibid., p. 112.
9. Rowe, C. J. (trans.). *Plato: Phaedrus*. England: Aris & Phillips, 1986, p. 57.
10. Ibid., p. 101.
11. Schimmel, Annemarie. *Mystical Dimensions of Islam*. USA: The University of North Carolina Press, 1975, p. 321–322.
12. Lovejoy, Arthur O. *The Great Chain of Being*. Cambridge, Massachusetts: Harvard University Press, 1964, p. vi.
13. Red Pine (trans.). *The Heart Sutra: The Womb of Buddhas*. Berkeley: Counterpoint, 2004, p. 70.
14. Verse 20 of the *Brahma Jnanavali Mala* by Adi Shankaracharya.

15. Okumura, Shohaku. *The Mountains and Waters Sutra: A Practitioner's Guide to Dogen's "Sansuikyo"*. USA: Wisdom Publications, 2018, p. 205.
16. Lovejoy, Arthur O. *The Great Chain of Being*. Cambridge, Massachusetts: Harvard University Press, 1964, p. 26.
17. Blake, William. *The Complete Poems*. England: Penguin Books, 1977, p. 183.
18. Idries Shah. *A Perfumed Scorpion*. London: The Octagon Press, 2000, p. 191.
19. Thomas Merton. *The Way of Chuang Tzu*. New York: New Directions, 1969, p. 154.
20. Lu K'uan Yu (Charles Luk). *Ch'an & Zen Teaching*. Berkeley: Shambhala, 1970, p. 129.
21. Plato (trans. Hamilton, Walter). *Phaedrus and the Seventh and Eighth Letters*. London: Penguin Books, 1973, p. 136.
22. Pseudo-Dionysius. *The Complete Works of Pseudo-Dionysius*. New York: Paulist Press, 1987, p. 139.
23. Pratchett, Terry / Stewart, Ian / Cohen, Jack. *The Science of Discworld*. New York: Anchor Books, 2014, p. 35.
24. Wei Wu Wei. *Ask the Awakened: The Negative Way*. Boulder: Sentient Publications, 2002, p. 23.
25. Snellgrove, D. L. *The Hevajra Tantra: A Critical Study*. London: Oxford University Press, 1959, p. 99.
26. Reps, Paul. *Zen Flesh, Zen Bones*. Great Britain: Penguin Books, 1957, p. 114.
27. Ibid., p. 118.
28. Pseudo-Dionysius. *The Complete Works of Pseudo-Dionysius*. New York: Paulist Press, 1987, p. 140–141.
29. Wittgenstein, Ludwig. *Tractatus Logico-Philosophicus*. London: Routledge & Kegan Paul Ltd., 1960, p. 189.
30. Tzu, Lao. *Tao Te Ching*. Boston & London: Penguin Books, 1963, p. 5.
31. Ibid., p. 28.
32. Ibid., p. 63.

33. Gurdjieff, George Ivanovitch. *Views from the Real World: Early Talks of G. I. Gurdjieff.* London: Arkana, 1984, p. 41.
34. Lu K'uan Yu (Charles Luk). *Ch'an & Zen Teaching.* Berkeley: Shambhala, 1970, p. 123.

CHAPTER 2: A CRY IN THE WILDERNESS
1. Ezekiel 4:9
2. Ezekiel 4:12
3. Hosea 1:2
4. Daniel 4:33
5. I Corinthians 4:9-10
6. I Corinthians 3:18-20
7. John 6:38
8. Luke 19:10
9. Luke 4:18
10. Matthew 10:34-36
11. Matthew 10:39
12. Meyer, Marvin (trans.). *The Gospel of Thomas: The Hidden Sayings of Jesus.* London: Harper Collins, 2004, p. 31.
13. John 6:53-56
14. John 6:60
15. Luke 14:33
16. Luke 14:26
17. Matthew 19:22
18. Matthew 19:21
19. Benedicta Ward (trans.). *The Sayings of the Desert Fathers.* Michigan: Cisternian Publications, 1975, p. 6.
20. Clarke, W. K. Lowther (trans.). *The Lausiac History of Palladius.* New York: The Macmillan Company, 1918, p. 35.
21. Ibid., p. 118.
22. Ibid., p. 118.
23. Ibid., p. 119.
24. Ibid., p. 119.
25. Ibid., p. 120.

26. Kempis, Thomas à. *The Imitation of Christ*. London and Glasgow: Collins Sons & Co. Ltd., 1974, p. 76.

27. Buber, Martin. *Tales of the Hasidim: Early Masters*. New York: Schocken Books, 1947, p. 150–151.

28. Ibid., p. 4.

29. Ibid., p. 7.

30. Ibid., p. 277.

CHAPTER 3: CHOP WATER, CARRY WOOD

1. Suzuki, Daisetz T. *Sengai: The Zen Master*. Greenwich, Connecticut: New York Graphic Society Ltd., 1971, p. 134.

2. Tzu, Lao. *Tao Te Ching*. Boston & London: Penguin Books, 1963, p. 7.

3. Wing-Tsit Chan. *A Source Book in Chinese Philosophy*. New Jersey: Princeton University Press, 1963, p. 136.

4. Tzu, Lao. *Tao Te Ching*. Boston & London: Penguin Books, 1963, p. 42.

5. Ibid., p. 54.

6. Ibid., p. 85.

7. Ibid., p. 77.

8. Merton, Thomas. *The Way of Chuang Tzu*. New York: New Directions, 1969, p. 118–119.

9. Wing-Tsit Chan. *A Source Book in Chinese Philosophy*. New Jersey: Princeton University Press, 1963, p. 136–137.

10. Tzu, Lao. *Tao Te Ching*. Boston & London: Penguin Books, 1963, p. 15.

11. Ibid., p. 48.

12. Feng, Gia-Fu & English, Jane (trans.). *Chuang Tsu – Inner Chapters*. London: Wildwood House, 1974, p. 9.

13. Reps, Paul. *Zen Flesh, Zen Bones*. Great Britain: Penguin Books, 1957, p. 98.

14. Hyers, Conrad. *Zen and the Comic Spirit*. Philadelphia: The Westminster Press, 1973, p. 103.

15. Idries Shah. *A Perfumed Scorpion.* London: The Octagon Press, 2000, p. 191.

16. Wei Wu Wei. *Ask the Awakened: The Negative Way.* Boulder: Sentient Publications, 2002, p. 92.

17. Red Pine (trans.). *The Zen Works of Stonehouse: Poems and Talks of a Fourteenth-Century Chinese Hermit.* Berkeley: Counterpoint, 1999, p. xii.

18. Reps, Paul. *Zen Flesh, Zen Bones.* Great Britain: Penguin Books, 1957, p. 95.

19. Cleary, Thomas (trans.). *A Buddha from Korea: The Zen Teachings of T'aego.* Boston & Shaftesbury: Shambhala, 1988, p. 87.

20. Blofeld, John. *Zen Teaching of Instantaneous Awakening: Master Hui Hai.* Devon, UK: Buddhist Publishing Group, 1995, p. 34.

21. Hyers, Conrad. *Zen and the Comic Spirit.* Philadelphia: The Westminster Press, 1973, p. 85.

22. Suzuki, Daisetz T. *Sengai: The Zen Master.* Greenwich, Connecticut: New York Graphic Society Ltd., 1971, p. 87.

23. Wei Wu Wei. *Why Lazarus Laughed: The Essential Doctrine, Zen-Advaita-Tantra.* Boulder, CO: Sentient Publications, 2003, p. 2.

24. Waddell, Norman (trans.). *Zen Words for the Heart: Hakuin's Commentary on the Heart Sutra.* Boston & London: Shambhala, 2013, p. 28–29.

25. Ibid., p. 28.

26. Red Pine (trans.). *The Collected Songs of Cold Mountain.* Washington: Copper Canyon Press, 2000, p. 67.

27. Ibid., p. 6.

28. Ibid., p. 261.

29. Ibid., p. 7.

30. Ibid., p. 287.

31. Ibid., p. 261.

32. Ibid., p. 257.

33. Ibid., p. 65.
34. Ibid., p. 295.
35. Ibid., p. 199.
36. Ibid., p. 57.
37. Arntzen, Sonja (trans.). *Ikkyū and the Crazy Cloud Anthology: A Zen Poet of Medieval Japan.* Japan: University of Tokyo Press, 1986, p. 119.
38. Ibid., p. 158.
39. Ibid., p. 138.
40. Ibid., p. 22.
41. Ibid., p. 90.
42. Ibid., p. 113.
43. Ibid., p. 25.
44. Ibid., p. 31.

CHAPTER 4: THE DHARMA OF THE INSIDERS

1. Kunsang, Erik Pema (trans.) / Schmidt, Marcia Binder (ed.). *Advice from the Lotus-Born: A Collection of Padmasambhava's Advice to the Dakini Yeshe Tsogyal and Other Close Disciples.* Boudhanath, Arhus & Hong Kong: Rangjung Yeshe Publications, 2004, p. 90.
2. Tsogyal, Yeshe. *The Lotus-Born: The Life Story of Padmasambhava.* Boston & London: Shambhala, 1993, p. 41.
3. Khenchen Palden Sherab Rinpoche. *The Eight Manifestations of Guru Padmasambhava.* (From a discourse at Padma Gochen Ling, in Monterey, Tennessee in May 1992.)
4. Dowman, Keith. *The Divine Madman: The Sublime Life and Songs of Drukpa Kunley.* Dzogchen Now! Books, 2014, p. 131.
5. Ibid., p. 33.
6. Ibid., p. 64.
7. Ibid., p. 65.
8. Ibid., p. 72.
9. Ibid., p. 50.

10. Trungpa, Chögyam. *Crazy Wisdom*. Boston & London: Shambhala, 1991, p. 12.
11. Dowman, Keith. *The Divine Madman: The Sublime Life and Songs of Drukpa Kunley*. Dzogchen Now! Books, 2014, p. 106.
12. Ibid., p. 107.
13. Ibid., p. xv.
14. Larsson, Stefan. *Crazy for Wisdom: The Making of a Mad Yogin in Fifteenth-Century Tibet*. Leiden & Boston: Brill, 2012, p. 161.
15. Dowman, Keith. *The Divine Madman: The Sublime Life and Songs of Drukpa Kunley*. Dzogchen Now! Books, 2014, p. 79.

CHAPTER 5: RIDING THE LION

1. Tsang Nyon / Stagg, Christopher (trans.). *The Hundred Thousand Songs of Milarepa: A New Translation*. Boston: Shambhala, 2016, p. 634.
2. Watts, Alan W. *The Way of Zen*. Great Britain: Penguin Books, 1968, p. 99.
3. Guenther, Herbert V. (trans.) *The Life and Teaching of Naropa*. London: Oxford University Press, 1974, p. 24.
4. Ibid., p. 30.
5. Ibid., p. 30.
6. Ibid., p. 31.
7. Ibid., p. 33.
8. Ibid., p. 33.
9. Ibid., p. 34.
10. Dowman, Keith. *Masters of Mahamudra: Songs and Histories of the Eighty-Four Buddhist Siddhas*. State University of New York Press, 1985, p. 142.
11. Guenther, Herbert V. (trans.). *The Life and Teaching of Naropa*. London: Oxford University Press, 1974, p. 50–51.
12. Tsang Nyon, (trans. Lobsang P. Lhalungpa). *The Life of Milarepa*. Boston & London: Shambhala, 1985, p. 50.

13. Ibid., p. 52–53.
14. Ibid., p. 53.
15. Ibid., p. 72.
16. Ibid., p. 139.

CHAPTER 6: THE LAND OF JAMBU TREES

1. Muṇḍaka Upaniṣad, Chapter 2, Verse 8.
2. Swami Madhavananda (trans.). *Bṛhadāraṇyaka Upaniṣad.* Calcutta: Advaita Ashrama, 1997, p. 369–370.
3. Cleary, Thomas (trans.). *The Flower Ornament Scripture: A Translation of the Avatamsaka Sutra.* Boston & London: Shambhala, 1993, p. 343.
4. Lama Chonam & Sangye Khandro (trans.). *The Guhyagarbha Tantra: Secret Essence Definitive Nature Just As It Is.* New York: Snow Lion Publications, 2011, p. 43.
5. Dowman, Keith. *Masters of Mahamudra: Songs and Histories of the Eighty-Four Buddhist Siddhas.* New York: State University of New York Press, 1985, p. 325.
6. Ibid., p. 34.
7. Ibid., p. 180.
8. Abhayadatta / Robinson, James B. (trans.). *Buddha's Lions: The Lives of the Eighty-Four Siddhas.* Berkeley: Dharma Publishing, 1979, p. 43.
9. Schaeffer, Kurtis R. *Dreaming the Great Brahmin: Tibetan Traditions of the Buddhist Poet-Saint Saraha.* New York: Oxford University Press, 2005, p. 21.
10. Guenther, Herbert V (trans.). *The Royal Song of Saraha: A Study in the History of Buddhist Thought.* Berkeley & London: Shambhala, 1973, p. 6.
11. Ibid., p. 7.
12. Khenchen Thrangu Rinpoche. *Essentials of Mahamudra: Looking Directly at the Mind.* Boston: Wisdom Publications, 2004, p. 74.

13. Khenchen Thrangu Rinpoche (commentary) / Martin, Michele (trans.) / O'Hearn, Peter (trans.). *A Song for the King: Saraha on Mahamudra Meditation.* Boston: Wisdom Publications, 2006, p. 105–106.

14. Abhayadatta / Robinson, James B. (trans.). *Buddha's Lions: The Lives of the Eighty-Four Siddhas.* Berkeley: Dharma Publishing, 1979, p. 43.

15. Dowman, Keith. *Masters of Mahamudra: Songs and Histories of the Eighty-Four Buddhist Siddhas.* New York: State University of New York Press, 1985, p. 314.

16. Ibid., p. 373.

17. Abhayadatta / Robinson, James B. (trans.). *Buddha's Lions: The Lives of the Eighty-Four Siddhas.* Berkeley: Dharma Publishing, 1979, p. 252.

18. Dowman, Keith. *Masters of Mahamudra: Songs and Histories of the Eighty-Four Buddhist Siddhas.* New York: State University of New York Press, 1985, p. 373.

19. Donkin, William. *The Wayfarers: An Account of the Work of Meher Baba with the God-intoxicated, and also with Advanced Souls, Sadhus, and the Poor.* South Carolina: Sheriar Press, 1988, p. 5.

20. Ibid., p. 45.

21. Ibid., p. 28–29.

22. Ibid., p. 31.

23. Lopez, Donald S. Jr. (ed.). *Religions of India in Practice.* New Jersey: Princeton University Press, 1995, p. 254.

24. Upendranath Bhattacarya. *Bānglār Bāul O Bāul Gan.* Calcutta: Orient Book Company, 1388, p. 911.

25. Lopez, Donald S. Jr. (ed.) *Religions of India in Practice.* New Jersey: Princeton University Press, 1995, p. 257.

26. Upendranath Bhattacarya. *Bānglār Bāul O Bāul Gan.* Calcutta: Orient Book Company, 1388, p. 1007.

27. Sri Anirvan. *Letters from a Baul: Life Within Life.* Calcutta: Sri Aurobindo Pathamandir, 1983, p. 119.

28. McDaniel, June. *The Madness of the Saints: Ecstatic Religion in Bengal.* Chicago & London: The University of Chicago Press, 1989, p. 157–158.

29. M. *The Gospel of Sri Ramakrishna.* Madras: Sri Ramakrishna Math, 1996, p. 265.

30. Isherwood, Christopher. *Ramakrishna & His Disciples.* Delhi: Advaita Ashrama, 2001, p. 85.

31. Ibid., p. 114.

32. Ibid., p. 89.

33. M. *The Gospel of Sri Ramakrishna.* Madras: Sri Ramakrishna Math, 1996, p. 18.

34. Ibid., p. 19.

35. Isherwood, Christopher. *Ramakrishna & His Disciples.* Delhi: Advaita Ashrama, 2001, p. 118.

36. Ibid., p. 124.

37. Hixon, Lex. *Great Swan: Meetings with Ramakrishna.* Delhi: Motilal Banarsidass, 2002, p. 273.

38. Rigopoulos, Antonio. *Dattātreya The Immortal Guru, Yogin, and Avatāra.* New York: State University of New York Press, 1998, p. 69.

39. Ibid., p. 65.

40. Debroy, Bibek (trans.). *The Markandeya Purana.* India: Penguin Random House India, 2019, p. 114–115.

41. Rigopoulos, Antonio. *Dattātreya The Immortal Guru, Yogin, and Avatāra.* New York: State University of New York Press, 1998, p. 69.

42. Feuerstein, Georg. *Holy Madness: The Shock Tactics and Radical Teachings of Crazy-Wise Adepts, Holy Fools, and Rascal Gurus.* New York: Arkana, 1992, p. 26.

43. Dass, Ram. *Miracle of Love: Stories About Neem Karoli Baba.* New York: E. P. Dutton, 1979, p. 291.

CHAPTER 7: DRUNK ON THE WINE OF THE BELOVED

1. Helminski Kabir, (ed.). *The Rumi Collection: An Anthology of Translations of Mevlana Jalaluddin Rumi.* Boston & London: Shambhala, 2000, p. 171.

2. Saiyid Athar Abbas Rizvi. *A History of Sufism in India (Volume One).* New Delhi: Munshiram Manoharlal Publishers, 1986, p. 22.

3. Matthew 13:10–13

4. Saiyid Athar Abbas Rizvi. *A History of Sufism in India (Volume One).* New Delhi: Munshiram Manoharlal Publishers, 1986, p. 26.

5. Vaughan-Lee, Llewellyn (ed.). *Travelling the Path of Love: Sayings of Sufi Masters.* California: The Golden Sufi Center, 1995, p. 185.

6. Saiyid Athar Abbas Rizvi. *A History of Sufism in India (Volume One).* New Delhi: Munshiram Manoharlal Publishers, 1986, p. 28.

7. Ibid., p. 57.

8. Luke 23:34

9. Shah, Idries. *The Sufis.* Great Britain: W. H. Allen & Co. Ltd, 1977, p. 375.

10. Shah, Idries. *The Way of the Sufi.* London: The Octagon Press, 1980, p. 167.

11. Schimmel, Annemarie. *Mystical Dimensions of Islam.* USA: The University of North Carolina Press, 1975, p. 40.

12. Attar, Farid al-Din / Arberry, A. J. (trans.). *Muslim Saints & Mystics: Episodes from the Tadhkirat al-Auliya ("Memorial of the Saints") by Farid al-Din Attar.* London & Boston: Routledge & Kegan Paul, 1973, p. 278.

13. Ibid., p. 279.

14. Ibid., p. 280.

15. Ibid., p. 282.

16. Vaughan-Lee, Llewellyn (ed.). *Travelling the Path of Love: Sayings of Sufi Masters.* California: The Golden Sufi Center, 1995, p. 31.

17. Ibid., p. 207.

18. Nicholson, Reynold. *Studies in Islamic Mysticism.* UK: Curzon Press, 2005, p. 12.

19. Ibid., p. 10–11.

20. Saiyid Athar Abbas Rizvi. *A History of Sufism in India (Volume One).* New Delhi: Munshiram Manoharlal Publishers, 1986, p. 72.

21. Ibid., p. 71.

22. Ibid., p. 73.

23. Okumura, Shohaku. *The Mountains and Waters Sutra: A Practitioner's Guide to Dogen's "Sansuikyo".* USA: Wisdom Publications, 2018, p. 205.

24. Sūra 5:59

25. Schimmel, Annemarie. *Mystical Dimensions of Islam.* USA: The University of North Carolina Press, 1975, p. 86.

26. Ibid., p. 86.

27. Attar, Farid al-Din / Arberry, A. J. (trans.). *Muslim Saints & Mystics: Episodes from the Tadhkirat al-Auliya ("Memorial of the Saints") by Farid al-Din Attar.* London & Boston: Routledge & Kegan Paul, 1973, p. 104.

28. Ridgeon, Lloyd (ed.). *Routledge Handbook on Sufism.* London & New York: Routledge, 2021, p. 263.

29. Ibid., p. 252.

30. Ibid., p. 255.

31. Lee, Rev. Samuel (trans./ed.). *The Travels of Ibn Battuta in the Near East, Asia and Africa 1325–1354.* New York: Dover Publications, 2004, p. 35–36.

32. Ridgeon, Lloyd (ed.). *Routledge Handbook on Sufism.* London & New York: Routledge, 2021, p. 254.

33. Smith, Margaret. *Rabi'a the Mystic and Her Fellow-Saints: Being the Life and Teachings of Rabia al-Adawiya Al-Qaysiyya of*

Basra Together with Some Account of the Place of Women Saints in Islam. UK: Llanerch Publishers, 1994, p. 3–4.

34. Farid al-Din Attar / Arberry, A. J. (trans.). *Muslim Saints & Mystics: Episodes from the Tadhkirat al-Auliya ("Memorial of the Saints").* London & Boston: Routledge & Kegan Paul, 1973, p. 50.

35. Widad El Sakkakini / Safwat, Dr. Nabil (trans.). *First Among Sufis: The Life & Thought of Rabia al-Adawiyya.* London: The Octagon Press, 1982, p. 2.

36. Attar, Farid al-Din / Arberry, A. J. (trans.). *Muslim Saints & Mystics: Episodes from the Tadhkirat al-Auliya ("Memorial of the Saints") by Farid al-Din Attar.* London & Boston: Routledge & Kegan Paul, 1973, p. 46.

37. Stoneman, Richard. *Legends of Alexander the Great.* London & New York: I. B. Tauris & Co, 2012, p. 44.

38. Attar, Farid al-Din / Arberry, A. J. (trans.). *Muslim Saints & Mystics: Episodes from the Tadhkirat al-Auliya ("Memorial of the Saints") by Farid al-Din Attar.* London & Boston: Routledge & Kegan Paul, 1973, p. 46.

39. Widad El Sakkakini / Safwat, Dr. Nabil (trans.). *First Among Sufis: The Life & Thought of Rabia al-Adawiyya.* London: The Octagon Press, 1982, p. 3.

40. Shah, Idries. *The Exploits of the Incomparable Mulla Nasrudin.* London: Picador, 1973, p. 13.

41. Shah, Idries. *The Sufis.* Great Britain: W. H. Allen & Co. Ltd, 1977, p. 56.

42. Borrow, George. *The Turkish Jester or The Pleasantries of Cogia Nasr Eddin Effendi.* Ipswich: W. Webber, 1884, p. 45.

43. Shah, Idries *The Sufis.* Great Britain: W. H. Allen & Co. Ltd, 1977, p. 57.

44. Osho. *The True Sage.* 1975, p. 123.

45. George Ivanovitch Gurdjieff. *All & Everything, or Beelzebub's Tales to his Grandson.* London and Henley: Routledge & Kegan Paul, 1950, First Book p. 349.

PART II

1. Stevens, John. *Three Zen Masters: Ikkyu, Hakuin, and Ryokan.* Tokyo, New York, London: Kodansha International, 1993, p. 131.
2. Reps, Paul. *Zen Flesh, Zen Bones.* Great Britain: Penguin Books, 1957, p. 40.
3. Adapted from: Dowman, Keith. *The Divine Madman: The Sublime Life and Songs of Drukpa Kunley.* Dzogchen Now! Books, 2014, p. 78–79.
4. Reps, Paul. *Zen Flesh, Zen Bones.* Great Britain: Penguin Books, 1957, p. 54.
5. Dowman, Keith. *The Divine Madman: The Sublime Life and Songs of Drukpa Kunley.* Dzogchen Now! Books, 2014, p. 60.

Bibliography

Abhayadatta / Robinson, James B. (trans.). *Buddha's Lions: The Lives of the Eighty-Four Siddhas.* Berkeley: Dharma Publishing, 1979.

Al-Amily, Hussain Mohammed. *The Book of Arabic Wisdom.* Northampton, Mass.: Interlink Books, 2004.

Arntzen, Sonja (trans.). *Ikkyū and the Crazy Cloud Anthology: A Zen Poet of Medieval Japan.* Japan: University of Tokyo Press, 1986.

Ashliman, D. L. *Nasreddin Hodja: Tales of the Turkish Trickster.* Pittsburgh: University of Pittsburgh, 2001.

Attar, Farid al-Din / Arberry, A. J. (trans.). *Muslim Saints & Mystics: Episodes from the Tadhkirat al-Auliya ("Memorial of the Saints") by Farid al-Din Attar.* London & Boston: Routledge & Kegan Paul, 1973.

Bahadur, Sri Jaya Chamarajendra Wadiyar. *Dattātreya: The Way and the Goal.* England: Coombe Springs Press, 1982.

Barks, Coleman. *The Essential Rumi.* New Jersey: Castle Books, 1997.

Barnham, Henry D (trans.). *Tales of Nasr-ed-din Khoja.* London: Nisbet & Co., 1923.

Blake, William. *The Complete Poems.* England: Penguin Books, 1977.

Blofeld, John. *Zen Teaching of Instantaneous Awakening – Master Hui Hai.* Devon, UK: Buddhist Publishing Group, 1995.

Boratav, Pertev Naili. *Nasreddin Hoca.* Istanbul: Kirmizi Yayinlari, 1995.

Borrow, George. *The Turkish Jester or The Pleasantries of Cogia Nasr Eddin Effendi.* Ipswich: W. Webber, 1884.

Brands H. W. *The First American: The Life and Times of Benjamin Franklin.* New York: Doubleday, 2000.

Broughton, Jeffrey L. *The Bodhidharma Anthology: The Earliest Records of Zen*. Berkeley, Los Angeles, London: University of California Press, 1999.

Buber, Martin. *Tales of the Hasidim: Early Masters*. New York: Schocken Books, 1947.

Clarke, W. K. Lowther (trans.). *The Lausiac History of Palladius*. New York: The Macmillan Company, 1918.

Claxton, Guy. *Wholly Human: Eastern & Western Visions of the Self and its Perfection*. London, Boston and Henley: Routledge & Kegan Paul, 1981.

Cleary, Thomas (trans.). *The Flower Ornament Scripture: A Translation of the Avatamsaka Sutra*. Boston & London: Shambhala, 1993.

_____. *A Buddha from Korea: The Zen Teachings of T'aego*. Boston & Shaftesbury: Shambhala, 1988.

Clemens, Samuel Langhorne / Howells, William Dean / Clark, Charles Hopkins. *Mark Twain's Library of Humor*. New York: Charles L. Webster & Co., 1888.

Conze, Edward. *Buddhist Scriptures*. Great Britain: Penguin Books, 1959.

Cornell, Rkia Elaroui. *Rabi'a From Narrative to Myth: The Many Faces of Islam's Most Famous Woman Saint, Rabi'a al-Adawiyya*. London: Oneworld Publications, 2019.

Dass, Ram. *Miracle of Love: Stories About Neem Karoli Baba*. New York: E. P. Dutton, 1979.

Dattatreya Avadhuta / Swami Chetanananda (trans.). *Avadhuta Gita: The Song of the Ever-Free*. Calcutta: Advaita Ashrama, 1998.

Davies, Oliver. *Meister Eckhart: Mystical Theologian*. London: SPCK, 1991.

Debroy, Bibek (trans.). *The Markandeya Purana*. India: Penguin Random House India, 2019.

DiValerio, David. *The Holy Madmen of Tibet*. New York: Oxford University Press, 2015.

_____. *The Life of the Madman of Ü.* New York: Oxford University Press, 2015.

_____. *Subversive Sainthood and Tantric Fundamentalism: An Historical Study of Tibet's Holy Madmen.* A Dissertation presented to the Graduate Faculty of the University of Virginia in Candidacy for the Degree of Doctor of Philosophy, 2011.

Donkin, William. *The Wayfarers: An Account of the Work of Meher Baba with the God-intoxicated, and also with Advanced Souls, Sadhus, and the Poor.* South Carolina: Sheriar Press, 1988.

Dowman, Keith. *The Divine Madman: The Sublime Life and Songs of Drukpa Kunley.* Dzogchen Now! Books, 2014.

_____. *Masters of Mahamudra: Songs and Histories of the Eighty-Four Buddhist Siddhas.* New York: State University of New York Press, 1985.

Drikung Kyabgon Chetsang Rinpoche. *The Practice of Mahamudra.* New York Press: Snow Lion Publications, 2009.

Duff, Lotsawa Tony. *Gampopa's Mahamudra: The Five-Part Mahamudra Practice Taught to Phagmo Drupa by Gampopa.* Nepal: Padma Karmo Translations, 2008.

Farid al-Din Attar / Arberry, A. J. (trans.). *Muslim Saints & Mystics: Episodes from the Tadhkirat al-Auliya ("Memorial of the Saints").* London & Boston: Routledge & Kegan Paul, 1973.

Feng, Gia-Fu / English, Jane (trans.). *Chuang Tsu: Inner Chapters.* London: Wildwood House, 1974.

Feuerstein, Georg. *Holy Madness: The Shock Tactics and Radical Teachings of Crazy-Wise Adepts, Holy Fools, and Rascal Gurus.* New York: Arkana, 1992.

Fisher, James F. (ed.). *Himalayan Anthropology: The Indo-Tibetan Interface.* The Hague/Paris: Mouton Publishers, 1978.

Fleming, Ursula (ed.). *The Man from Whom God Hid Nothing.* UK: Gracewing, 1995.

Graham, A. C. (trans.). *The Book of Lieh-tzu: A Classic of Tao.* New York: Colombia University Press, 1990.

Guenther, Herbert V (trans.). *The Life and Teaching of Naropa.* London: Oxford University Press, 1974.

_____. *The Royal Song of Saraha: A Study in the History of Buddhist Thought.* Berkeley & London: Shambhala, 1973.

Gurdjieff, George Ivanovitch. *All & Everything, or Beelzebub's Tales to his Grandson.* London and Henley: Routledge & Kegan Paul, 1950.

_____. *Views from the Real World: Early Talks of G. I. Gurdjieff.* London: Arkana, 1984.

Hatengdi, M. U. *Nityananda: The Divine Presence.* Cambridge, Mass.: Rudra Press, 1984.

Helminski Kabir, (ed.). *The Rumi Collection: An Anthology of Translations of Mevlana Jalaluddin Rumi.* Boston & London: Shambhala, 2000.

Hixon, Lex. *Great Swan: Meetings with Ramakrishna.* Delhi: Motilal Banarsidass, 2002.

Hyers, Conrad. *Zen and the Comic Spirit.* Philadelphia: The Westminster Press, 1973.

Isherwood, Christopher. *Ramakrishna & His Disciples.* Delhi: Advaita Ashrama, 2001.

Jackson, Roger R. *Tantric Treasures: Three Collections of Mystical Verse from Buddhist India.* New York: Oxford University Press, 2004.

Jones, Franklin. *The Method of the Siddhas.* California: The Dawn Horse Press, 1973.

Jones, Franklin (Bubba Free John). *Garbage & the Goddess.* California: The Dawn Horse Press, 1974.

_____. *The Paradox of Instruction.* California: The Dawn Horse Press, 1977.

Jones, Franklin (Da Free John). *God is Not a Gentleman and I Am That One.* California: The Dawn Horse Press, 1983.

Karamustafa, Ahmet. *God's Unruly Friends: Dervish Groups in the Islamic Later Middle Period 1200-1550*. Salt Lake City: University of Utah Press, 1994.

Karn, Rahul. *Zen Stick: A Collection of 91 Weird Zen Stories*. Milton Keynes: Lightning Source UK Ltd., 2019.

Kempis, Thomas à. *The Imitation of Christ*. London & Glasgow: Collins Sons & Co. Ltd., 1974.

Khenchen Thrangu Rinpoche (commentary) / Martin, Michele (trans.) / O'Hearn, Peter (trans.). *A Song for the King: Saraha on Mahamudra Meditation*. Boston: Wisdom Publications, 2006.

Khenchen Thrangu Rinpoche. *Essentials of Mahamudra: Looking Directly at the Mind*. Boston: Wisdom Publications, 2004.

Kunsang, Erik Pema (trans.) / Schmidt, Marcia Binder (ed.). *Advice from the Lotus-Born: A Collection of Padmasambhava's Advice to the Dakini Yeshe Tsogyal and Other Close Disciples*. Boudhanath, Arhus & Hong Kong: Rangjung Yeshe Publications, 2004.

Lama Chonam & Sangye Khandro (trans.). *The Guhyagarbha Tantra: Secret Essence Definitive Nature Just as It Is*. New York: Snow Lion Publications, 2011.

Larsson, Stefan. *Crazy for Wisdom: The Making of a Mad Yogin in Fifteenth-Century Tibet*. Leiden & Boston: Brill, 2012.

Lee, Rev. Samuel (trans./ed.). *The Travels of Ibn Battuta in the Near East, Asia and Africa 1325–1354*. New York: Dover Publications, 2004.

Legge, James (trans.). *The Texts of Taoism – Part 1*. New York: Dover Publications, 1962.

_____. *The Texts of Taoism – Part 2*. Oxford: Clarendon Press, 1891.

Lévi, Eliphas. *The Key of the Mysteries*. London: Rider & Company, 1977.

Lopez, Donald S. Jr. (ed.). *Religions of India in Practice*. New Jersey: Princeton University Press, 1995.

Lovejoy, Arthur O. *The Great Chain of Being.* Cambridge, Massachusetts: Harvard University Press, 1964.

Lu K'uan Yu (Charles Luk). *Ch'an & Zen Teaching.* Berkeley: Shambhala, 1970.

M. *The Gospel of Sri Ramakrishna.* Madras: Sri Ramakrishna Math, 1996.

McDaniel, June. *The Madness of the Saints: Ecstatic Religion in Bengal.* Chicago & London: The University of Chicago Press, 1989.

Merrell-Wolff, Franklin. *The Philosophy of Consciousness Without an Object: Reflections on the Nature of Transcendental Consciousness.* New York: The Julian Press, Inc., 1973.

_____. *Pathways Through to Space: A Personal Report of Transformation in Consciousness.* New York: Warner Books, 1976.

Merton, Thomas. *The Way of Chuang Tzu.* New York: New Directions, 1969.

Messer, Sarah (trans.) / Smith, Kidder (trans.). *Having Once Paused: Poems of Zen Master Ikkyū (1394–1481).* USA: University of Michigan Press, 2015.

Meyer, Marvin (trans.). *The Gospel of Thomas: The Hidden Sayings of Jesus.* London: Harper Collins, 2004.

Nesin, Aziz. *The Tales of Nasrettin Hoca.* Istanbul: Dost Yayinlari, 1988.

Nicholson, Reynold. *Studies in Islamic Mysticism.* UK: Curzon Press, 2005.

Nisker, Wes. *Crazy Wisdom.* California: Ten Speed Press, 1990.

Okumura, Shohaku. *The Mountains and Waters Sutra: A Practitioner's Guide to Dogen's "Sansuikyo".* USA: Wisdom Publications, 2018.

Osho. *The True Sage.* 1975.

_____. *The Tantra Experience.* Great Britain: Element, 1998.

Pelikan, Jaroslav. *Fools for Christ: Essays on the True, the Good, and the Beautiful.* Philadelphia: Muhlenberg Press, 1955.

Plato (trans. Hamilton, Walter). *Phaedrus and the Seventh and Eighth Letters*. London: Penguin Books, 1973.

Pratchett, Terry / Stewart, Ian / Cohen, Jack. *The Science of Discworld*. New York: Anchor Books, 2014.

Prebish, Charles S. / Baumann, Martin (ed.). *Westward Dharma: Buddhism Beyond Asia*. Berkeley: University of California Press, 2002.

Pseudo-Dionysius. *The Complete Works of Pseudo-Dionysius*. New York: Paulist Press, 1987.

Red Pine (trans.). *The Zen Teaching of Bodhidharma*. New York: North Point Press, 1997.

_____. *The Diamond Sutra: The Perfection of Wisdom*. Berkeley: Counterpoint, 2001.

_____. *The Collected Songs of Cold Mountain*. Washington: Copper Canyon Press, 2000.

_____. *The Heart Sutra: The Womb of Buddhas*. Berkeley: Counterpoint, 2004.

_____. *The Platform Sutra: The Zen Teaching of Hui-Neng*. Berkeley: Counterpoint, 2006.

_____. *The Zen Works of Stonehouse: Poems and Talks of a Fourteenth-Century Chinese Hermit*. Berkeley: Counterpoint, 1999.

Reps, Paul. *Zen Flesh, Zen Bones*. Great Britain: Penguin Books, 1957.

Ridgeon, Lloyd (ed.). *Routledge Handbook on Sufism*. London & New York: Routledge, 2021.

Rigopoulos, Antonio. *Dattātreya The Immortal Guru, Yogin, and Avatāra*. New York: State University of New York Press, 1998.

Saiyid Athar Abbas Rizvi. *A History of Sufism in India (Volume I): Early Sufism and its History in India to AD 1600*. New Delhi: Munshiram Manoharlal Publishers, 1986.

_____. *A History of Sufism in India (Volume II): From Sixteenth Century to Modern Century*. New Delhi: Munshiram Manoharlal Publishers, 1992.

Schaeffer, Kurtis R. *Dreaming the Great Brahmin: Tibetan Traditions of the Buddhist Poet-Saint Saraha*. New York: Oxford University Press, 2005.

Schimmel, Annemarie. *Mystical Dimensions of Islam*. USA: The University of North Carolina Press, 1975.

Serle, Jason Brett. *Kissing Achilles' Heel: The Joyful Unmasking of Delusion*. North Carolina: Lulu Press, 2007.

_____. *Abide As That: Ramana Maharshi & the Song of Ribhu*. UK: John Hunt Publishing, 2019.

Shah, Idries. *The Sufis*. Great Britain: W. H. Allen & Co. Ltd, 1977.

_____. *The Way of the Sufi*. London: The Octagon Press, 1980.

_____. *The Exploits of the Incomparable Mulla Nasrudin*. London: Picador, 1973.

_____. *The Pleasantries of the Incredible Mulla Nasrudin*. London: Picador, 1975.

_____. *The Subtleties of the Inimitable Mulla Nasrudin*. London: The Octagon Press, 1983.

_____. *Thinkers of the East*. Great Britain: Penguin Books, 1977.

_____. *The World of Nasrudin*. London: The Octagon Press, 2003.

Smith, Margaret. *Rabi'a the Mystic and Her Fellow-Saints: Being the Life and Teachings of Rabia al-Adawiya Al-Qaysiyya of Basra Together with Some Account of the Place of Women Saints in Islam*. UK: Llanerch Publishers, 1994.

Snellgrove, D. L. *The Hevajra Tantra: A Critical Study*. London: Oxford University Press, 1959.

Sri Anirvan. *Letters from a Baul: Life Within Life*. Calcutta: Sri Aurobindo Pathamandir, 1983.

St. Athanasius. *St. Anthony of the Desert*. North Carolina: TAN Books, 2014.

Stevens, John. *Three Zen Masters: Ikkyu, Hakuin, and Ryokan.* Tokyo, New York, London: Kodansha International, 1993.

Stoneman, Richard. *Legends of Alexander the Great.* London & New York: I. B. Tauris & Co, 2012.

Suzuki, Daisetz T. *Sengai: The Zen Master.* Greenwich, Connecticut: New York Graphic Society Ltd., 1971.

Swami Madhavananda (trans.). *Bṛhadāraṇyaka Upaniṣad.* Calcutta: Advaita Ashrama, 1997.

Thaye, Jampa. *A Garland of Gold: The Early Kagyu Masters in India & Tibet.* Bristol: Ganesha Press, 1990.

Thrangu, Rinpoche / Martin, Michele (ed.). *A Song for the King: Saraha on Mahamudra Meditation.* Boston: Wisdom Publications, 2006.

Trungpa, Chögyam. *Journey Without Goal: The Tantric Wisdom of the Buddha.* Boston & London: Shambhala, 1985.

_____. *Crazy Wisdom.* Boston & London: Shambhala, 1991.

_____. *The Life of Marpa the Translator (by Tsang Nyon Heruka).* Boulder: Prajna Press, 1982.

_____. *Illusion's Game: The Life and Teaching of Naropa.* Boston & London: Shambhala, 2010.

Tsang Nyon / Lobsang P. Lhalungpa (trans.). *The Life of Milarepa.* Boston & London: Shambhala, 1985.

_____. / Stagg, Christopher (trans.). *The Hundred Thousand Songs of Milarepa: A New Translation.* Boston: Shambhala, 2016.

Tsogyal, Yeshe. *The Lotus-Born: The Life Story of Padmasambhava.* Boston & London: Shambhala, 1993.

Tzu, Lao. *Tao Te Ching.* Boston & London: Penguin Books, 1963.

Van de Wetering, Janwillem. *The Empty Mirror.* Great Britain: Arkana, 1987.

Vaughan-Lee, Llewellyn (ed.). *Travelling the Path of Love: Sayings of Sufi Masters.* California: The Golden Sufi Center, 1995.

Waddell, Norman (trans.). *Zen Words for the Heart: Hakuin's Commentary on the Heart Sutra*. Boston & London: Shambhala, 2013.

_____. *The Essential Teachings of Zen Master Hakuin*. Boston & London: Shambhala, 1994.

Ward, Benedicta (trans.). *The Sayings of the Desert Fathers*. Michigan: Cisternian Publications, 1975.

Watts, Alan W. *Beyond Theology*. New York: Vintage Books, 1973.

_____. *The Way of Zen*. Great Britain: Penguin Books, 1968.

_____. *Tao: The Watercourse Way*. Great Britain: Penguin Books, 1979.

Wei Wu Wei. *Ask the Awakened: The Negative Way*. Boulder: Sentient Publications, 2002.

_____. *Why Lazarus Laughed: The Essential Doctrine, Zen-Advaita-Tantra*. Boulder: Sentient Publications, 2003.

_____. *All Else is Bondage: Non-Volitional Living*. Hong Kong: Hong Kong University Press, 1982.

_____. *Open Secret*. Hong Kong: Hong Kong University Press, 1982.

Widad El Sakkakini / Safwat, Dr. Nabil (trans.). *First Among Sufis: The Life & Thought of Rabia al-Adawiyya*. London: The Octagon Press, 1982.

Wilber, Ken. *Sex, Ecology, Spirituality: The Spirit of Evolution*. Boston & London: Shambhala, 2000.

_____. *Integral Spirituality: A Startling New Role for Religion in the Modern and Postmodern World*. Boston & London: Integral Books, 2006.

_____. *The Simple Feeling of Being: Embracing Your True Nature*. Boston & London: Shambhala, 2004.

Wing-Tsit Chan. *A Source Book in Chinese Philosophy*. New Jersey: Princeton University Press, 1963.

Wittgenstein, Ludwig. *Tractatus Logico-Philosophicus.* London: Routledge & Kegan Paul Ltd., 1960.

Xu Yun / Luk, Charles (trans.). *Empty Cloud: The Autobiography of the Chinese Zen Master Xu Yun.* Shaftesbury: Element Books, 1988.

O-BOOKS

SPIRITUALITY

O is a symbol of the world, of oneness and unity; this eye
represents knowledge and insight. We publish titles on general
spirituality and living a spiritual life. We aim to inform and
help you on your own journey in this life.
If you have enjoyed this book, why not tell other readers
by posting a review on your preferred book site?

Recent bestsellers from O-Books are:

Heart of Tantric Sex
Diana Richardson
Revealing Eastern secrets of deep love and
intimacy to Western couples.
Paperback: 978-1-90381-637-0 ebook: 978-1-84694-637-0

Crystal Prescriptions
The A-Z guide to over 1,200 symptoms and their healing crystals
Judy Hall
The first in the popular series of eight books, this handy
little guide is packed as tight as a pill bottle with
crystal remedies for ailments.
Paperback: 978-1-90504-740-6 ebook: 978-1-84694-629-5

Shine On
David Ditchfield and J S Jones
What if the after effects of a near-death experience were
undeniable? What if a person could suddenly produce
high-quality paintings of the afterlife, or if they
acquired the ability to compose classical symphonies?
Meet: David Ditchfield.
Paperback: 978-1-78904-365-5 ebook: 978-1-78904-366-2

The Way of Reiki
The Inner Teachings of Mikao Usui
Frans Stiene
The roadmap for deepening your understanding
of the system of Reiki and rediscovering
your True Self.
Paperback: 978-1-78535-665-0 ebook: 978-1-78535-744-2

You Are Not Your Thoughts
Frances Trussell
The journey to a mindful way of being, for those who want
to truly know the power of mindfulness.
Paperback: 978-1-78535-816-6 ebook: 978-1-78535-817-3

The Mysteries of the Twelfth Astrological House
Fallen Angels
Carmen Turner-Schott, MSW, LISW
Everyone wants to know more about the most misunderstood
house in astrology — the twelfth astrological house.
Paperback: 978-1-78099-343-0 ebook: 978-1-78099-344-7

WhatsApps from Heaven
Louise Hamlin
An account of a bereavement and the extraordinary
signs — including WhatsApps — that a retired
law lecturer received from her deceased husband.
Paperback: 978-1-78904-947-3 ebook: 978-1-78904-948-0

The Holistic Guide to Your Health
& Wellbeing Today
Oliver Rolfe
A holistic guide to improving your complete health,
both inside and out.
Paperback: 978-1-78535-392-5 ebook: 978-1-78535-393-2

Cool Sex
Diana Richardson and Wendy Doeleman
For deeply satisfying sex, the real secret is to reduce the heat,
to cool down. Discover the empowerment and fulfilment
of sex with loving mindfulness.
Paperback: 978-1-78904-351-8 ebook: 978-1-78904-352-5

Creating Real Happiness A to Z
Stephani Grace
Creating Real Happiness A to Z will help you understand
the truth that you are not your ego
(conditioned self).
Paperback: 978-1-78904-951-0 ebook: 978-1-78904-952-7

A Colourful Dose of Optimism
Jules Standish
It's time for us to look on the bright side, by boosting
our mood and lifting our spirit, both in
our interiors, as well as in our closet.
Paperback: 978-1-78904-927-5 ebook: 978-1-78904-928-2

Readers of ebooks can buy or view any of these bestsellers by
clicking on the live link in the title. Most titles are published
in paperback and as an ebook. Paperbacks are available in
traditional bookshops. Both print and ebook formats are
available online.

Find more titles and sign up to our readers' newsletter at
www.o-books.com

Follow O-Books on Facebook at **O-Books**

For video content, author interviews and more, please subscribe to our YouTube channel:

O-BOOKS Presents

Follow us on social media for book news, promotions and more:

Facebook: O-Books

Instagram: @o_books_mbs

X: @obooks

Tik Tok: @ObooksMBS

www.o-books.com